The First Century

The First Century:
The Chicago Bar Association
1874-1974

ILLUSTRATED WITH PHOTOGRAPHS

By HERMAN KOGAN

RAND McNALLY & COMPANY

Chicago   New York   San Francisco

Library of Congress Cataloging in Publication Data

Kogan, Herman.
   The first century.

   Bibliography: p.
   1.   Chicago Bar Association—History.   I.   Title.
KF334.C52C545   340'.06'277311   74-788
ISBN 0-528-81974-7

Printed in the United States of America
by Rand McNally & Company

First printing, 1974

Other Books
by Herman Kogan

The Great EB

The Long White Line

Lending Is Our Business

A Continuing Marvel

Lords of the Levee
  with Lloyd Wendt

Bet a Million!
  with Lloyd Wendt

Give the Lady What She Wants
  with Lloyd Wendt

Big Bill of Chicago
  with Lloyd Wendt

Chicago: A Pictorial History
  with Lloyd Wendt

The Great Fire: Chicago 1871
  with Robert L. Cromie

Contents

The First Century

Foreword

In this narrative, I seek to fulfill the role of chronicler rather than formal historian, reporter rather than legal scholar.

During my many years in journalism, my interest has been intense and steadfast in the manifold aspects of our legal system and in the deeds, activities, and careers—for better or worse—of scores of lawyers and judges, and I have covered hundreds of hearings and trials in courts of varying jurisdictions. Consequently, when I was asked by the Chicago Bar Association early in 1972 to consider writing a centennial volume that would encompass for the individual lawyer and the general reader the decades from its origins to its present, I responded with considerable enthusiasm and with certain stipulations. Prime among the latter were that I would be given full access to all Association records and documents and that I would have freedom to record as fully as time and space permitted whatever seemed to me most significant and most vital in the Association's initial century—its conflicts and failures as well as its successes and accomplishments. With these stipulations readily granted, I have delved deeply into all such data, have interviewed dozens of members and officials, and have read intensively in a widely ranging mass of publications dealing not only with the specific subject but also with the general field of American law. A questionnaire sent to most of the membership of 11,000, extending from officers and intensely active participants on some 75 standing committees to far less sedulous members, elicited frankly enunciated views, opinions, and estimates that have been of great value, however much they differed from each other in virulence and attitude.

My hope, of course, is that I have achieved my sought-for aim of producing an authentic, informative, and readable account. I am realistically aware that some readers will disagree with my basic concepts or feel that certain events and personalities have been given undue emphasis or that profound discussion has been diminished for the sake of revealing anecdote and incident. I respect such disagreement—it is a characteristic of virtually everything that has happened in the Association's lifetime on all levels of endeavor—yet I must here give ready assurance that my judgments have been based on careful examination and study of all that occurred in the past century and of those who played their parts, large or small. Much more remains to be written about specific aspects of the Association—indeed, of the legal profession in Chicago—and my involvement in this project prompts me to express the wish that scholars and authorities in the field will produce important and instructive volumes in the years ahead.

A listing of all who aided in this endeavor appears in an Acknowledgments section, but I would be remiss here were I not to make special mention of a number of persons without whose unstinting assistance and guidance this project could not possibly have reached completion: Judge Robert E. English of the Appellate Court of Illinois, whose counsel was invaluable and whose wit helped to lighten the occasional weight of the task; Circuit Court Judge George Fiedler, who made available to me his monumental work *The Illinois Law Courts in Three Centuries 1673–1973* while it was still in manuscript form; Jacques G. Fuller, former executive director of the Chicago Bar Association, and Stephen Czike, director of the Association's excellent library, and his staff, particularly Donna Wisniewski, Margaret Seline, and Jack Liebovitz; Bessie Louise Pierce, professor emeritus of history of the University of Chicago; and Willard L. King and George W. Gale, attorneys and historians of distinction, for their diligence in reading and commenting on the manuscript; and Shirlee De Santi, whose formidable secretarial skills and organizational talent were of inestimable value. Gratitude must be expressed to the Association's Chicago Bar Foundation for aiding in this project without, in any way, placing restrictions on me.

HERMAN KOGAN

Origins

1.

AT HER STURDY oaken desk one early December morning in 1873, Myra Bradwell composed an editorial for her *Chicago Legal News*, a fascinating and instructive weekly compendium of cases, opinions, gossip, aphorisms, anecdotes, and information about a miscellany of matters dealing with the law.

Instead of another strident demand that women be accorded rights equal to those of men in diverse sectors of society, the doughty editor noted emphatically that although there were associations of doctors, ministers, printers, shoemakers, masons, the English, the Irish, the Scotch, and the representatives of many other nations, professions, and occupations in every large city of the United States, "the members of the bar, although numerous in every large city and excelling every other class in intelligence, ability and power, have not half a dozen strong, healthy associations in America."

She welcomed,. therefore, the news that a group of lawyers had met to form an association. An effective organization, she declared, might do much to elevate the standard of professional conduct "and the disreputable shysters who now disgrace the profession could be driven from it." And she added: "We hope the Bar of this city, which as already commenced, will lead off in this matter of organization, and that every county in the State will follow. Chicago with its five hundred lawyers could form an association strong enough to have regular monthly meetings and an annual reunion which, if properly conducted, would be an honor to our city."

The action to which she referred had taken place a month earlier, on November 3, when 42 men convened in the rooms of the Chicago Law College in response to a resolution introduced at a previous meeting by John S. Cooper, a young Ohio-born lawyer, that cited "a great need in this city of an organized association of the practicing members of the Bar." All 42 put their signatures to a document underscoring a solemn intent: "The undersigned members of the Bar of the City of Chicago, believing that the organized action and influence of the legal profession, properly exerted, would lead to the creation of more intimate relations than now exist, and would, at the same time, sustain the profession in its proper position in the community, and thereby enable it in many ways to promote its own interests and the welfare of the public, do hereby mutually agree to unite in forming an association for such purposes."

At another meeting, held on the following March 7, an eight-man committee was named to draft a constitution and bylaws. One after another, a dozen men arose to enumerate objectives: the desirability of an association for its own protection and for the elevation of the character of the profession ("both as to its learning and morals"); the securing of proper discipline of "unworthy members of the bar"; the exercise of influence in matters of legislation and the administration of justice; the attainment of a better social life among the members of the profession; the establishment of an *esprit de corps*, which, all avowed, did not exist. There was considerable discussion—and explanation—for what some might construe as "exclusivity" by those gathered to create the association. "The assumption of those present to move in this matter, without calling upon a larger number of the profession," reported the *Chicago Legal News*, "was alluded to, but it was conceded that someone was compelled to take the lead, and that such an association, to a certain extent, must be exclusive, or the objects to be attained would be defeated at the very outset, and that, in assuming to act, those present did not pretend they were more worthy members of the profession than many others who would un-doubtedly unite with them in carrying forward this undertaking, but that an organization must be accomplished by someone, into which the more worthy members of the profession would be invited to come—at the same time reserving the power to keep out the unworthy, and thus make it an association of honorable gentlemen of the legal profession, having the best interests of the profession at heart."

And, reflecting on the recent 28th anniversary dinner of the Illinois St. Andrews Society in the Sherman House and the abilities of its president, Robert Hervey ("the finest specimen of a Scottish lawyer in America. His voice is silvery and his tongue is eloquent"), Myra Bradwell expressed the wish that Chicago's impending bar association would be one "as well organized as this society, that could meet for an annual dinner, be presided over with the same ability, and have its members act as orderly."

2.

At that important November meeting were men who would loom large not only in the city's courts of law but also in various phases of the city's history. Some would attain great fame and distinction and rise to high judicial office in the land, and some would grow rich in material possessions or in public adulation, and some would fight strenuously for impassioned causes and rise to triumphs or sink into the despair of defeat. And a few would be tainted ignominiously as the city, growing feverishly and recklessly in the years to come, offered temptations difficult to resist.

There had been licensed lawyers—of varying repute—in Chicago even before the city was officially incorporated in 1837. The very first was Charles Jouett, who came in 1805, not to practice law, but to serve as Indian agent, a post he had filled creditably in Detroit by effecting a treaty with the Wyandot, Ottawa, and other tribes in southeastern Michigan. Russell E. Heacock, who had studied law in St. Louis after working as a carpenter in his native Connecticut, arrived on Independence Day, 1827, six years after being admitted to practice in Illinois. Heacock lived first inside Fort Dearborn, then in a log cabin near the area that later became Bridgeport. He served as a justice of the peace and an election clerk in the early 1830s, prospered in real estate until the Panic of 1837, and, although his practice was minimal, annually advertised himself as an attorney in city directories until he died during a cholera epidemic in 1849. A native Kentuckian, Richard Jones Hamilton engaged in little private practice after arriving at what was still a village in 1831 but held a great number of official positions. An inveterate orator fond of declaiming, "A public office is a public trust," Hamilton served simultaneously as a judge in probate cases, clerk of the Cook County Circuit Court established the year of his arrival, recorder of deeds, commissioner of school lands, and notary public. Yet as one of the most public-spirited of early settlers, he found ample time to participate in varied social, political, and religious activities.

First to actually earn their living, however meager, as lawyers were John Dean Caton and Giles Spring, both of whom came in mid-June 1833, within a few days of each other. Caton, from upstate New York, had switched to law after contemplating a career as a surveyor. Spring came from Ohio, where, although of limited education, he had taken avidly to the law while clerking in an Ashtabula office.

With only $14 in his pockets, Caton leased living quarters and a small office in a building owned by Dr. John Temple and rented part of the space to Spring. The two men agreed that when one had a client to talk to, the other would leave so that business could be transacted. Their library consisted of two tomes: *Persdorf's Abridgement* and *Chitty's Pleadings*. To these, Hamilton contributed a bound copy of the Illinois statutes of 1833.

Shortly after their arrival, Caton and Spring were involved in the first case ever entered on the docket of the Cook County Circuit Court. James C. Hatch charged that Nathaniel Murdoch, a fellow lodger at a local inn, had stolen $36 from him. Caton was engaged to prosecute the alleged thief and secured a warrant from Heacock, then one of three justices of the peace

in the community. When the defendant was brought before
Heacock in his makeshift courtroom—the shop where he continued to practice carpentry—and denied all, Caton demanded
he be stripped to his underclothing. This was done, but no
money was found. But as the defendant began dressing, Caton
noticed a lump in one of his stockings. He seized the lump,
turned down the stocking, and found the missing bills. The
case was set for hearing on the next morning, and the prisoner
ordered to lie beneath a carpenter's bench under a constable's
watchful eye. When Spring and Hamilton showed up as defense attorneys, they secured a change of venue to the court of
Isaac Harmon, another justice of the peace. Harmon usually
held court in his tannery, but so intense was the interest in this
first known case of larceny in the fledgling community that the
hearing was shifted to the front porch of Wattles' Tavern on
the West Side, before which virtually the entire population of
some 150 gathered. In the style of the day, Caton made an
impassioned speech to the jury, sounding a theme that would
often be reiterated in ensuing years: "The courts must take the
responsibility of determining whether Chicago is to become a
den of thieves or an honest community where life and property
are to be protected by a rigorous administration of the law."
He painted a roseate picture of what glories could accrue to a
law-abiding Chicago and urged the presiding magistrate to
impose just punishment. "Imagine the effect if a theft of this
sort were to go unpunished. The criminals, the dregs of society
from every part of the country, would stream here in ever-
increasing numbers until neither man nor woman could walk
the streets of the city with safety. The answer is plain. Give
notice to the criminal class that Chicago is an unwholesome
place to practice their arts." Bail was set for the culprit, who
promptly fled and was never seen again. For his labors, Caton
received $10; it was a fee, as he was fond of recalling in later
years, "I never received with more satisfaction, for it just paid
my two weeks' board up to that time."

Caton also figured in a case involving ten black men who had
emigrated to Chicago from the East. State statutes were

predicated on the assumption that all blacks were born slaves and that this condition could be overcome only by documentary evidence showing their right to freedom. A warrant was sworn out against the newcomers by a merchant—"some person badly troubled by what we then called 'Negrophobia' on the brain," Caton later wrote—and the ten black men were brought before Harmon to compel them to produce their "free papers" or be sold as the statute required. Caton volunteered to defend them and asked Harmon for permission to appear before the county commissioners to request that they issue free papers, although there was no statute authorizing such a proceeding. Harmon assented, and Caton marched his clients to the commissioners' office, where he made a speech in which he declared that a monstrous wrong and a disgrace to the village and state would result if the charge were upheld. Impressed with Caton's oratory, the commissioners drew up for each of the ten men elaborately formal documents attesting to their free status, and with these in hand, Caton led the group back to Harmon, who promptly discharged the prisoners and assessed court costs against the plaintiff.

Toward the end of 1833, after the community's 150 inhabitants were mustered out to incorporate Chicago officially as a town, Caton was appointed corporation counsel, and in half a year more, he won his first elective office when, after a rather fierce contest, he defeated Josiah C. Goodhue, 182 to 47, for justice of the peace. In ensuing years, he was an alderman, gained statewide fame as a practicing attorney—in one notable case, he successfully defended 112 citizens of Ogle County charged with lynching three desperadoes who had shot and killed a leading citizen—and in 1842 began 22 uninterrupted years of service as a member of the Illinois Supreme Court, the years from 1855 to 1864 as its chief justice. In the decades before he died, honored and revered, in 1895, Caton traveled widely over the world, wrote a number of books, including the authoritative *Early Bench and Bar of Illinois,* and orated often and colorfully about his origins as a lawyer and about his almost sanctified concept of the law. A typical effusion, in an

1868 speech at Hamilton College in Ohio, went: "When God stood on quaking Sinai, from out the fiery cloud He declared His laws for the government of His peculiar people, and with His divine finger He registered these in visible characters on slabs of stone, and by the hand of His chosen instrument published them to all the tribes of Israel. Worthy indeed is it that the first of all the written codes to control the conduct of fallen man should come from that Divine Legislator who had already, and from the beginning, graven on all human hearts the fundamental principles of right and wrong. Till then, not only the descendants of Abraham but also, as I have no doubt, the polished people of Egypt, as well as the people and tribes of Asia and of Europe, were governed by a few simple laws, told only from the mouth of man, which were often perverted and distorted by rulers to satisfy their ambition, their avarice or their pleasures."

3.

In the decade that followed the arrival of Caton and Spring, more lawyers streamed into Chicago. By 1833, there were enough of them to constitute a formal meeting called to commemorate the death of United States Supreme Court Justice John Marshall. The newcomers, also primarily from the East, included Isaac N. Arnold, Alexander Fullerton, Grant Goodrich, Thomas Hoyne, Norman B. Judd, George Manierre, Buckner S. Morris, and Jonathan Young Scammon. Most of these men, however diversified their economic and social origins, had already been admitted to practice in their native states and found it easy to be licensed in Illinois. Many handled transactions involved in the land boom that raged throughout most of the 1830s. So frenzied was this activity that a parcel of real estate worth $300 at the start of 1833 soared to $30,000 at year's end. Within two years, Joseph N. Balestier, a lawyer freshly arrived from the East, recorded that he often averaged $500 a day for five successive days preparing titles to land: "The physicians threw physic to the dogs and wrote promissory notes instead of prescriptions. Even the day laborer became learned in the mysteries of quit-claim and warranty. Few cared to work and the price of labor was exorbitant."

At this time, the only requirements for licensing were that the applicant study law in the office of a reputable attorney and pass a brief oral examination by a presiding Circuit Court judge. In 1847, with the ranks increased tenfold and swelled by a high percentage of poorly educated men, John J. Brown, who had come a year earlier from downstate Danville, was persuaded by leading lawyers and judges to open a school. Brown instructed pupils in basic law, supplementing lectures with sessions presided over by practicing lawyers. A teacher with piercing eyes, a massive shock of hair, and vehement gestures, Brown was described in a contemporary account as a "retiring and misanthropic man, undoubtedly the greatest master of withering and remorseless irony, when aroused, of satirical and scornful gibe then at the Chicago Bar, and of sarcasm that, when given full rein, had something almost sardonic in it." More formal law training became available in 1859 when the law department of the first University of Chicago opened in the Larmon Building at Clark and Washington streets. Its initial class of 12 students had Henry Booth as its professor with Superior Court Judges John M. Wilson and Grant Goodrich as instructor-lecturers. By 1873, this school, with a greatly increased student body, would join with the new law department of Northwestern University to form the Union College of Law, which remained the city's foremost law school until after the turn of the century.

From the early efforts of lawyers who banded together informally to organize a study group in 1848 came the establishment by legislative act of the Chicago Law Institute in 1857, with several hundred legal volumes and general reference books gathered and organized into a library by Julius Rosenthal, a young lawyer who had fled his native Germany in the Revolution of 1848 and had already established a reputation as a legal scholar. Rosenthal had come to know Abraham Lincoln in Lincoln's circuit-riding days and was fond of repeating

Lincolnian aphorisms, his favorite among them, "If in your judgment you cannot be an honest lawyer, resolve to be honest without being a lawyer." In 1854, a commercial reporter, Edward Bean, created the first court paper in the country in the offices of the *Democratic Press.* He called it the *Daily Report* and in it, for the benefit of the city's multiplying business and financial houses, he printed a daily list of suits filed, judgments rendered, and chattel mortgages issued; later it was renamed the *Chicago Law Bulletin* and is still published as the official source of notice of the setting of cases in all courts in Cook County.

The legal community was expanding. In its earliest years, the County Courthouse had been a brick structure built in 1835, with a 200-seat courtroom on the first floor and a basement for offices and prisoners' lodgings. Pigs often gathered in the court-yard and blocked the entrances. The Saloon Building, whose one huge room served as the center of culture and political life in early Chicago, housed the City Hall from 1837 to 1843, then the post office for a time, and the United States District Court until 1857. A new courthouse at Clark and Randolph streets was completed in 1853, an ornate, ugly building containing city and county offices and a number of courtrooms. In this year too, a new Cook County Recorders' Court was established by the state legislature to try all crimes except murder and treason and civil suits involving more than $100. This court, later called Criminal Court, came 22 years after the Cook County Circuit Court—established the year the county had been created by legislative act—and preceded by a year the Court of Common Pleas, which in 1859 became the Superior Court. In addition, there were local justices of the peace and the Mayor's Court.

Whatever the jurisdiction, a kind of frontier informality seemed to prevail. A bemused visitor in 1856 noted in *Putnam's Magazine* the practices and procedures: "There is more free-dom of illustration, and more frequent use of phrases which, of themselves, mean little or nothing but as delivered with a tone and manner implying great import. There is also a much more frequent reference to general principles, and to organic laws, than in those states where precedents are more abundant. This feature, when able counsel are employed, frequently gives to the argument a breadth and scope which render the proceedings more attractive to a casual spectator than the dry citation of authorities usually heard in our Eastern courts." The writer told how a lawyer ("an old settler residing in one of the country towns") tried to make good his client's preemption title against a more recent claimant under a tax sale by describing with great eloquence his client's sufferings in the days of the Black Hawk War, a tactic that, however dramatic, failed to impress the jury. As for court decorum: "The judges, jury and lawyers patronize the apple-boys rather more frequently than would be considered proper in some places, and on one occasion, when a military company passed in the street, lawyers, sheriff, jury and spectators—in fact, everybody except the judge—made a general stampede to the windows to see them go by."

4.

Few members of the legal community were more actively involved on various levels or were abler chroniclers of the times than the Bradwells.

British-born, James B. Bradwell had been brought to the Chicago area by his parents from downstate Jacksonville in a prairie schooner in May 1834 when he was six years old. After working his way through Knox College in Galesburg, he read law and handled cases before local justices of the peace even before he was admitted to practice. In 1852, he married Myra Colby, a bright and bubbly schoolteacher from Vermont and a woman of strong opinions on everything from abolition of slavery to equal rights for women. After a two-year interlude in Memphis, Tennessee, where he was head of a private school in which she served as a teacher, they returned to Chicago, where he was admitted to the bar and set out to build a good practice and a long career as lawyer, judge, and legal historian.

Myra Bradwell began to study law in her husband's office,

24

not because she had any intention of practicing, but because she felt she could be helpful to him in preparing briefs, doing research, and interviewing clients. But the longer she delved into lawbooks, the more assured she was that she did want to become a licensed lawyer. Before she could make a move in that direction, the Civil War came, and Mrs. Bradwell characteristically threw herself into varied home-front activities ranging from the soldiers' fairs of 1863 to the Northwestern Sanitary Fair. After the war, she worked vigorously in behalf of projects to aid crippled soldiers and established a sewing exchange to teach needy and new immigrants a way to earn a living. During this period, her husband served notably as County Court judge and in other judicial posts.

In 1868, she established the *Chicago Legal News,* affixed to its masthead the motto "Lex vincit" and announced her intention to "do all we can to make it a paper that every lawyer and business man in the Northwest ought to take." Not only did Mrs. Bradwell promise to offer in her weekly publication a record of cases decided in various United States courts and the Illinois Supreme Court, headnotes to important cases in advance of publication in the reports of regional courts, and liberal dollops of legal information and general news, but also, starting with her very first issue, she made it clear that she would use her publication to battle for improvements in everything directly or indirectly connected with the practice of law. At once, she began to inveigh against the condition of the courthouse. The grass in Courthouse Square had been trampled out by boys, cows, and goats. The fountains, dry and waterless, were monuments to the neglect and inefficiency of those in charge of the courthouse. The corridors were covered with accumulated filth, and the walls were defaced and dilapidated. "The windows are so dirty," she wrote, "that one in attempting to look through them towards the Sherman House would be unable to tell whether it was built of brick or stone."

Even more persistently did she carry on a fight for equal rights for women. Under the catchall heading "Laws Relating to Women," she campaigned for women's suffrage, maintaining that the issue was not a question of politics but of necessary reform: "We have never said anything in the columns of the *News* and never intend to, from which any person could tell whether we were in favor of the Democratic or Republican party—the Methodist, Baptist, Universalist or Catholic churches. But one thing we do claim—that woman has a right to think and act as an individual—believing that if the Great Father had intended it to be otherwise—he would have placed Eve in a cage and given Adam the key." She incessantly called on the state legislature to consider passage of laws affording women just property rights and barring sex discrimination in employment, sought to persuade J. C. Burroughs, president of the first University of Chicago, to admit women to its law department, and printed scores of stories about women in other states who served, unlike those in Illinois, as jurors, justices of the peace, and deputy sheriffs. As the city's most ardent feminist, she helped to set up the Middle West's first women's suffrage convention, held in Chicago on February 11–12, 1869, and, of course, reported copiously on its sessions in the columns of the *Chicago Legal News.*

All this was a kind of prelude to her most dramatic battle. It began that August when she passed her examination creditably before Circuit Court Judge E. S. Williams and was certified to the state Supreme Court for admission to the bar. But the high court rejected her because she was married. "The court instructs me to inform you," read the letter from Norman L. Freeman, the Supreme Court reporter, "that they are compelled to deny your application for a license to practice as an attorney-at-law in the courts of this state upon the ground that you would not be bound by the obligations necessary to be assumed where the relation of attorney and client shall exist, by reason of the DISABILITY IMPOSED BY YOUR MARRIED CONDITION—it being assumed that you are a married woman.

"Applications of the same character have occasionally been made by persons under twenty-one years of age, and have always been denied upon the same ground—that they are not bound by their contracts, being under a legal disability in that regard.

"Until such DISABILITY shall be removed by legislation, the court regards itself powerless to grant your application."

In a quick counterassault, Mrs. Bradwell filed a detailed and scholarly brief citing innumerable cases holding views contrary to that of the state Supreme Court. She included reports of recent admissions of women to law schools and medical colleges in many sections of the country, the granting of licenses to practice law in Iowa and Missouri, and trades and professions newly available to women. By referring to "the disability imposed by your married condition," she wrote, the jurists had struck "a blow at the rights of every married woman in the great State of Illinois who is dependent on her labor for support and say to her, you cannot enter into the smallest contract in relation to your earnings or separate property that can be enforced by you in a court of law."

To this, the high court responded by going beyond its original reason for denying her admission to the bar and once again rejected Mrs. Bradwell, not because she was a married woman but simply because she was a woman. Asserting that inasmuch as women were not known as attorneys at common law, the court stated it could not exercise its discretion and admit them, because, in its opinion, this was possible only if state statutes were changed. Chief Justice C. B. Lawrence expressed perfunctory and mild approval of current campaigns for women's rights but then intoned: "Whether, on the other hand, to engage in the hot strifes of the bar, in the presence of the public, and with momentous verdicts the prizes of the struggle, would not tend to destroy the deference and delicacy with which it is the pride of our ruder sex to treat her, is a matter certainly worthy of her consideration. But the important question is what effect the presence of women as barristers in our courts would have upon the administration of justice, and the question can be satisfactorily answered only in the light of experience."

Myra Bradwell offered curt reply: "What the decision of the

Supreme Court of the United States in the Dred Scott case was as to the rights of Negroes as citizens of the United States, this decision is to the political rights of women in Illinois—annihilation." And she countered with a petition to the United States Supreme Court for a writ of error. A close friend of the Bradwells and one of the country's ablest constitutional lawyers, Sen. Matt H. Carpenter of Wisconsin argued that it was contrary to the Fourteenth Amendment and the Fourth Article of the Constitution to deny her admission for the stated reasons. The argument failed to convince. After holding the case for two years, the United States Supreme Court, in May 1873, affirmed the judgment of the state Supreme Court, declaring that admission to the courts of a state was not a privilege belonging to citizens of the United States which individual states were prohibited from abridging, emphasizing it was not one of the privileges of women citizens, and maintaining that "the Laws of the Creator" placed limits on the functions of womanhood. Such a philosophy was not unusual for the times. In denying the petition of a woman applicant from Wisconsin, the United States Supreme Court expressed what was a widely held feeling among conservative jurists: "It is a public policy to provide for the sex, not for its superfluous members; and not to tempt women from the proper duties of their sex by offering the duties peculiar to ours. The peculiar qualities of womanhood, its gentle graces, its tender susceptibility, its purity, its delicacy, its emotional impulses, its subordination of hard reason to sympathetic feeling are surely not qualifications for forensic strife. Nature has tempered woman as little for juridical conflicts of the courtroom as for the physical conflicts of the battlefield. Woman is moulded for gentler and better things, and it is not the saints of the world who chiefly give employment to our profession."

The immediate effect of the high court's ruling was to enjoin Mrs. Bradwell from practicing law. It did not, however, keep her from continuing her agitation in behalf of other applicants. She had already taken an intense interest in the efforts throughout 1871 of a brilliant young woman, Alta M. Hulett, to gain admittance to the bar. At only 18, Miss Hulett had applied for admission after spending a year as a student in the office of a Rockford lawyer but was refused. Promptly, Miss Hulett prepared a bill providing that no person could be precluded or debarred from any occupation, profession, or employment, except military, on account of sex. With considerable encouragement from Mrs. Bradwell, not only in the columns of the *Chicago Legal News* but also during sessions of the legislature in Springfield, she secured the bill's passage in March 1872. On her 19th birthday, June 4, 1873, Miss Hulett became the first woman in Illinois admitted to the bar, starting a brilliant practice in Chicago that ended with her sudden death in 1877.

Myra Bradwell, increasingly involved in the women's rights movement and busy with her weekly newspaper, never again sought to secure admission. But in 1890—four years before her death—the Illinois Supreme Court righted the previous wrong by granting Mrs. Bradwell a license on its own motion, and two years later, she was admitted to practice before the United States Supreme Court. Despite this overdue action, she did not practice in the courts, but she continued to carry on her drive for legal reform and improvements.

5.

That there was need for reform and improvements had become increasingly evident.

From its beginnings, the pages of the *Chicago Legal News* were studded with accounts of faulty admission standards, the ineptness and low character of some lawyers and justices of the peace, filthy and noisy courtrooms, and flagrant activities of unlicensed practitioners. In May 1869, a seven-man committee, headed by Circuit Court Judge E. S. Williams, imposed stiffer admission requirements; prime among them was that an applicant had to submit either a diploma from a recognized law college or a certificate from a practicing attorney stating that the applicant had studied law for at least two consecutive years, six months of them in Illinois. Mrs. Bradwell welcomed this as a measure "to decrease the vast number of incompetent persons who are yearly admitted to the bar," but within a few months, she had an additional complaint: "The crude and vulgar course of study pursued in law offices has been the means of placing the names of many very poor lawyers upon the roll of the profession who, if they had taken a thorough and well-digested course of reading, might have been numbered among its most useful members." She did more than complain, however, and printed the suggestions of William H. Underwood, a highly regarded attorney, for a reading list that would aid clerks and others aiming for admittance; it included several volumes of *Blackstone's Commentaries, Puterbaugh's Pleading and Practice, Mitford's Pleadings in Equity Law, Kent's Commentaries, Paschal's U.S. Constitution in U.S. Jurisprudence, Gross' Statutes,* and the Illinois Constitution of 1848. To assist students, she published a 100-page book ("50 cents for a paper-covered copy, $1.50 for one on heavy, tinted paper bound in law sheep") that contained a full report of the examination of candidates appearing before the Illinois Supreme Court: all questions asked by the examiners, the answers of the candidates, remarks of the judges, and the court's final determination. In a light vein, she reported anecdotes about unusual answers in examinations in other states; one such told of a young law student before the Indiana Supreme Court who, when asked by the presiding judge what the first duty of a lawyer was, responded, "To secure his fees, sir!" "This answer to a question strangely general and indefinite, so apt and unexpected," reported the *Chicago Legal News,* "produced an irrepressible burst of laughter at the judge's expense who, blushing and indignant, cried out to the clerk, 'Prepare a license for the applicant. I find him well qualified to practice law in the state of Indiana!'" And she sought to provide a kind of inspiration for applicants by printing in considerable detail admonitions and messages by judges presiding at various sessions at which candidates appeared. "You must remember that 'the law is a jealous mistress' and will bear no rival," read a characteristic statement by Sidney Breese, chief justice of the Illinois Supreme Court. "By constant assiduity you may win her approbation and partake of her triumphs. No man has ever risen to eminence in our profession save by unceasing study. It is a life of labor, and in proportion to your efforts will be your success. The best wishes of the court attend you upon your entrance upon the labor of a profession so useful and so honorable. May you become its distinguished ornaments."

Indeed, hardly an issue passed without an article idealizing the profession. "A truly great lawyer," wrote Charles C. Bonney, an especially prolific contributor to Mrs. Bradwell's pages early in 1871, "is one of the highest products of civilization. He is a master of the science of human experience. He sells his clients the results of that experience and is thus the merchant of wisdom. . . . He has outlived the childish ambition of display before courts and juries. He loves justice, law and peace. He will not do a mean thing for money. . . . He proves that honesty is the best policy and that peace pays a lawyer and client better than controversy. . . . The gift of eloquence is as dangerous to a lawyer as that of beauty is to a woman. It tempts its possessor to build his house upon the sand of a mere accomplishment instead of an enduring rock of an informed and cultivated judgment. . . . Officers of the judicial courts, counselors even of the highest judges, sworn upholders of the constitution and laws, defenders of private rights, ministers of justice, the character and conduct of lawyers can never be a matter of indifference to the public mind."

Examples of lawyers' character and conduct, for good or ill, were duly noted in Myra Bradwell's journal. She was well aware of the presence in the city of reputable lawyers but she took special pains to deplore all lapses of behavior in or out of courtrooms, hesitating not at all in printing blunt news items: "Newel Pratt, one of the divorce attorneys of this city, died last week. It was the liquor killed him." In the year of the Great Chicago Fire of 1871, heavy drinking among the city's 1,000 lawyers seemed to be especially prevalent, and Mrs. Bradwell lamented the fact: "We remember quite a number of men who, in their day, were distinguished at the bar, had all the clients they desired and wealth sufficient to make them comfortable for life. We have seen them take to drink, neglect their business and client after client left them to return no more. Their wealth would, day by day, drop from their nerveless hands, their friends would forsake them and, at last, they would die a miserable death, and be saved from filling a pauper's grave only through the kindness of some surviving friend who would collect enough money to give them Christian burial."

Nor did she spare those who sat in judgment. Chiding judges who were late in opening sessions, she wrote, "A judge has no more right, morally speaking, by his tardiness to take an hour from the time of a lawyer than he has to put his hand in the attorney's pocket and extract five dollars." Late in 1872, when the state Supreme Court reversed the conviction of a man who had killed a policeman, the *Chicago Evening Journal* published an article attacking "corrupt and mercenary shysters—the jackals of the legal profession who feast and fatten on human blood spilled by the hands of other men"—and implying that bribery had been used to obtain the reversal. The paper's owner, Charles L. Wilson, and its editor, Andrew Shuman, were held in contempt and respectively fined $100 and $200. In the discussions that ensued among the city's lawyers, Mrs. Bradwell was unequivocally opposed to the findings, criticizing the high court as "wanting in dignity" and expressing fears for the liberty of the press. On a lower judicial level, she inveighed against justices of the peace who not only had little or no training for their jobs and imposed outlandish fines to obtain greater fees but also failed to maintain even a minimum of decorum. With considerable approval, she reprinted a report from the *General Illinoisan* that said, in part: "In an upper room, reached by a rickety pair of stairs, in a slimy, weather-beaten, tumble-down frame structure, this dispenser of justice is found, dealing out law, cheap in quality and price. . . . The most ludicrous spectacles are here presented. Usually as many as can gain admittance elbow each other in their efforts to draw attention, thinking their success or defeat depends on their physical exertions to obtain a prominent position in the estimation of the dirty court and its chief centre."

Small wonder, then, that as the plan for an association of lawyers progressed, Myra Bradwell, who had so steadfastly trumpeted the need for such an organization, had words of approval and, typically, of counsel. "If the Association adheres to the objects for which it was created, as declared in its constitution, it will certainly do a good work, and should have the hearty support not only of every member of the bar but of the public in general, for all are interested in whatever tends to promote the due administration of justice. We hope to see the members of the bar of this city work honestly, earnestly and fearlessly to make this Association a success. Let its affairs be administered with a view of making our laws better, elevating the profession, aiding our judges in the administration of justice and bringing about a better feeling between the professional and non-professional citizen by discountenancing the conduct of those members who disgrace the profession. We hope to see it remain free from political influences, and no rings formed for its management."

A Number of Crises

1.

THE 42 LAWYERS who had gathered in the initial meetings to create a Chicago Bar Association had varied precedents for their action. The concept of such an organization in the United States dated back to pre-Revolutionary War days, when there was sporadic formation of "societies" or "assemblies of gentlemen of the bar" or "legal alliances" designed to discuss mutual problems, set up collections of legal tomes, take action against errant members of the legal community, or adopt resolutions on the death of a respected practitioner or distinguished judge. But few of these endured for very long. The first such group that maintained continuity came into being in 1802 as the Law Association of Philadelphia, later and forever known as the Philadelphia Bar Association. It was followed in the next 25 years by a number of similar groups, but of them only the Philadelphia organization survived in a period that legal historians came to call the "Era of Decadence" because it was a time, as Roscoe Pound later described it, in which there were "so many hundred or so many thousand lawyers, each a law unto himself, accountable only to God and his conscience—if any." By 1870, this dismal situation had more or less ended. The birth that year of the Association of the Bar of the City of New York in the wake of the scandals and civic brigandage of the Boss Tweed ring helped to stimulate the serious drive to form a similar organization in Chicago.

Beyond the formation of the Chicago Law Institute, there had been attempts at unified action in Chicago in the two years before the fire of 1871. In 1869, John S. Cooper, James L. High, and a few other lawyers and judges formed a club, mostly social and partly professional, that met from time to time in rooms at Monroe and Dearborn streets. And in 1870, after adoption of the new state constitution among whose many provisions was the addition of three Circuit Court judges, 88 lawyers held a long meeting in the courthouse to arrange for a vote among the city's 400 lawyers that would produce for the citizenry a nonpartisan list of suitable candidates. Despite the good wishes of local newspapers in this effort—most joined the *Chicago Tribune* in expressing the hope that the populace would heed the recommendations of the legal assemblage—and for all the noble motives and a plea from Myra Bradwell ("Let there be no party conventions—no man taken because he is a Democrat or a Republican, but simply because he is honest, and will make an able and impartial judge"), there were 336 ballots proposing no fewer than 69 candidates, with no clear majorities for anyone; and nominations subsequently were made along strict party lines. Despite the lack of consensus, the event was significant historically because it marked the first time on record that a judicial poll among the city's legal community was conducted, and a precedent was thus established for active participation of the city's lawyers in the selection of judges. In 1873, leading members of the bar joined with business, professional, and political leaders to back successfully five incumbent Circuit Court judges in a campaign devoid of political partisanship.

These instances of collective action had been for specific purposes. The aims of the new organization of 1874 were for permanence, solidity, professionalism, and the fostering of loftiest ambitions. "The Association is established," read its constitution adopted that March 14, "to maintain the honor and dignity of the profession of the law, to cultivate social intercourse among its members, and to increase its usefulness in promoting the due administration of justice."

Eligible for membership was any member of the legal profession who had been approved by the Admissions Committee and had paid a fee of $25. The bylaws provided for four five-member standing committees—Grievance, Amendment of the Law, Judiciary, and Legal Education—and nine-member Executive and Admissions committees. On May 27, 1874, a corporate charter was issued, and the Association's initial headquarters was established, with payment of a year's rent in advance, in a suite of rooms in Brown's Building at Clark and Madison streets. One room was to serve as a dining hall open from noon to 3:30 P.M. daily, another was for weekly Saturday meetings, and two small parlors were "for relaxation and smoking" from 9:00 A.M. to 9:00 P.M.

2.

The first president of the Association was William C. Goudy, who had come to Chicago from Springfield in 1859 already an experienced lawyer with a solid record of practice not only in local courts but also before the Illinois and United States Supreme Courts and a career as an officeholder, having served in the state Senate and as state's attorney in downstate counties. As an active Democratic candidate for various offices in the early 1860s, Goudy had been vociferously opposed to much that Abraham Lincoln stood for. During his campaign for the United States Senate, Goudy vied with other Democratic hopefuls in what the *Tribune* characterized as "expressions of disloyalty," declaiming in speeches that if the president refused to withdraw his recently issued Emancipation Proclamation, "I am in favor of marching an army to Washington and hurling the officers of the present administration from their positions!" Later he was revealed to have been a member of the Chicago branch of the secret pro-South organization known as the Knights of the Golden Circle, but after the war's end and the lessening of tensions, Goudy abandoned politics and concentrated only on legal matters, gradually achieving renown as one of the city's most proficient lawyers and evoking an encomium from Franc B. Wilkie, the *Times'* popular columnist "Poliuto," in his *Sketches and Notices of the Chicago Bar,* an 1871 volume of perceptive profiles of some 150 of the city's lawyers and judges: "As a general practitioner and real estate lawyer, Mr. Goudy takes no second position at the Chicago bar. . . . One of his marked qualities is an intense secretiveness. He is reticent, and is always a sort of locomotive enigma. . . . As a counsellor he is a very prudent man, and he will never give a client an opinion that will be likely to involve him in a losing litigation. He prepares a case with the utmost care, tries it closely, discusses legal questions arising with great clearness, is perfectly unmoved during its progress and accepts defeat or victory with a passionless face and an imperturbability that are adamantine in their character."

Equally prominent were the two vice-presidents, Lyman Trumbull and Thomas Hoyne, both members of the committee named to draw up the Association's constitution and bylaws. Trumbull had been among the city's legal pioneers and by now had achieved national distinction as an important figure in the politics of eras before, during, and after the Civil War. In direct contrast to Goudy's political stand, Trumbull, after going to Washington as junior senator from Illinois in 1855, had been a stern foe of the extension of slavery and a foremost sponsor of wartime confiscation acts, the Thirteenth Amendment abolishing slavery, and the Civil Rights Act of 1866, the first piece of legislation pledging equality to black citizens. Trumbull's active political career had more or less ended in 1872, when his chances for the presidential nomination of the Republican Party had been thwarted by former Lincoln lieutenants still smarting over Trumbull's 1855 election to the United States Senate and his later vote to acquit President Andrew Johnson of impeachment charges.

Hoyne, by now more or less retired from active daily practice, had come from his native New York in 1837, worked for a time in the Circuit Court clerk's office, taught school, and gained admittance to the bar after studying in the offices of Jonathan Young Scammon, foremost among the members of the city's original law establishment and reporter, after 1839, of four volumes of state Supreme Court decisions. Prominent in manifold civic affairs, Hoyne had been involved in everything from the presidency of the Young Men's Christian Association to cooperating with Stephen A. Douglas in establishing and sustaining the first University of Chicago in 1856 and had held offices ranging from city clerk to United States district attorney to federal marshal to acting mayor—in all, a man, as Wilkie wrote, "thoroughly respected, not only as a lawyer but as a citizen" whose life was "a model which every young man of Chicago can safely study and imitate with profit."

Another charter member, Melville Weston Fuller, a protégé of Goudy's despite an earlier gap in political views and a highly regarded lawyer ("A bulldog in pertinacity, never surrenders, and always pushes his cases to the last extremity," was Wilkie's pithy estimate), was deep into a career whose eventual climax would be the position of chief justice of the United States Supreme Court. The Association's other 164 charter members included Robert Todd Lincoln, who, having trained for the law with Fuller, had embarked on a respectable if not especially brilliant career and was described in the *Chicago Legal News* as "a worthy son of a loved and eminent father"; Stephen Strong Gregory and William Perkins Black, kinetic young men who in later years, amid hysteria and hatred, would valiantly defend men involved in intensely unpopular causes; Murray F. Tuley, Richard Hamilton's stepson and a former corporation counsel heading for many years of service as an unusually wise and understanding jurist; Julius Rosenthal; Adolph Moses, a German immigrant who had served in Confederate ranks; Ezra B. McCagg, a pioneer citizen and a partner of Scammon's until the fire of 1871, after which he was a leading spirit in the city's reconstruction as a leader in the Chicago Relief and Aid Society; and Wirt Dexter, young and dashing ("With his great torso and long arms," wrote Wilkie, "he would have made a cavalry officer of the most magnificent presence") personal lawyer for the city's prime merchant, Marshall Field, and known rather uniquely for being one of the first attorneys to abandon the habitual silk hat and Prince Albert coat, worn by most of the lawyers of the day, for a soft hat and a sack coat.

3.

The new organization's activities in its first year were mainly fraternal in nature. "This Association," noted the *Chicago Legal News,* "is doing much to cultivate a friendly and social feeling between the members of the bar." By September, the Association could report that many judges and lawyers patronized its dining hall, whose meals were catered by the city's prime restaurateur, H. M. Kinsley. But no sooner did such a report appear in Myra Bradwell's journal than Kinsley notified the Association that there was not enough business to warrant his continuing to serve lunches and that he intended to discontinue the practice until patronage improved considerably. Mrs. Bradwell joined in the resultant controversy, insisting that the apparent drop in business was caused by high prices and slow service: "A lawyer is the last man that wants to wait half an hour for his dinner. We have no doubt that the officers of the Association, who are all capable men, will see that Mr. Kinsley lives up to his contract, whatever it may be. If these bar dinners were furnished at a reasonable rate and properly conducted, they would be well attended, and both agreeable and beneficial to those attending." Despite Mrs. Bradwell's counsel, the Association officers let Kinsley out of the contract, and when the first annual dinner was held on December 30, 1874, the site was not Kinsley's restaurant, a five-story establishment on Adams Street in the design of a Moorish castle and self-acclaimed as the city's most fashionable eating place, but the spacious ballroom of the ornate Grand Pacific Hotel at Jackson Boulevard and La Salle Street.

In attendance at this major debut event were not only many of the Association's membership but also other lawyers and local judges and jurists from the Supreme Courts of Illinois, Indiana, and Wisconsin and legislators and varied political dignitaries. Inevitably, the speeches were plentiful and lengthy and filled with naught but the loftiest sentiments about the legal profession. Goudy set the tone with opening remarks to the effect that the mission of all lawyers was to maintain justice among men: "It is no idle boast to say that the followers of our profession are an indispensable element of every free and enlightened people and its usefulness is attested by every page of history." He sustained the mood with his toasts to the judiciary ("The safeguard of constitutional right and the bulwark of civil liberty, may its future resemble its past in the exhibition of that wisdom, integrity and intrepidity upon which the preservation of constitutions and laws, the due administration of justice and the maintenance of personal security and private property depend") and to the legal profession ("Devoted to that sublime science whose object it is to extend the domination of justice and reason and to contract within the narrowest limits the domain of brutal force and arbitrary will") and to pioneer lawyers ("From the sessions of sweet, silent thought, we summon up remembrance of things past"), and, of course, to clients ("The Scriptures assure us much may be forgiven to flesh and to blood by the mercy of heaven, but we've researched all the books, and texts we find none that pardon the man whom his attorney must dun"). There was a good deal of reminiscing about an earlier Chicago by Thomas Hoyne and Lyman Trumbull and other pioneers. Orville H. Browning, former United States secretary of the interior, pleased the entire assemblage with his ultimate and hyperbolic tribute: "Lawyers are, in the best and highest sense, the peacemakers and the conservators of order in all civilized communities. They are not, as is vulgarly supposed, the fomentors of strife and dissension. Their best mission in life is to pour the oil of peace upon the billows of passion and soothe them into repose before their turbulence has wrecked the peace of families and neighborhoods."

4.

Browning and others who spoke of noble practitioners avoided reference to disreputable lawyers who advertised their ability to obtain cheap divorces or were not averse to bilking hapless clients. Most prominent and affluent of the "divorce shysters" was Alphonso Goodrich, whose advertisements read:

> Divorces legally obtained, without publicity, and at small expense. Address P.O. Box 1037. This is the P.O. Box advertised for the past seven years and the owner has obtained five hundred and seventy-seven divorces during that time.

To solicit business, Goodrich also distributed printed circulars, which showed the figure of Justice with one hand resting on a sword and the other bearing aloft the scales.

After a thorough investigation by the Grievance Committee into Goodrich's machinations, the Association filed disbarment proceedings before the Illinois Supreme Court. But even before this, the Association had taken action against others it deemed to be malefactors. The very first recorded disbarment case, on February 5, 1875, was against D. James Leary for filing in Superior Court an affidavit he knew to be false. This disbarment proceeding was successful, but the second, against E. J. Hill, was rejected. The move against Goodrich was the third on record and drew from the high court a disbarment order in which Justice Sidney Breese excoriated Goodrich. "The wiles and arts and contrivances to which defendant has resorted in his most disgusting course," he said, "are not only not denied but justified. Such shameless effrontery has never before, to our knowledge, been manifested by any member of this or any other bar, and it should stigmatize their author with enduring shame and contumely. No honorable, high-minded lawyer, alive to the dignity of his profession and emulous of its honors, would stoop so low as this defendant has. That he should embellish his papers, contrived in a spirit of barratry, with the emblem of Justice is singularly inappropriate. He is an unworthy member and must be disbarred."

Quite naturally, Goodrich contested the ruling and so prolonged the case that it was still pending when the Association's Grievance Committee, in its year-end report for 1876, noted that since its birth, the Association had taken in $8,625 in admission fees and dues and $1,500 for three annual dinners. "For all this, what have we to show? A little furniture, rarely used; a few legal periodicals, never read; one divorce lawyer disbarred and pursuing his nefarious traffic with more brazen impunity than before; three dinners, eaten in the past; and the absolute proprietorship of a janitor *in praesenti* and *in futuro*. This, and nothing more." The report also complained of a lack of cooperation from lawyers who were quick to make general charges against alleged miscreants but reluctant to give specific shape to such charges and cited "a growing conviction, shared both by the bar and public, that the Association has fallen far short of the high mission which it assumed in the outset of its career and that its efforts at law reform and the elevation of the profession have been by no means commensurate either with its promises, its professions or with its expenditures."

5.

By this time, the membership had decreased to little more than half of the city's 500 lawyers, and the Association's headquarters had moved several times, finally ensconcing itself in the second floor of the Young Men's Christian Association Building at an annual rental of $1,200 for five years. As if in response to the Grievance Committee's harsh criticism, the Association—during the presidency of John N. Jewett, a forceful lawyer especially noted for the bitterness of the language in his briefs—spurted into activity throughout 1877, but, except in two instances, without marked success. Action against jury bribery, quite rampant then, was steadily discussed at Saturday meetings but to little avail. Myra Bradwell ventured to propose a reason for the lack of solid results: "If the Association would investigate some of these cases of attorneys improperly influencing jurors and deal with offenders without regard to whether they are men of ability, who are celebrated for gaining their points or belong to the shyster class, it would greatly aid the officers who have charge of enforcing the jury law." Discussions extended into the next year, with strong attacks on the entire jury system by some Association members and equally able defenses by others. It would be two decades more before really effective action would put a crimp into widespread jury bribery. Meanwhile, with startling naiveté, the Association appointed a committee to meet with the County Board and by reasoning with members and appealing to whatever they retained of their civic virtue somehow induce them to comply with the law and select panels of jurors with better reputations. "Many of them," declared the *Chicago Legal News,* "are now bummers and vagabonds .... No punishment can be too severe for a juryman who accepts a bribe or the person who bribes them. They are both outside the law regulating legitimate legal warfare, and were it not for the possibility of mistake, should, when caught, be either shot or hung on the nearest lamp-post by an indignant public whose justice they have outraged."

Another failure was in connection with the Association's attempt to influence the appointment of a new United States Supreme Court justice to replace David Davis when Davis was named to the United States Senate by the Illinois legislature. The Association's choice, proposed in a resolution by William Perkins Black, was Thomas Drummond, a United States District Court judge for 25 years and described as a man of "exalted and spotless character." Although copies of the resolution were sent to President Rutherford B. Hayes, all members of the Supreme Court, every senator, other bar associations in the area, and legal journals throughout the country, the seat was given to John Marshall Harlan, who had served as chairman of the Kentucky delegation to the Republican convention that had nominated Hayes the previous year; at 44, Harlan became the youngest man up to that time to receive such an appointment. In good grace, the Association honored the new associate justice early in 1878 with a reception at the Palmer House, an event marked by the interesting and rather astounding development, considering the high degree of volubility at other Association dinners (in 1876 the annual dinner had lasted until four o'clock in the morning), that not a single speech was delivered other than the brief toast of the Association's vice-president, William H. King: "Gentlemen, fill your glasses. I propose the health of Mr. Justice Harlan."

Two solid accomplishments did do credit to the Association. Shortly after the start of 1877, Julius Rosenthal, who was already performing valuable service to the city's lawyers as librarian of the Chicago Law Institute, submitted for the Association's sponsorship a bill creating the Probate Court of Cook County. Until then all probate matters had been under the jurisdiction of county courts. First of the judges to handle probate matters in 1831 had been the ubiquitous Richard Hamilton, serving in the post at the same time he was cashier of the State Bank of Illinois set up by the legislature, clerk of Cook County Circuit Court, recorder of deeds, and commissioner of school lands. Among Hamilton's successors in hearing probate cases had been Mahlon D. Ogden—brother of the city's first mayor, William B. Ogden—and the venerable Thomas Hoyne.

Rosenthal's bill called for establishment by the legislature of a separate unit for adjudication of all probate matters in accord with provisions of the 1870 state constitution. With the backing of the Association, the bill became law April 27, 1877, and the first sessions of the Probate Court of Cook County were held that December, with Joshua C. Knickerbocker as presiding judge. The initial action before Judge Knickerbocker involved a petition for letters of administration in the estate of William F. Coolbaugh, a well-known banker whose body had been found early one morning on the steps leading to the tomb of Stephen A. Douglas on the Lake Michigan shore at 35th Street. The first will filed was that of the onetime Indian agent Alexander Wolcott, whose marriage to Nell Kinzie had been the earliest of a non-Indian couple in the Chicago of 1823. (Four years after the Probate Court came into being, a challenge to its constitutionality was raised on highly technical grounds, but Judge Knickerbocker, with such Association stalwarts as William C. Goudy, Julius Rosenthal, and Abram M. Pence, took the case to the state Supreme Court, which ultimately upheld the creation of the Probate

45

Court, and as the *Tribune* stated, "breathed judicial life into the nostrils of the probate judge, enabling him to resume his labors.")

Another advancement in the court system that bore strong support from the Association also had its origins in the 1870 state constitution. During the constitutional convention, there had been considerable agitation for the creation of Appellate courts to relieve the Supreme Court of its immense case load and an equal amount of opposition from delegates who claimed that creation of such an intermediate system would encourage litigants to appeal all kinds of trifling cases. The new constitution carried a provision that called for Appellate courts to be set up after 1874, but delays and procrastination followed. The intolerable situation confronting the overworked high court justices was dramatized in November 1875, when Justice William K. McAllister resigned his seat in protest against increasing burdens—the rise in cases stemming mainly from Chicago—and was elected a Cook County Circuit Court judge at a higher salary. Continued pressure by the Association and other groups led to the legislature's passage, on June 2, 1877, of an act that organized the Appellate Court into four districts: one for Cook County, another for northern Illinois exclusive of Cook County, a third for central Illinois, and the fourth for southern Illinois. In subsequent decades, the Appellate Court system underwent various revisions, but of importance then was that for the first time in the annals of the state's legal history, Chicago and the remainder of Cook County were accorded meaningful separate treatment from the rest of the state by having their own reviewing court. Its first location was in rented rooms in the Grand Pacific Hotel, with subsequent sites including the Chicago Opera House at Clark and Washington streets; the Ashland Block at Clark and Randolph streets, which housed dozens of lawyers; and finally atop the towering Chicago Civic Center near the City Hall. With every move, appropriations for payment of rent had to be made by the state legislature. In the Grand Pacific quarters, Justice Joseph Bailey of Freeport began to teach law in his chambers to clerks, and these classes grew so popular that they were expanded and shifted to his courtroom in off-hours. These classes soon assumed the name of the Chicago Evening College of Law and were the genesis for the Chicago College of Law, later renamed the Chicago Kent College of Law.

6.

Except for sponsorship and backing of these major bills, the Association meanwhile seemed to be infected with a kind of lassitude. Meetings, often attended by only a dozen members, were devoted primarily to a mass of technical matters of no great import, except for periodic verbal assaults against justices of the peace and constables who exacted excessive and illegal fees from defendants. Annual dinners continued to be held, with the customary long speeches—and recurring complaints about their arduous length—and a new adjournment call of "To your tents, O, Israel!" Despite a reduction in annual dues from $25 to $10 and then to only $2, few new members were acquired, and the existing membership declined. "It appears," reported the *Chicago Legal News* in 1878, "that the number of members of the Association, for some reason, is on the decrease. Of the 227 who have joined it since its organization, only 166 are now members, and proceedings have been commenced against a number of these to forfeit their membership for non-payment of dues. There being over five hundred lawyers at the Chicago Bar, it will be seen that less than one-third of the members of the Bar are members of the Association." Nor, evidently, was the quality of the membership universally high. "It would be folly to say," lamented William C. Goudy, "that the remainder who are members comprise the cream of the bar."

Worse yet, a new crisis was approaching that would further disrupt the membership and debilitate the organization.

Henry W. Blodgett was one of the community's most highly regarded judges, having been named to the United States District Court by President Ulysses S. Grant in 1870 after a

20-year career as a lawyer and state legislator who had helped frame many of the early laws of Illinois. In the summer of 1878, the Association began an inquiry into charges that Homer N. Hibbard, for eight years a registrar in bankruptcy cases in Judge Blodgett's court, had failed to report some $11,000 in fees received in performance of his duties, as required by United States Supreme Court rules, and had collected excessive —and unreported—expense funds.

In a four-hour meeting on June 8, stern-minded members led by John S. Cooper, now the Association's secretary, orated against Hibbard. Others, more tolerant, defended him as a reasonably efficient administrator about whom no real evidence of wrongdoing had been presented other than a certain amount of carelessness in not adhering to a set of rules that many authorities thought ought to be abandoned as unworkable. "I do not believe," said William H. King, speaking for this group, "that Mr. Hibbard, while possibly guilty of some irregularities, ever intended to do anything dishonest."

The Association offered a vote of confidence in Hibbard, 37 to 18. And a week later, his supporters fought off, by an extremely close vote of 40 to 39, an attempt to reconsider the action on the grounds that not even one-third of the membership had been present at the June 8 session. A minority protest by Henry G. Miller, S. W. Packard, and Ira O. Wilkinson charged a whitewash: "The members of the Association, by saying in their associated capacity that . . . they deem it proper to express their confidence in Homer N. Hibbard, have, in the opinion of these protestants, prescribed a standard of official integrity which the most dishonest person in the community can scrupulously observe without in the slightest degree improving his character or reputation and have placed the profession to which we belong in apparent sympathy with that spirit of lawlessness which to such an alarming extent characterizes the administration of public and private trusts."

For a while, the Hibbard case was shoved into the background, but that autumn, charges were carried in several local newspapers and in others elsewhere that Judge Blodgett, who had presided over most of the bankruptcy cases, had conducted himself improperly by engaging in murky dealings with Hibbard and had, moreover, shown gross favoritism toward his friends and exerted severe pressure against his foes, had ruled persistently in favor of railway corporations and big business enterprises, and had conducted his court in a manner that obstructed justice. The judge issued a blanket denial, but the city seethed with report and rumor.

In December, John S. Cooper, Henry Sheldon, and John J. Knickerbocker sent to Carter H. Harrison, then a member of the Illinois delegation in the United States House of Representatives, a letter charging Judge Blodgett with official misconduct and urging Congress to impeach him. Within days, another Association group, headed by the previous year's president, John N. Jewett, demanded to know from Harrison and from Cooper, Sheldon, and Knickerbocker the specific charges against Judge Blodgett. When Harrison replied that he had not yet received the details of the overall charge and the jurist's accusers declined to specify further the reasons for their accusation, Jewett, at a heated meeting during Christmas week, offered fervent defense of Judge Blodgett: "I have had the highest estimation of his honor and integrity as a man and as a judge, and a very exalted appreciation of his capacity and business ability as a judge." He urged, nevertheless, that because of the widespread publicity given to the accusation, a committee be named to inquire into the charges.

Several men denounced Cooper, Sheldon, and Knickerbocker for violating their duties as Association members by taking such unilateral action instead of first laying their case before the Association and demanded passage of a resolution directing them to specify the charges.

"Is it not a wrong," cried Stephen A. Goodwin, one of the Association's charter members, "that when a gentleman high in official position takes his place upon the bench he should find hissing throughout the length and breadth of the union charges to his dishonor and against his integrity? Is not this a wrong? What has he a right to say? He has a right to say that

49

if any gentleman has any such fact against him, let him bring it out in the open day and not smuggle it up to a Congressional committee and keep it a secret while the brunt of it went broadcast throughout the land."

Lyman Trumbull, while praising Judge Blodgett ("Of his purity and integrity I have never known the slightest suspicion"), advised against hasty conclusions and attempts to thwart the demand for congressional inquiry. "It is idle to talk about stopping a thing of this kind by any action here keeping it from the records of the country. The right of petition is guaranteed by the Constitution of the United States to the humblest citizen in it." He was critical of the acrimonious nature of the resolution: "Whatever we do, we should do it in a calm and considerate spirit, without acrimony and without denunciation at this time."

Passage of the resolution came readily, but by now a congressional committee, headed by Proctor Knott, had been named to investigate the case. Throughout January 1879, hearings were held in the Association's rooms, and the results, for all the hullabaloo and fervid meetings, were rather anticlimactic. The prime evidence indicated that Hibbard had lent money to Judge Blodgett presumably out of funds of bankrupt estates under his jurisdiction but that the jurist had made prompt repayment. By March, the investigating committee issued a report to the United States House of Representatives' Judiciary Committee mildly censuring Judge Blodgett but recommending that no further action be taken and that all charges against him be tabled. The *Chicago Legal News* rejoiced—"It must be a satisfaction to him to know that the great mass of the bar who knew him best and appreciated his worth and ability as a judge most never doubted his integrity"—and neighbors gathered at the judge's home in suburban Downers Grove to conduct him by torchlight to the Baptist church, where various tributes were paid to him. He again asserted his innocence of any wrongdoing, and, referring to his accusers, intoned: "If it was their intention to do what they could to break my heart and to wring from me the utmost anguish that human nature can bear, then they certainly must have been abundantly gratified, for they could have taken no surer means to accomplish that end. The storm came, falsehood did its worst, but finally truth asserted itself and I now stand before my friends without an extra furrow in my face and with my health unbroken!"

7.

Absolved, Judge Blodgett went on to enjoy an exemplary judicial career and various appointive positions before he died at 84, but the tensions and bitterness over his case and the Association's role in it disrupted the organization to the extent that for nearly six years, little of consequence was accomplished. The Association did sustain its campaign against jury bribers, in 1882 reinstituting cases that had been dropped against two prominent offenders and winning a conviction against one of them. For a time, it continued to hold annual dinners but canceled them after the one at the end of 1880, which was notable for being the first to have women guests and for a remarkably lavish menu that included oysters on the half shell; green-turtle soup; boiled salmon with small potatoes; filet of beef with mushrooms, baked potatoes, and asparagus; stuffed roast turkey with cranberry sauce, green peas, and stewed tomatoes; cutlets of partridge; escalloped oysters baked in shells; saddle of venison; roast quail on toast, with jelly; boned turkey; chicken; fruit; Edam and Roquefort cheese; and coffee and punch. The Association moved its headquarters again and again, each time into less expensive quarters. In 1882, it moved to a single room in the County Courthouse. Membership continued to dwindle. In the three years after the Hibbard-Blodgett case, not a single new member was added, and in the 1882 election of officers, with membership below 200, only 24 members cast ballots.

One outgrowth of all this was the formation of the Law Club of Chicago, conceived in 1883 by a bright young lawyer of 27 named Eugene E. Prussing, an athletic fellow who made a practice of jogging one mile and walking four miles every day. He felt that the local Association and the Illinois State Bar Association, in existence since 1877, had become too stuffy, that "the old fellows" had got control of both, and that younger men were not being given an opportunity to participate prominently even in the few events taking place in this period of relative inactivity, especially in the local group. Consequently, Prussing put forward the idea of a club for practicing lawyers not more than 40 years old at the time of election to membership. The Law Club's constitution stated its purpose as one of "advancing, by social intercourse and a friendly exchange of views, the condition of the law and the interest of its practitioners in this city." Only 16 others joined Prussing in the new club, most of them already members of the Association and several destined to become presidents of both organizations. Thomas Maclay Hoyne, one of the sons of the legal pioneer, just made the age-limit requirement; most of the others were in their 30s. The youngest member, at 27, was John H. Hamline, who had achieved earlier fame by entering Northwestern University when he was only 12 years old. This initial aggregation included Stephen Strong Gregory, an early member of the Association and a future president of it and the American Bar Association; Frank J. Loesch, then in the early phases of a full and interesting legal career that would involve him for many years in civic affairs ranging from membership on the Board of Education to heading powerful anti-crime organizations; and Charles E. Kremer—popularly known as the "Admiral" because he specialized in admiralty law and was a founder of the Chicago Yacht Club—who regaled subsequent annual dinners of the Law Club with his stories about a mythical Mike Monaghan, through whom, in broad Irish dialect and with gentle wit, he told of cases involving Great Lakes shipowners, captains, and crewmen. Although the Law Club's constitution provided for as many as 150 active and 150 privileged members, there appeared to be no great rush to join. Until 1900, when membership numbered 112, the largest number to sign up was 10 in two years and 8 in four other years.

Law Club meetings tended to be less formal than those of the Association. In its earliest years, members, especially after joyous imbibing of spirits, enjoyed heckling speakers. This practice began when one of the more serious-minded members arose to read a paper. No sooner had he announced the title "Why Are We Lawyers?" than there came the cry "Because we can't all be judges!" The laughter and shouting kept the hapless speaker from continuing, and heckling became a feature of subsequent sessions, directed principally at anyone endorsing an application of a new member or proposing the acceptance of the treasurer's report; in the latter instance, the customary gibe was to suggest that the membership disapprove the report and request the state's attorney to take the matter before the grand jury. Even at the jolliest gatherings, however, serious attention was always paid—and continues to be—to speakers discoursing on the law, education, government, politics, literature, international affairs, historical events, the press, and a vast variety of other subjects.

The Law Club has persisted alongside the Association, with many of the latter's members on its roster. One of the Law Club's most notable contributions to the lighter side of the legal profession was the development of planned frivolity and annual satirical programs that inspired, in 1924, the first of the Association's famous Christmas Spirits shows. As for the Law Club's founder, he gained a smidgen of legal fame in 1886 when, as a witness in a Superior Court trial, he was permitted to testify even though he stoutly declared that he had no fixed belief in the existence of God, a response that should have disqualified a witness from taking the stand in those days. There was discussion in legal circles pro and con on this issue, but most agreed with the conclusion reached by Boston's *Daily Law Record*: "These old inhibitions have lingered too long into the light of the nineteenth century." In 1912, Prussing organized trial lawyers in the short-lived Chicago Society of Advocates and later went off to Hollywood, where he achieved some renown and wealth representing movie stars.

First Cook County Courthouse, built in 1835 at Clark and Randolph streets, with a 200-seat courtroom on the first floor and prisoners' cells in the basement. Pigs not only roamed in the streets but often strayed into the courthouse hallways.

Author's collection

Richard Jones Hamilton (top), a
pioneer Chicago lawyer of the
1830s, actually practiced little law
but held several official positions
ranging from clerk of the Cook
County Circuit Court, established
in 1831, to commissioner of school
lands.

Chicago Today

John Dean Caton (bottom), another pioneer, who rose from lawyer to chief justice of the Illinois
Supreme Court in his long career.

Chicago Historical Society

Myra Bradwell and James B. Bradwell as they looked in 1868, when their *Chicago Legal News* began publication.

Alta M. Hulett, first woman lawyer in Illinois, in 1873.

The prefire Cook County Courthouse and Chicago City Hall, built in 1853.

1

2

4

3

5

6

Group of Charter Members
of the Chicago Bar Association

7

Julius Rosenthal (1), who organized the library of the Chicago
Law Institute.   Chicago Bar Association

Robert Todd Lincoln (2), son of
the martyred president.
Chicago Bar Association

Thomas Hoyne (3), legal pioneer
and founder of family of famed
lawyers.   *Chicago Today*

Adolph Moses (4), German immigrant and former Confederate
Army officer.   Chicago Historical Society

Lyman Trumbull (5), former United States senator.   *Chicago Tribune*

William C. Goudy (6), the Association's first president.
Chicago Historical Society

Melville Weston Fuller (7), later
chief justice of the United States
Supreme Court.   Willard L. King

Clark Street, looking north from Randolph Street, the year the Chicago
Bar Association was founded.

A Matter of Great Concern

1.

THE REVIVAL of the Association began in 1886, with a determined campaign for new members but with apparently no slackening in admission standards; when Charles S. Cutting, later a judge and Association president, applied for membership, his application was referred back to the Admissions Committee to recheck his qualifications. At year's end, 45 new members had been added to the rolls, and no year thereafter, unlike the period since its origin, saw any diminution in the ranks. During that year, meetings, still held in the single room in the County Courthouse, were livelier than most of those in the preceding few years. The March meeting was sparked by a rather critical speech by James L. High, shortly to become the Association's president, entitled "Certain Tendencies in the Legal Profession," in which he deplored what he considered a growing inclination to make the legal calling an art rather than a science. "The scientific and philosophical," he declared, "is giving way to the money making and commercial. The bar of this country is becoming a sort of trades union, lacking even the elements of cohesion which belong to most trades unions. The vicious system of an elective judiciary and the unseemly scramble among lawyers for every vacant judicial position are among the surest signs of the decadence of the professional spirit. The bar is coming to occupy no higher rank than that of ordinary business avocations!" The *Chicago Legal News'* comment seemed rather uncharacteristically designed to offend no one: "Mr. High believes more in the sages of the past than in the lawyers of the present. It is well that this is so, for there is no doubt the lawyers of the future will count among the sages many members of today. Sometimes with lawyers 'tis distance lends enchantment to the view."

As if to signalize its revitalization, the Association resumed its annual banquets December 30, 1886, with a gathering in the Grand Pacific Hotel of men the *Chicago Legal News* happily referred to as "the legal lights of the bench and bar of this great city." President Frederic Ullmann profusely welcomed the resumption of the banquets, seeking to link the period of the Association's major deeds with that in which the annual dinners had been held. "During the seven years that we annually satisfied our hunger and thirst together," he reflected, "we made a record with which any such organization might well be satisfied." That record, he was proud to say, included legislation creating the Appellate and Probate courts and the disbarment of a number of practitioners "whose unprofessional conduct could never have been successfully attacked, except through such organized effort as an Association like this could bring to bear." In accordance with the tradition of previous dinners, there were toasts, and there were other speeches, including one by Judge Henry W. Blodgett—now on the state Supreme Court bench with the disputes of a few years back long forgotten—in which he expressed sympathy for a federal judiciary that was "overworked and underpaid." The final oration, by Wirt Dexter, set the tone of the holiday week: "Gentlemen, standing now at the close of the year, how profitable to recall the memories of the past year, for which we should be thankful, and also how profitable to leave the unpleasant unremembered! It is a happy circumstance of our nature that the disagreeable is so soon forgotten. Standing upon the verge of this old year, let its receding waters sweep away into oblivion every vestige of enmity and uncharitableness. Then what a new and almost heavenly clean sheet to start the coming year with! Thus begun, the harmony of its days will leave sweet music in Cathay."

2.

For all of Dexter's dithyrambs, the disagreeable had not yet been forgotten nor had "every vestige of enmity and uncharitableness" been swept into oblivion.

Indeed, at the very moment Dexter spoke, the city and the legal community were still in the throes of turmoil aroused on the evening of May 4, 1886, when some 2,000 persons gathered in a drizzle at Haymarket Square to listen to orators excoriate the police and those they held responsible for a murderous clash the night before at the strike-bound McCormick harvester works on Blue Island Avenue. Samuel Fielden, an avowed British-born anarchist known as "Good-natured Sam," was addressing the crowd when from the nearby Desplaines Street station came a force of 176 policemen, each armed with a club and an extra revolver and led by Captain William Ward, who shouted, "In the name of the people of the State of Illinois, I command this meeting immediately and peaceably to disperse." Just as Fielden replied, "We are peaceable," a bomb was thrown; in the explosion, several policemen were killed and other policemen and bystanders were injured.

In an atmosphere of frenzy and hysteria, Police Captain Michael J. Schaack, a zealous foe of agitators and unionists, took command of a roundup of acknowledged anarchists, suspected anarchists, radicals of every hue, and even laborites who opposed anarchists but had campaigned for nearly a decade in behalf of such daring ideas as an eight-hour day and sanitary factory conditions. Many innocent Chicagoans were taken from their homes without warrants and held without bail, and for days station-house cells were jammed, some with women and children. Out of the hundreds seized, Fielden and seven other men—Albert R. Parsons, a Confederate Army veteran, a writer, and a leader in the Central Labor Council, an aggregation of left-wing unions; August Spies, a fiery editor of a German workers' newspaper, the *Arbeiter Zeitung;* Adolph Fischer, a printer; George Engel, a toy maker; Louis Lingg, a carpenter; Oscar W. Neebe, a beer-wagon driver; and Michael Schwab, an editorial assistant on the *Arbeiter Zeitung*—were held without bail to the grand jury under the jurisdiction of John G. Rogers, chief justice of the Criminal Court. On May 27, these eight men were indicted for being accessories to the murder of Policeman Mathias J. Degan, for murder by pistol shots, and for general conspiracy to murder.

The prevailing atmosphere was incredibly tense. Day after day, the accused were condemned in the city's newspapers, some of whose editors cried out for public hanging without trial. The *New York Times* called for "death for the cowardly savages," and the *Philadelphia Inquirer* demanded "a mailed hand" to teach anarchists that the United States was not a "shelter for cutthroats and thieves." Even liberal clergymen joined the cry: "We need a careful definition of what freedom is," intoned David Swing of the Central Church. "If it means the license to proclaim the gospel of disorder, to preach destruction and scatter the seeds of anarchy and death, the sooner we exchange the Republic for an ironhanded monarchy the better it will be for all of us!" Charles C. Bonney, a lawyer who had for years often criticized industrialists and inveighed frequently against "the greed, the selfishness, the neglect and folly of wealth and power," now maintained that labor was responsible for its ills, that labor and anarchism were genuine allies, and that the use of the bomb, no matter by whom thrown, was literally "a waiver of trial and a plea of guilty."

In an aura of fear and depression, it seemed next to impossible to secure legal counsel for the accused. Yet, even while the grand jury was in session, the task of organizing a legal defense committee was undertaken by Dr. Ernst Schmidt, a prominent physician who had run for mayor a few years earlier on the Socialist ticket and had spoken out against the use of force in securing gains for workers. Two young attorneys for the Central Labor Council, Sigmund Zeisler and Moses Salomon, headed the committee but realized they were too inexperienced for so monumental and controversial a trial. Dr. Schmidt first sought to retain Luther Laflin Mills, a former state's attorney of Cook County, but Mills swiftly declined. William S. Forrest, highly experienced in the technicalities of criminal law, asked for a fee that was far beyond the capacity of the committee, most of whose contributions had been from $1 to $5.

3.

The next man approached was William Perkins Black, as bright and promising a lawyer as any in the city and presumably destined for an affluent future as the partner of Thomas P. Dent in the practice of corporate law. Before the Civil War, Black had studied in Danville to be a Presbyterian minister like his father, but with the coming of the conflict, he and his older brother, John, enlisted in the Eleventh Indiana Zouaves, whose commander was Lew Wallace. Later both men organized a company of Illinois volunteers in the Thirty-seventh Illinois Infantry, popularly known as the Fremont Rifles, and within months were in fierce combat at Pea Ridge, Arkansas. William, a captain, performed so valiantly there that he was awarded the Congressional Medal of Honor. John's bravery in a battle later at Prairie Grove, Arkansas, won him the Medal of Honor and a promotion to general. After the war, both men studied law and came to Chicago early in the 1870s. John ran unsuccessfully for lieutenant governor on the Democratic ticket. William, after campaigning in behalf of Horace Greeley's futile presidential bid in 1872 as candidate of the short-lived Liberal Republican party, turned Democrat and ran for Congress in 1882 but was defeated by only 2,400 votes.

William's practice with Dent, an old friend from their days in Danville, was rapidly expanding when he was approached by Dr. Schmidt to join the defense team. Black's immediate response was negative, stressing that he had no great experience in criminal law and advising that a specialist in that kind of practice be hired. Dr. Schmidt told him of the fruitless efforts to retain Mills and Forrest. Black promised to secure an expert in defending men accused of serious crimes but failed incessantly. The longer he tried, the more indignant he became that the defendants might go to trial without adequate counsel.

He went to see Circuit Court Judge Murray F. Tuley, respected and admired as one of the city's prime jurists.

"I've been applied to by the friends of the anarchists to undertake their defense," Black said. "I advised them to try to employ someone who made criminal law their specialty. But they came back a second time and said they were still unable to get any such person to undertake their defense because they had very little money and again pleaded with me to take the case. The amount of money they have offered me is not worthy of consideration, but it is their all—all they can raise. I told them I would consider the matter and give them my decision. You know what undertaking their defense means to me or any lawyer of position at the bar."

"You have counted the cost?" asked Judge Tuley.

"Yes, I think I can foresee the result to me if I undertake their defense. I think I can foresee that he who undertakes the defense of these anarchists will be looked upon with at least great disfavor. It means to some extent social ostracism and, I believe, an almost total sacrifice of my business and possibly of my future prospects. Now, Judge, what shall I do? What would you do?"

To this Judge Tuley replied, "Captain Black, your question is a very serious one, and probably one that you should solve yourself. But as you ask my opinion, I shall give it to you. As these men have offered a retainer and that to the extent of their ability, I have no hesitation in saying that your duty to your profession, your duty to yourself, demands that you accept it and undertake their defense. I must say to you that you have rather underestimated than overestimated the cost to yourself. But yet, Captain, it is always expedient to do one's duty."

"I do feel," said Black, "that it is my duty to take the case, and your advice has encouraged me to do so."

Aware that Judge Rogers' charge to the grand jury was so filled with prejudice that the *Chicago Legal News* was moved to comment, "It gives guilty anarchists no reason for hope," Black sought a change of venue, hoping the case might be assigned to Judge Tuley, whose reputation for impartiality and sound judgment was of the highest. But the case was assigned instead to Judge Joseph E. Gary, who, as a practicing lawyer in Chicago since 1856, had been a partner of Tuley's and had been elected to the Superior Court in 1863. Gary had a reputation as a strict but fair judge, a man with a strong sense of humor, and a stickler for punctuality and court decorum, so much so that he never permitted a lawyer or litigant to see him in his chambers for any reason, explaining that people were already so suspicious of lawyers and judges that he did not want to stimulate public curiosity and stir more suspicion by transacting judicial matters except in open court. "Judge Gary is a very independent, experienced, able, impartial, judicial officer," stated the *Chicago Legal News*. "There is no man on the bench in this country that exceeds him in executive ability. He allows no nonsense in his court. He calls things by their right name, proceeds at once to business. He is not flattered at the praise of counsel or frightened at their threats. In fact, he allows neither. He governs his court in a quiet way with a strong hand and a clear head, never descending to wrangling with counsel."

The trial, unsurpassed in drama and tension in the city's legal annals, began on July 15, 1886. It took 21 days to pick a jury from among 982 talesmen, during which Parsons, appalled at what he considered Judge Gary's prejudice in permitting potential jurors to state that they were opposed to anarchism, passed Zeisler a note that read, "In taking a change of venue from Judge Rogers to Lord Jeffries, did not the defendants jump from the frying pan into the fire?"

Julius S. Grinnell, still basking in the fame of his recent convictions of a ring of thieving Cook County commissioners and of Joseph "Chesterfield Joe" Mackin, a powerful Democratic politician, for vote stealing, was chief prosecutor. Through witnesses and evidence, he sought to connect the defendants to Rudolph Schnaubelt, the man who, though still missing, was generally believed to have hurled the bomb. Grinnell offered the argument, among many, that even if Schnaubelt were not the actual bomb thrower, the defendants were guilty of engaging in a conspiracy against established society. At one point, he declared that the Confederate attack on Fort Sumter in 1861 "was nothing compared with the insidious, infamous plot to ruin our laws and our country secretly and in this cowardly way." And in his final summation, he cried: "I say to you, the law demands now, here, its power . . . that law which the exponents of anarchy violated to kill Lincoln and Garfield, that law that has made us strong today and which you have sworn to obey, demands of you a punishment of these men. . . . Don't try, gentlemen, to shirk the issues. Law is on trial! Anarchy is on trial! The defendants are on trial for treason and murder!"

Black's defense—in which he was aided not only by Zeisler and Salomon but also by a tough, tobacco-chewing Iowan, William A. Foster—was based on the lack of specific evidence to prove the charges in the indictment. The men were being tried, he asserted, because they were radicals. "The defendants are not charged with anarchy, they are not charged with Socialism. They are not charged with the fact that anarchy or Socialism is dangerous or beneficial to the community. . . . They had the right to gain converts, to make anarchists and Socialists, but whether Socialism or anarchy shall ever be established never rested with these defendants, never rested in a can of dynamite or in a dynamite bomb. It rests with the great mass of people, with the people of Chicago, of Illinois, of the United States, of the world. If they, the people, want anarchy, want Socialism, if they want Democracy or Republicanism they can and they will inaugurate it." Black's closing summation, in which he challenged virtually every point made by prosecution witnesses, ended with: "Gentlemen, the last words for these eight lives. They are in your hands, with no power to whom you are answerable but God and history, and I say to you in closing only the words of that Divine Socialist, 'As ye would that others should do to you, do you even so to them.'"

In his charge, Judge Gary instructed the jury that the defendants could be adjudged guilty if the evidence showed that they had agreed to overthrow the law by force and also if

Policeman Degan had been killed "in pursuance of such con-spiracy." The jury needed only three hours to decide that seven of the defendants were guilty and an hour more to agree that Neebe was guilty too. Next morning, all but Neebe, who received 15 years, were sentenced to death, the date of execution set for that December 3.

From that point on, a series of legal steps were taken to save the men from the gallows. Leonard D. Swett, Abraham Lincoln's legal associate, joined Black early in 1887 in an unsuccessful appeal to the Illinois Supreme Court, and later that year, appeared with Gen. Ben Butler in a hearing before the United States Supreme Court, which resulted in the high tribunal's refusal to intervene. Agitation for executive clemency for the condemned men, led by Lyman J. Gage, a prominent banker, over the strenuous opposition of such leading citizens as Marshall Field, Cyrus McCormick, George M. Pullman, and Philip D. Armour, prompted the commutation by Gov. Richard J. Oglesby of Fielden's and Schwab's sentences to life imprisonment. Lingg killed himself by exploding a detonating cap in his mouth, and the remaining four—Parsons, Spies, Fischer, and Engel—were hanged on November 11, 1887, in the Cook County jail yard. On that day, there appeared on the bulletin board of the Palmer House the notice: "Trap fell. Spies Parsons Fischer & Engel expiate their crime & the law vindicated."

4.

In the immediate aftermath of the hanging, the issue refused to die. Judge Gary remained aloof from the still-continuing controversy except at a dinner tendered him by the Chicago Bar Association several weeks after the hangings. At this dinner, Wirt Dexter presumed to speak not only for the Association but for the legal profession with this astounding statement: "We offer the bulwark of a conservative element. How needful is this bulwark at the present time I need not say, with the deep unrest that exists about us. When men armed with destructive theories seek their enforcement, which would speedily make for us an earthly hell, other professions will expostulate, but the law—and I say it with Judge Gary sitting in our midst—will hang! I mention his name in obedience to an impulse of the heart too strong to resist, for I don't believe he will ever know how we feel towards him, and how we love him!"

After the applause subsided, Judge Gary responded with a slashing attack on those he considered labor agitators. He scored the "arrogant assumption of the labor organizations to control the acts of every man who lives by manual labor," and while he deplored political corruption and monopolistic capitalism, he noted that such evils did not deprive people of life's necessities. "The tyranny under which labor groans stops industry and takes bread from the mouths of hungry women and children. What can we do to break it down?"

Yet Judge Gary was increasingly—and irritatedly—aware of the growing reaction, even among some who had been at that very dinner, against the outcome of the heated trial. Now among some 60,000 names on a petition for clemency for the surviving defendants were those of prominent Association members. The petition was presented to the state's new governor, John Peter Altgeld, shortly after his election in 1892. Although he had a reputation as a man of liberal views, Altgeld had taken no part in any of the earlier action in behalf of the anarchists, despite the urging of his close friend George Schilling, a labor union leader. After his election, Altgeld began to study the voluminous trial record. He was still examining it when the April 1893 issue of *The Century* magazine appeared, and in it was an article headed "The Chicago Anarchists of 1886. The Crime, The Trial, and The Punishment. By the Judge Who Presided at the Trial. And The Law is Common Sense."

In the startling, embittered article, Judge Gary emphasized that the anarchists were convicted not for their political creed but for "horrible deeds." He denounced each of the defendants and accused them of being insincere men who actually had little sympathy with the workers they exhorted to follow their counsel. He reiterated the main points of his decision overruling a motion for a new trial. He made several misstatements about what the defendants had said and about events at the McCormick harvester works. Worst of all, he attacked not only Black but also Black's wife, Hortensia. After Judge Gary had imposed the death sentence on seven of the defendants, Mrs. Black had written a letter to the *Daily News* in which she expressed sympathy for the anarchists: "During all that long trial a kind of soul crucifixion was imposed upon me. Often, as I took up one or the other of the daily papers, I would recall reverently those words of my Divine Master: 'For which of my good works do you stone me?' Anarchy is simply a human effort to bring about the millenium. Why do we want to hang men for that, when every pulpit has thundered that the time is near at hand?" Quoting from the letter, Judge Gary implied that Mrs. Black and her husband were bound by some kind of spell to the anarchists, that they were unduly fascinated by them, and that the words they spoke and wrote were motivated, not by social consciousness or deep feelings about society, but by that peculiar fascination. He was even rougher on Black for having declared, in his funeral oration for the hanged anarchists at Waldheim Cemetery: "I loved these men. I knew them not until I came to know them in the time of their sore travail and anguish. As months went by and I found in the lives of those with whom I talked the witness of their love for the people, of their patience, gentleness and courage, my heart was taken captive in their cause. . . . I saw that whatever fault may have been in them, these, the people whom they loved and in whose cause they died, may well close the volume, and seal up the record, and give our lips to the praise of their heroic deeds, and their sublime sacrifice."

Judge Gary had privately expressed his indignation over these remarks when they were first made, and now, nearly six years later, he was still outraged. He scoffed at such phrases as "supreme sacrifice" and interpreted Black's reference to the men's "cause" to mean "rebellion, to prosecute which they taught, and instigate murder." The Blacks were guilty not only of falling under the anarchists' spell, but also of maudlin sympathy.

Commenting on the article, the *Tribune* decreed, "It is

timely," but a youthful Clarence Darrow denounced it in a speech to the Law Club of Chicago, with Judge Gary stony-faced in a nearby chair. As for Governor Altgeld, he was spurred to a decision to pardon Fielden, Neebe, and Schwab; and his official document, "Reasons for Pardoning," issued on June 26, 1893, was a direct assault on Judge Gary and the conduct of the trial, from the faulty method of picking the jury to the failure of evidence to prove guilt. Judge Gary, concluded the governor, had conducted the trial "with malicious ferocity," had ruled without exception on every contested point in favor of the prosecution, had made "insinuating remarks" in the jurors' presence to sway them to his way of thinking, and had made speeches that were "much more damaging" than any by Grinnell. The article in *The Century* Altgeld considered "full of venom" because of the attacks on Mr. and Mrs. Black. "It is urged," the governor wrote toward the conclusion of the statement, "that such ferocity of subservience is without a parallel in all history, that even Jeffries of England contented himself with hanging his victims and did not stoop to berate them after death."

The furor and frenzy following Altgeld's decision would long persist—such staunch admirers of Altgeld's as Darrow and Jane Addams deplored his personal attack on Judge Gary, although the governor insisted, "I denounced not Gary the man but Garyism"—but Black could derive scant personal satisfaction from the result. He was desperately striving to rebuild his law practice, while Judge Gary was on his way to reelection later that year in a Republican landslide and Black's erstwhile partner, Thomas P. Dent, was slated to assume the presidency of the Chicago Bar Association in 1895.

5.

Except for the dinner to Judge Gary, no official attention was paid the tumultuous case by the Association in the seven years from the horrendous explosion in the Haymarket to the ultimate pardon by Governor Altgeld. But informally, hardly a member failed to express opinions at meetings and at lunches, and frequently legalistic discussions resulted in shouting and a waving of fists. Conservative-minded members, fearful of people they considered dangerous to national institutions, upheld every phase of the proceedings against the anarchists and were quick to spring to the defense of Judge Gary during and after the trial and most certainly after Altgeld's decision to pardon the men still jailed. In the immediate wake of the arrest of the accused, many agreed with the more strident of the newspapers, the *Chicago Times* crying, "No time for parleying!" and the *Daily News,* after first calling for forbearance and self-control, shrilling, "These anarchists are amenable to no reason except that taught by the club and the rifle. . . . No mercy should be shown them." John Barton Payne, prominent in Association affairs and in later years head of the American Red Cross, took the lead in organizing a vigilante committee prepared to take the law into its own hands and put down what he was certain was a radical revolution touched off by the Haymarket explosion. But a considerable segment of Association members came gradually to believe that Judge Gary's sentences had been unduly severe, and many were among signers of the petitions for clemency. Judge Tuley and such other Circuit Court judges and Association stalwarts as William C. Goudy, Judge Lambert Tree, Edward Osgood Brown, Judge William K. McAllister, Frank Baker, and Thomas A. Moran joined with the Association's second president, Benjamin F. Ayer, and a future president, Stephen Strong Gregory, in these pleas.

Indeed, Gregory, who had till then been an establishment-minded partner in several solid firms, seems to have been spurred in the aftermath of the Haymarket case to assume the role of a defender of unpopular causes. In October of the year of Altgeld's pardons, Patrick Eugene Prendergast, angered over being rejected by Mayor Carter H. Harrison for the corporation counsel's post, accosted Harrison on the steps of his Ashland Avenue mansion and fatally shot him. The slaying, shortly after the closing of the World's Columbian Exposition and on the eve of a fearful economic depression, at once stirred passions almost akin to those after the Haymarket affair. "It would seem from all reports of the case," stated the *Chicago Legal News,* "that Prendergast, at the time of the shooting, was in a condition of mind to know right from wrong, and if so, he was responsible for his acts and ought to be hung with as little delay as possible. It should take strong evidence to establish insanity in the, case of a man who attends to his regular business and is never suspected of insanity by his relatives and friends until after he kills a man. Chicago is the greatest law abiding city in the world. Had this crime been committed in Mr. Harrison's native state, Kentucky, his murderer would never have reached the jail—and many people would have said *Amen.*"

In the face of such sentiments—even the *Tribune,* which had persistently and sometimes savagely fought Harrison in his previous mayoral terms, declared that the death of no other Chicagoan by such an act of violence could arouse more regret or sympathy—Gregory took an intense interest in the case, aiding in a fruitless defense, and after Prendergast was sentenced to hang, leading the drive to persuade Governor Altgeld to commute the sentence. This proved futile, and so did a series of legal moves by Clarence Darrow and Gregory to prove Prendergast insane at the time he assassinated the beloved mayor. Prendergast was hanged, thereby gaining the dubious distinction of being the only client Darrow ever lost to the gallows.

Within a year, Gregory was again involved in a highly charged case when he joined Darrow in defending, in United States District Court, Eugene Victor Debs and seven associates on conspiracy charges stemming from the turbulent strike of Debs' American Railway Union against George M. Pullman's massive railroad-car works. Darrow had resigned his post as general attorney for the Chicago and North Western Railway to lead the defense, and in Gregory he found a man who, as he later wrote in his autobiography, "was emotional and sympathetic . . . devoted to the principles of liberty and always fought for the poor and oppressed." In a month-long trial before Judge Peter S. Grosscup early in 1895, Gregory ably furnished Darrow, superb as a courtroom orator but less than thorough in amassing legal data and precedents, with copious information and cases relating to the history of labor unions and conspiracy laws.

The trial ended indecisively. Darrow sought to subpoena Pullman, who promptly left town, and called several members of the General Managers' Association, representing the two-dozen railroads running out of Chicago, to ask them about their companies' connections with the hiring of strikebreakers. Pullman could not be found, and the railroad officials avowed they could remember nothing about what was said at their meetings. In the midst of this, a juror became ill, and Judge Grosscup, over the strong objections of Darrow and Gregory, discharged the jurors—who filed out after shaking hands with the defendants and the two lawyers—and continued the case until May. It was never reopened, but Debs served six months in a Woodstock jail for having violated an injunction against continuing the strike and thereby interfering with delivery of the mails, a sentence affirmed by the United States Supreme Court despite cogent arguments by Darrow, Gregory, and the aged Lyman Trumbull. "It seems strange to me, except that it has ever been thus," Gregory wrote to his friend Henry Demarest Lloyd after the Pullman strike was broken and Debs was lodged in his cell, "that the railroads did not realize as well as public officials how it would disarm Debs to treat him justly—to show that the courts and judges whom he denounced as corporate tools could yet, calm and unruffled, administer the law justly, unmoved by the demand of the wealthy and influential classes for vengeance upon him."

This was not the first time Gregory was critical of the judiciary, and in his later years—as president of the Chicago Bar Association in 1900, president of the Illinois State Bar Association in 1904, and president of the American Bar Association in 1911—he would be foremost among those crying out for a judiciary as free as possible from prejudices, political affiliations, bigotry, and rigidity of mind.

Setting Higher Standards

1.

THAT MANY in the Association were of the same mind as Gregory had long been apparent but never more vividly and excitingly than in the summer of 1887. Two days before the scheduled meeting on May 23 of leaders of the Republican and Democratic parties in the Sherman House to name a "fusion ticket" of six candidates for a special Circuit Court election Association President Frederic Ullmann met with Gregory and such other members as William C. Goudy, Abram M. Pence, and Frederick W. Tourtellotte to discuss a course of action if the fusion candidates were inferior. When the names were announced on what was promptly dubbed the "Sherman House ticket," the three Democratic nominees—Adolf Kraus, Clayton E. Crofts, and W. J. English—were immediately denounced by editorialists as "poor" and "unpopular" and "shameful." The *Tribune* was especially critical of the nonpartisan system of judicial nominations that had prevailed for some time, hinting at illicit payments to influence nominations and asserting, "Better that the candidates for judges should be nominated in political conventions and fought over on party lines than to have either weaklings or men whose nominations may have been secured by improper means."

Gregory, Pence, and Goudy promptly called on three men to oppose the Democrats: Julius S. Grinnell, recently victorious in the Haymarket trial, I. K. Boyesen, and Richard Clifford.

Association members and nonmembers circulated petitions throughout the city for a general meeting of lawyers, obtaining over 3,000 signatures in a single day. The meeting, on May 28, was a riotous one, for many in attendance disagreed with the Gregory-Pence-Goudy group, which had assumed the name of the Citizens' Campaign Committee of Fifty. The *Daily News* called "the so-called meeting of the Chicago Bar a disgraceful affair in every way" and blasted the "howling bullies whose long experience in yelling at saloon political meetings befitted them perfectly for their job at controlling the meeting with noise." The *Chicago Legal News* cited the meeting and another two days later as "the most exciting of any ever held by the Bar of this city." Out of these meetings came a resolution by which members of the bar would select three Republicans and three Democrats from 12 candidates proposed at the meetings and from those already picked by the party chieftains. The balloting, conducted for seven hours in the Union League Club, resulted in the naming of the same Republicans endorsed by the party and of Grinnell, Clifford, and Frank Baker. Boyesen withdrew, one of the first—and rare—instances of a candidate dropping out of a judicial race because of a denial of an Association endorsement.

Only a few days remained for those in support of the bar-endorsed ticket to electioneer. As the last act of his presidency, Ullmann named 25 members to work with the committee in campaigning for votes and distributing sample ballots. Two of them, John H. Hamline and Adolph Moses, prepared a circular that lawyers were asked to distribute to clients. Mass meetings held on the weekend before the June 6 election were addressed by Association members and other lawyers. The result was a complete triumph for the candidates backed by the Citizens' Campaign Committee of Fifty. It was a notable victory, showing that concerted actions for a better quality of judicial candidate could yield good results. And it was a precedent-setting triumph that the Association would seek, with varying degrees of success, to emulate in years to come.

2.

Thereafter, Stephen Strong Gregory was almost always in the forefront of criticism not only of political parties' domination in the selection of judicial candidates and the methods used, but, even more, of inept judges and those who continued, after ascending the bench, to participate in political activities. Invariably in this decade, the Association's Judiciary committees saw fit, in their annual reports, to comment adversely on conditions in the courts, especially crowded calendars and excessively long trials. Many special Association meetings, often acrimonious, were called specifically to discuss an assortment of judicial matters, and at each, judges were present to agree, disagree, or propose legislation to increase their ranks or lengthen court hours.

At an 1896 session, one typical response to criticism was that of John Barton Payne, then a Superior Court judge: "The courts have had to deal with a tremendous number of men who ought to be working on the street or plowing corn. They never prepare the cases or know what they want. If a lawyer comes into court knowing what he wants and sets about to do it, he will have no complaint about the question of dispatch." At another meeting, after he became the Association president in 1900, Gregory was especially irate about judges who censured juries for bringing in verdicts that, in their opinions, were wrong. "This practice," he said, "is wholly without the warrant of the law, is subversive of the provisions of the Constitution and destructive of the guarantee of the right of trial by jury. It can not be justified under the law and should be condemned." And at a later meeting, toward the close of his presidency, Gregory called attention to other judicial defects. Too many men on the bench, he asserted, were lax in granting certificates of good moral character to attorneys. "It has been found possible for a gentleman of the bar, just from the penitentiary of a sister state, to come here and secure from the court of this county a cordial and flattering testimonial to the excellence of his moral character. It is disgraceful that this should be possible, it is still more disgraceful that when the attention of the judges has been called to this grave abuse and an apparently practicable and efficient remedy suggested they should refuse to put it into effect." Commenting on long delays in disposing of cases in the Superior and Circuit courts, Gregory minced few words: "The truth is, our two courts of general jurisdiction are in an acephalous, anarchic condition. The judges seem unable to agree, except with the greatest difficulty, on anything, and when they act in a collective capacity and with a divided responsibility, the results of their deliberations are sometimes little short of scandalous." And on a matter that would vex and occupy the attention of the Association in the future, Gregory was especially to the point: "Our judges take too much part in politics. I can not think that a judge on the bench is justified in carrying on an active campaign, either for a nomination or an election to a political office. When he does so, his judicial duties must necessarily be neglected and that calm judicial temper of mind so desirable in a judge is certain to be more or less ruffled."

3.

Other matters of importance to the legal profession in these years occupied the time and attention of many Association members, acting mostly in committee.

One accomplishment—raising standards for admission to the bar—was the culmination of a long and sustained drive. Not until 1841, precisely 23 years after Illinois became a state, and for over three decades thereafter was there any specific rule concerning such admission. Even then, the rule adopted was simple: Admission was granted after oral and often cursory examination in open court. This prevailed until a year after the formation of the Chicago Bar Association, one of whose earliest goals was not only to attack unlicensed practitioners but also to improve requirements of those seeking legitimately to become lawyers.

For over 20 years, the Association persisted in this campaign. Typical of its efforts was a resolution, drawn in 1878 by its Committee on Legal Education, that described the method of examination of candidates for admission as "defective and wholly inadequate" and went on to say that as a consequence, "many incompetent persons, not learned in law, are licensed as attorneys and counselors and thereby the profession and the public are alike injured." The resolution called on the state Supreme Court to set new standards and methods, notably the appointment of three learned and competent members of the bar in each of the state's three judicial divisions to constitute boards of examiners who would test all applicants. These examinations would be in writing, encompassing not only legal studies but also "the common branches of an English education." Moreover, each applicant would be required to have studied three years in the office of a practicing lawyer or in an established law school or partly in each.

The resolution aroused brisk argument. Some scorned it as an insult to the judges of the Appellate Court, then in charge of such examinations, and others sought to soften this implied affront by proposing that the Appellate Court appoint the examiners. The requirement of written questions and answers was criticized by some as too severe a test, and Myra Bradwell objected particularly to the resolution's suggested criticism that examinations by the Appellate Court in respective districts localized them: "The local bar would be more likely to know of an improper person making application for admission than they would if an examination were conducted 200 miles away. Many of the young men making application for admission are poor and it is quite a task upon their impoverished pockets to require them to pay railroad fare and hotel bills in a foreign city, in order to be examined by the Supreme Court."

The outcome was a compromise in which educational requirements were fulfilled with a law school diploma after two years of study or a certificate attesting to an equal period spent in a reputable law office. In 1889, the Committee on Legal Education, headed by James B. Bradwell, approved the two-year rule but offered additional counsel: "Your committee is strongly of the opinion that a general education is of great advantage to a young man intending to fit himself for the bar and while they do not make this as a recommendation, they incline to the opinion that perhaps those who have enjoyed the advantages of such an education might properly be admitted to the bar upon a shorter period of professional study than those who have not had such training."

The subject provoked much discussion at many meetings of the Association. At one meeting in 1893, such educators as Henry Wade Rogers, president of Northwestern University, and his stellar law professor, John H. Wigmore, came out in favor of a three-year college course of legal studies along with immersion in general subjects. But others were not so sure of the value of such a course or even of a college diploma. Thomas A. Moran, president of the Chicago College of Law, offered the suggestion that some men who could not spell well and were not blessed with much education sometimes became excellent lawyers. "I had a young man in my classes," he recalled, "who was not a good grammarian, could not spell all the words in the spelling book, worked at plumbing days and studied law nights, but had an excellent legal mind and will make his mark in the profession." Superior Court Judge James Goggin scorned the value of an American college diploma entirely. "A diploma from a college here," he declared, "is not equal to one from a college in Canada or England. No one who holds a diploma from a college here can recite twenty lines in the original from the Latin text books. Too much attention is paid to training in football, baseball, banjo practice and secret societies. A student who has a finger broken or receives a scar in saving a game of baseball considers it a higher honor than to receive a college diploma."

Continued discussion and work were carried on by subsequent Legal Education committees. One of them, in 1894, pushed especially hard for a commission with authority to control and supervise examinations, for the three-year course of study plus high school training or its equivalent in general education to be shown by a diploma or examination, and for abolition of admission to the bar on mere evidence of a law school diploma without examination. "We are convinced that three years is not too long a time," wrote its chairman, William Eliot Furness, "for a young man of average education and intelligence to prepare for the practice of law. Practice by men without sufficient training leads to mismanagement of cases, wastes the time of courts and juries and tends to bring the law into contempt in the eyes of the public. . . . It is doubtless true that practical experience under the eye of older advisers is a most valuable part of legal education. But this can be had without license as with it. The license to practice is not intended merely as a passport to the presence of the court but it certifies to the public that the holder is competent to manage legal business. If granted to incompetent persons, it becomes a snare to the client and an injury to the community at large."

The long campaign was climaxed on October 27, 1897, when the Association memorialized the state Supreme Court to take definite action. Julius Rosenthal, as chairman of a new Admissions Committee, itemized the results of innumerable defects in the existing system: "Unfit and unworthy men have been admitted. The time of the courts has been uselessly consumed. Progress has been impeded. Litigation has increased and justice has been delayed." He severely criticized the lack of uniform standards in the various Appellate Court districts and noted that students too often chose to take their examinations in districts where questions were known to be less difficult than in other districts: "Not even a fundamental knowledge of the three R's is necessary for admission." Too many fly-by-night law schools existed, giving two-year diplomas whether the recipients had attended classes diligently or not: "The lazy student desirous of becoming a professional man seeks the law as the easiest entrance gate. This is doubtless one of the chief causes of the great increase in the number of lawyers, many of whom are entirely unfitted for the exercise of their professional obligations to the client and to the state."

The Association's proposal was for the establishment by the

Supreme Court of a State Board of Law Examiners, with one member from each of the Appellate Court districts and one from the state at large, to hold examinations as before on the first Tuesday of each March, May, September, and December in Chicago, Springfield, Ottawa, and Mount Vernon. More significantly, the length of the required course of study for all applicants was to be extended from two to three years.

The proposal was adopted by the high court as Rule 39. Rosenthal, by this time head of one of the city's foremost firms and a specialist in probate and real estate law while still serving ably as librarian of the Chicago Law Institute, was named by the state Supreme Court to be the board's secretary, and George W. Wall, for two decades a Circuit Court judge, its president. The other members were Nathaniel W. Branson, a former state legislator and a lawyer of varied experience, and two County Court judges, James H. Stearns of Stephenson and William B. Wright of Effingham.

Even before the board met for the first time on December 7, 1897, in Mount Vernon, there was an outcry against Rule 39, notably from scores of students then enrolled in two-year courses who had expected to be admitted to practice on presentation of diplomas and now felt themselves victims of injustice unless Rule 39 was modified to exempt them from the three-year requirement. Nor were their minds put at ease when, of the six applicants who appeared at the board's initial two-day meeting, only one, William H. Craig of Shelbyville, passed the examination. In the *Chicago Legal News*, Judge Bradwell, its editor since the death of Myra Bradwell three years earlier, expressed his awe that Craig was so "strong in mind and body." For the possible benefit of other aspirants, he recorded what Craig had read to prepare himself: volumes by Blackstone and Kent and *Story on Contracts, Story's Equity Pleading, Smith and Bishop on Contracts, Gould and Stephenson on Pleadings, Bishop's Criminal Law, Greenleaf on Evidence, Underhill on Evidence, Martindale on Conveyances and Abstracts, Chitty's Pleadings,* and the statutes of the state. "Strictly speaking, Mr. Craig is the only one of his kind. He has had to pass through

an ordeal that no one in the state was ever subjected to before.
... He stands alone in his law examination, but it will not be
long before he will have hundreds of followers."

Agitation continued for modification of Rule 39. Protest
meetings were held by students, petitions were drawn up, and
organizations were formed. Many established members of the
profession expressed sympathy with the protesters. With super-
charged rhetoric, William F. Wiemers, a Circuit Court master
in chancery, wrote in Judge Bradwell's weekly: "All who have
had experience in the matter of making a 'bed rock' start in life
and who know the difficulties which beset those endeavoring,
by dint of their own efforts and practically without means, to
enter any one of the professions will realize that many of the
students affected by the new rule have struggled through years
of pinching poverty, practiced most heroic self-denial, sub-
sisted upon ten-cent meals, slept in garrets, mortgaged future
possibilities to furnish them the scant means to reach the
coveted prize of professional dignity and an opportunity for
a livelihood. After having almost completed this long and trying journey over the dreary waste of their preparatory struggles,
tottering from fatigue as it were, and with their resources
exhausted, to find, suddenly, their journey's end has been removed from them by another year, will work a hardship which
must draw forth a protest from every person capable of sym-
pathizing with them."

The students took their case to the state legislature. Toward
the close of the decade, that body, with but one dissenting
vote, passed an act requiring the Supreme Court to admit anyone who had been in the process of earning a two-year diploma
prior to the adoption of Rule 39. Thereupon, a group of those
who had been two-year students at the time of the new rule's
imposition filed a motion before the high court for admission
on presentation of their diplomas and also challenged the
court's right to prescribe rules for admission to the bar without
authority of the state legislature. Countering this action on
behalf of the Association were Julius Rosenthal, Abram M.
Pence, and Blewett Lee. The court's ruling was that it did have

the power to deal with admissions to the bar, and Rule 39 remained steadfast as a base from which other moves were instituted in subsequent years to raise standards of admission.

4.

Ironically, although the number of lawyers was increasing—by the century's end, there were 4,000 in Chicago—the average practitioner was finding no great financial boons. Many were entering law not as a means to gain wealth but as a quick way to achieve political influence. Changes were coming about swiftly. The development of corporations and the trend toward business monopolies in the century's final decade led to almost a parallel situation in law practice. When a number of companies combined to form one corporation, there was need for only a single law firm instead of several. Yet even the law firms, each with a specialist in a specific field, had the advantage over the individual practitioner engaged in general practice, for these hapless fellows were hampered by new institutions cutting into their ability to make money: Abstract and title-insurance companies were invading the field of real estate law, banks and trust companies were handling the settlement of estates, insurance firms were beginning to indemnify policyholders against risks that formerly needed the services of lawyers, and there was an increasing tendency of many litigants to make out-of-court settlements instead of engaging in prolonged and expensive lawsuits. Indeed, as he prepared to assume the presidency of the Chicago Bar Association in the first year of the new century, Stephen Strong Gregory deplored the conditions of the individual lawyer and noted regretfully that many good men were leaving the law for other professions and trades that would earn them more money.

Yet, for all the changing aspects of the profession, certain verities existed for the organization that, 25 years earlier, had been formed for the purpose of improving the administration of justice and the standards of the legal profession.

In this busy period, the long fight to suppress widespread

bribing of jurors was marked by notable victories. There had been some small triumphs in earlier years, but not until the election of Charles S. Deneen in 1896 as Cook County state's attorney was the widespread practice quelled to a substantial degree.

A member of a pioneer Illinois family, a graduate and trustee of the venerable McKendree College in downstate Lebanon, and a former state legislator, Deneen, a forceful and vigorous man, came to his new office with the largest vote ever cast for any county officer. Dutifully, Judge Bradwell reminded him in the *Chicago Legal News* that hundreds of prisoners languished in the pestilential Cook County jail awaiting trial, and while he cautioned Deneen that his was an office "that has been the ruin of quite a number of originally honest men for want of genuine firmness," he expressed confidence: "We believe that Mr. Deneen, when the tempter comes, as come he will, has firmness to say, as the Savior did when he was taken up to the top of an exceedingly high mountain by a nameless individual, 'Get thee behind me, Satan.'"

The Association had sought to put a halt to jury bribery not only by urging some of Deneen's predecessors to investigate intensively lawyers suspected of involvement on a wide scale—without any appreciable results—but also by passing resolutions calling for improvements in the method of selecting jurors; too often, according to complaints received by the Association, jury panels included persons who could not speak or understand English and some who were former inmates of penitentiaries and reform schools. In a swirl of activity, Deneen set out to put a considerable crimp in the ranks of jury bribers, and by the time his first four-year term was drawing to a close, he had broken up a rather formidable combine by sending several men to jail and forcing others to flee the state. Much of the information on which Deneen based his investigations and subsequent prosecutions resulted from a resolution of an Association Grievance Committee, headed by Frank Asbury Johnson, asking members who believed that verdicts in cases prosecuted or defended by them were obtained by unlawful evidence to furnish Deneen with every bit of pertinent information about such cases, principally the names of opposing attorneys, their clerks, and assistants or "all other persons present in the interest of such opposing party." Deneen also pressed forward, on urging of the Association, against unlicensed practitioners then plying a lucrative trade and obtained convictions against several disbarred attorneys charged with defrauding clients and with embezzlements.

Actually, his forays against the jury bribers and crooked lawyers were part of a vast pattern of convictions, ranging from those of a number of wife murderers—including Adolph Luetgert, who chopped his spouse into sausage stuffing—and dishonest election judges to embezzling bankers and such notorious aggregations of robbers as the Maxwell Street Gang, the Shevlin Gang, and the Market Street Gang. Reelected in 1900, Deneen built a powerful following and went on to a distinguished career, serving two terms as governor from 1905 to 1913 and as United States senator from 1925 to 1931.

The Chicago Bar Association

OBJECTS

1—To Maintain the Honor and Dignity of the Profession of the Law.

2—To Cultivate Social Intercourse among its Members.

3—To Increase its Usefulness by Promoting the due Administration of Justice.

THE CHICAGO BAR ASSOCIATION.—In this issue we publish the Constitution, By-Laws, Address of the Executive Committee, Names of the Officers, Committees and Members of the Bar Association, recently formed in this city. We have frequently in these columns urged the formation of bar associations in the county seats throughout the country, and of State associations, made up from the principal officers of the county associations, and an annual National Convention of lawyers, composed of delegates from the State associations. With a view of aiding in this work, we place before our readers the entire history of the formation of the Chicago Bar Association. The objects of the Association are by the II. Article of the Constitution declared to be " to maintain the honor and dignity of the profession of the law, to cultivate social intercourse among its members, and to increase its usefulness in promoting the due administration of justice."

Cover of Association charter (left). A notice (right) in the *Chicago Legal News* about formation of the Association. Chicago Bar Association

Farwell Hall, on Madison Street
west of Clark Street, to which the
Association moved in 1875.

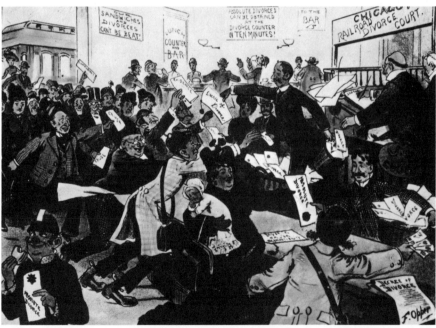

Criminal Courts Building and county jail in 1875 at Hubbard and Dearborn streets. Here Mary Todd Lincoln's insanity hearing was held, and Haymarket anarchists were sentenced to hang.

A cartoon about the "easy divorce" system in late 1870s.

The Union College of Law's 1877 graduating class.

94

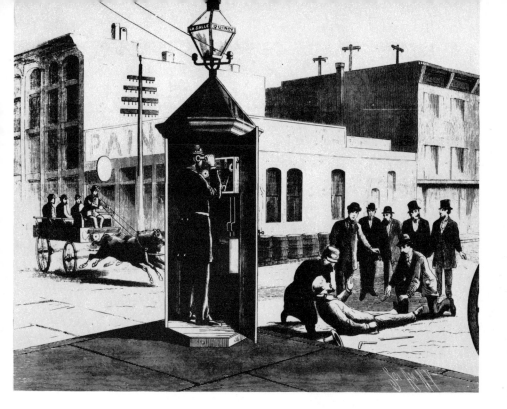

Early (1880) police alarm box (top). Chicago was the first city to adopt this telephone patrol system, two years after the telephone was put into service. This illustration from a contemporary magazine shows a patrol box at Quincy and La Salle streets. Illinois Bell Telephone Company

Grand Pacific Hotel (bottom), scene of early annual Association dinners and home of early Appellate Court of Illinois. Author's collection

Artist's sketch (top) of the bomb exploding in Haymarket Square.
Anarchy and Anarchists

Police Captain Michael J. Schaack (left), zealous foe of all radicals, commanded the roundup of anarchists, following the Haymarket bombing.
Anarchy and Anarchists

Judge Joseph E. Gary (top left), who presided over the trial of the Haymarket anarchists.

Chicago Historical Society

William Perkins Black (top right), Association member who forsook promising career to defend the Haymarket anarchists.

Chicago Historical Society

Governor John Peter Altgeld (right), as he appeared in 1893 when he pardoned the three remaining defendants convicted in Haymarket trial. Four others had been hanged; the eighth committed suicide.

Author's collection

Henry W. Blodgett, the United States District Court judge who was the central figure in an early controversy that shook the Association.

Chicago Historical Society

Typical courtroom of 1880s.

Chicago Bar Association

New Courts and New Hopes

1.

BEFORE THE CENTURY ENDED, the Association played a central role in what then seemed to be—and, indeed, was hailed as such—one of the brightest and most progressive social advances in American history.

For decades, concern had grown over the plight of Chicago children arrested by police for offenses ranging from robbery and assault with a deadly weapon to filching coal along railroad tracks, building bonfires in which to roast potatoes, playing ball in the streets, or stealing rides on railroad freight trains. Most of the youngsters—half under 14—were from poor families, a preponderance of them from new immigrant groups. When arrested, boys and girls—some already confirmed cocaine addicts or prostitutes—were thrown, however serious or slight the offense, into grimy police station cells. The rigidity of existing laws tended to treat young offenders as adult criminals, although some judges sought to circumvent these statutes by granting probation. Police courts had jurisdiction over most of those arrested, and children unable to furnish bail until their cases could be heard were kept in police station cells, often for as long as two weeks. Then they were tried by a justice of the peace or a police magistrate and if found guilty and could not pay assessed fines, were sent to the Chicago Reform School or to the noxious correctional institution known as the Bridewell, where they were placed in the same section with hardened criminals to serve sentences that were—in the term of the era—

"laid out" at the rate of 50 cents a day. In 1871, Myra Bradwell inveighed against the Chicago Reform School's "unwarranted and illegal practice of seizing poor children in the streets of our city whose only crime was poverty and against the protest of their parents and in defiance of the law of the land, confining them for years within the walls of this prison and making them work for its benefit." Her investigation into the institution had an ancillary effect by calling attention to the activities of its superintendent, Robert Turner, who pleaded guilty that June to smuggling silks and was fined $300 in United States District Court.

Not much was done by the city's officialdom to assuage these conditions, although the Board of Education established the John Worthy Manual Training School at the Bridewell. After 1879, several "industrial schools" were set up to teach children a trade, but thievery was the prime trade learned there by many children picked up for as minor an offense as staying out late at night and assigned to the schools with young toughs reared by prostitutes, pimps, and gangsters.

The local organization most concerned was the Chicago Woman's Club. Beginning in 1883, its membership, which included society leaders and ardent feminists, pressed for improvements in the treatment of jailed children, organized school classes in the Bridewell, persuaded authorities to hire several matrons, campaigned against placing delinquent children in the county poorhouse, and continued to agitate for progressive laws in children's behalf. In 1891, an Association member, Timothy D. Hurley, prominent in Catholic charities, drafted a bill providing for a separate court to hear cases involving children and persuaded Rep. Joseph A. O'Donnell to introduce it in the state legislature. The bill provided, among other things, that if the child were dependent, neglected, or delinquent, the court could commit custody to one of several organizations devoted to caring for such youngsters. It failed to pass, primarily because of the opposition of such representatives of officialdom as John G. Shortall, president of the Illinois Humane Society, and Oscar L. Dudley, superintendent of the

Glenwood Industrial School, who denounced Hurley's bill as a flagrant example of "advanced legislation." In 1895, the Chicago Woman's Club drew up a bill that proposed not only a separate court but also a system of probation to replace incarceration, but because of technical flaws certain to have it declared unconstitutional, it was abandoned.

At a joint meeting on October 28, 1898—when no less than 575 youngsters were locked up in the Bridewell—the club, the Illinois State Board of Charities, and other organizations, all led by Julia Lathrop and Lucy Flower of Jane Addams' Hull House, passed a resolution asking the Chicago Bar Association to name a committee to survey the situation and propose passable legislation. A committee named by President George Follansbee was headed by Harvey B. Hurd, who, in his variegated career since becoming a lawyer in 1848, had been a fervid abolitionist in pre-Civil War days, a founder of the suburb of Evanston, the reviser over a five-year period from 1869 to 1874 of the state statutes and their annual editor ever since, the originator in 1886 of legislation creating the Chicago Sanitary District and in 1892 of the Torrens system of registering land titles, and a humanist concerned with child welfare as a pioneer organizer of the Children's Aid Society of Chicago. Hurd and the other committee members—Ephraim Banning, John W. Elg, Edwin Burritt Smith, and Merritt Starr—met frequently to discuss how to frame workable legislation. Hurd called on Hurley for support from the organization he headed, the Catholic Visitation and Aid Society. "I've had too much experience in legislation," he told Hurley, "not to realize I'll need all the help I can get and I need your help and the backing of your society."

On December 10, the committee met in Hurd's office with a large group of interested parties, including Hurley; Misses Flower and Lathrop; Dr. Hastings H. Hart, superintendent of the Illinois Children's Home and Aid Society; A. G. Lane, superintendent of schools; John L. Whitman, superintendent of the county jail; and Rep. John F. Newcomer, who had indicated he would introduce in the state legislature whatever

bill was ultimately drawn. Out of this and subsequent discussions, Hurd prepared the draft of a bill for submission to
his fellow committee members. Revised and amended after
three weeks of intensive work, a bill was hammered out and
made public as Association sponsored. It provided for establishment of a Juvenile Court, in which a Circuit Court judge
would hear cases involving offenses charged to children 16
years or younger. No court or magistrate was to commit a child
under 12 unable to post bail to a jail or police station but instead to a suitable place elsewhere. The law took great pains
to avoid the trappings of a typical court action. Instead of a
complaint or indictment against a child, a petition would be
presented to the court; instead of a warrant, a summons would
be issued. No child accused of an offense would be seized
by police but would be brought in by a parent, guardian, or
a probation officer. The bill expressly forbade keeping any
child in a jail or any enclosure in which adults were confined.
Children found guilty of a charge would not be sent to a prison
or reformatory but would be committed to the care of a probation officer or to a friendly institution. Court proceedings
would be decidedly informal, with no strict adherence to the
rules of evidence. The prime objective would be to determine
what course of action was best for the child and to follow
through, if possible.

On February 7, 1899, Newcomer introduced the bill—officially
"An Act to Regulate the Treatment and Control of Dependent,
Neglected and Delinquent Children"—in the Illinois House of
Representatives, and Solon H. Case introduced it in the Senate.
Hurd, Banning, and Smith testified on behalf of the Association
at hearings before a joint legislative judiciary committee. Support came from many quarters, and Albert C. Barnes, first
assistant to State's Attorney Charles S. Deneen, spoke for most
of the backers of the bill when he told the State's Attorneys
Association in Ottawa: "The fundamental idea of the law is
that the state must step in and exercise guardianship over a
child found under such adverse social or individual conditions
as develop crime. To that end it must not wait to deal with

him as now in jails, Bridewells or reformatories or after he has become criminal in tastes and habits, but must seize upon the first indications of the propensity." Barnes urged treatment of a young offender not as a criminal but as "a ward of the state, to receive practically the care, custody and discipline that are accorded the neglected and dependent child and which, as the act states, shall approximate as nearly as possible that which should be given by its parents. Embodying, as it does, the ripest thought upon this question, the results of scientific inquiry and special study of the causes and conditions of crime, and the lessons from practical experience with various corrective and repressive agencies employed not only in this country but in Europe, this act, unless thwarted by persistent and unnatural foes, by niggardly means for carrying out its provisions or by the assaults of those who seek to defeat rather than promote beneficial legislation, will prove the dawn of a new era in our criminal history and of a brighter day for the people of Illinois."

Duly passed with scant debate by both legislative houses, the act establishing a Juvenile Court was signed into law on April 21, 1899, by Gov. John R. Tanner and became effective on July 1. The court it provided for was not only the first of its kind in the United States—within four years similar legislation would be passed in Wisconsin, New York, Maryland, Ohio, Indiana, and Colorado—but also in the world, with spreading acceptance of its basic principle of specialization in the treatment of children's behavior problems.

Symbolic of its distinctive role, the first courtroom was set up not in the courthouse in the center of the city, but in a building on Halsted Street, across from Hull House, that had schoolrooms and a gymnasium and was furnished so amply that angry critics of the court denounced it as "a swell boarding house for boys." Circuit Court Judge Richard S. Tuthill, with a solid record of judicial service, was selected to preside, and highest hopes were expressed, especially by those praised or derided as "the child-savers," for the court's future. Much still needed to be done, however, for the bill, despite its virtually revolutionary features, provided for no supplementary agencies to compel enforcement. Without sufficient appropriations to hire probation officers, it became necessary for private organizations to provide such personnel; Hurley's Catholic Visitation and Aid Society furnished some funds for salaries, and he himself served as the chief probation officer, with Alzina Parsons Stevens, a kinetic Hull House resident prominent in the labor union movement of the early 1890s, as his first appointee. The new mayor, Carter H. Harrison, Jr., offered his cooperation and assigned an officer from each of the city's 16 police districts to serve as probation officers in their areas. Mrs. Joseph T. Bowen, a wealthy society woman who was one of Jane Addams' closest friends and was devoted to social causes, raised money to supplement probation officers' salaries, and, as president of the Juvenile Court Committee, rented an old house used by the Illinois Industrial Association as a detention home and paid workmen to refurbish it as a haven for neglected or abandoned children awaiting hearings before Judge Tuthill.

For all its innovative character and laudable intentions, the Juvenile Court system, as the years progressed, accumulated external and internal problems. Despite official Association approval and its deep involvement in drafting and passing the landmark law, some lawyers objected to it because their services were not needed since the bill did not provide for adversary proceedings. Many politicians increasingly disliked the new system because they could no longer do favors for worried families whose children had been apprehended and because Judge Tuthill and court officers opposed all efforts to inject politics into the selection of probation officers and caseworkers. Some considered the new law "socialistic" because they claimed the state took children from their parents.

As time went on, many directly involved in the court's creation and administration came to take much broader views about juvenile delinquency and crime. While agreeing that the Juvenile Court system was a massive step forward in substituting treatment of children's behavior problems for imprisonment with adult criminals, they were aware that it was not a final solution. Julia Lathrop, who went on to become first head of the Federal Children's Bureau, saw the court and system as "wise contrivances," but she knew they were hardly substitutes for a wholesome, orderly, decent family life: "These contrivances wholly restore some children, partly restore others and sometimes fail, but they never seal up the sources of delinquency." Hurley, when he was elected to the Superior Court bench in 1921, vowed to do what he could in eliminating conditions that bred the social and family ills leading to juvenile truancy, dependency, and delinquency: "These, as a rule, are disorderly houses, gambling houses and ill-governed houses and are all classed under the law of nuisances and can be abated by the long arm of this court. No ill-governed house that encourages the visitation of either boys or girls or has been instrumental in their downfall should be permitted to operate."

Judge Julian W. Mack—who succeeded Judge Tuthill and proved, in his years on the Juvenile Court bench, to be one of the most sympathetic, social-minded, and understanding jurists with children who appeared before him—knew he could do only so much by the time cases came into his courtroom. The Juvenile Court, for all its benefits, was only a palliative for social ailments, he told the Minnesota Bar Association. "The great thing is to prevent reaching that condition in which they have to be dealt with in any court, and we are not doing our duty to the children of today when we fail to uproot the evils that are leading them into careers of delinquency, when we fail not merely to uproot the wrongs, but to implant, in place of it, the positive good." Judge Mack was especially adamant in defending the court against lawyers who objected to their exclusion from proceedings. He often pointed out at Association meetings that children before him were not being tried in the strict sense nor were they defendants in a legal battle. They were really wards of the state, by terms of the new law, and the judge more or less acted as the parent. Occasionally he did permit a lawyer to take part informally in a case but only as a friend of the family involved. Judge Mack was so effective that in 1906 when the Illinois Supreme Court ordered him transferred to the Appellate Court, a flood of letters from social reformers led by Jane Addams' Hull House contingent compelled a reversal of the decision, and he continued for another year, during which he helped in the development of what came to be known as the "Chicago school" of social welfare, which spawned such notable and energetic leaders as Jessie Binford and her Juvenile Protective Association, Sophonisba Breckinridge and the Abbott sisters, Edith and Grace, and the construction of the Juvenile Detention Home and the start of psychiatric-counseling research.

Other judges followed Judge Mack, but longest in years of service—from 1923 until her retirement in 1933—was one of Myra Bradwell's protégés, Mary Margaret Bartelme. After winning her bachelor of laws degree from Northwestern University Law School in 1894 with a thesis on spendthrift trusts, she had practiced law, then served as public guardian of Cook County, and with formation of the Juvenile Court, was appointed a judicial assistant. Following ten years' service, she was elected a Circuit Court judge in 1923—the first woman jurist in the state's history—and she was assigned fully to the Juvenile Court. In the next decade on the Juvenile Court bench, she achieved worldwide fame. Social workers and civic leaders from many countries gave a visit to her courtroom top priority. The philosophy that guided her decisions was idyllic and uncomplicated: "There are no bad children, there are confused, neglected children, love-starved and resentful children. These are the ones who find their way into the court, and what they need most I try to give them—understanding and a fresh start in the right direction." Active in Association work as a member of the Public Service and Delinquent Children committees, she organized what came to be called the Mary Bartelme Club by transforming her West Side dwelling in 1914 into a home for dependent girls; by the time she retired in 1933, there were three such establishments in which close to 2,000 troubled adolescent girls had been helped to assume better lives.

In subsequent years, in an increasingly complex society, the original concepts of the Juvenile Court remained steadfast, but there were many changes, ranging from adjustments in the age limits of juvenile offenders to new commitment procedures that, critics charged, did little to bring about the desired result of rehabilitation. Having been so closely involved in the court's creation, the Association, through its various Juvenile Delinquency committees, kept close surveillance on the system and made proposals for improvements, some of which were adopted and some of which were rejected. It pressed constantly for better methods of rehabilitation, for the establishment of a public agency to coordinate efforts of voluntary social agencies, and for clarification of contradictions in laws dealing with youthful offenders. In 1948, the name of the court was changed to Family Court, but in 1965, after various studies by legal and sociological groups and recommendations by Association committees, a new Juvenile Court Act was passed by the state legislature restoring the original name, setting age limits of boys at 17 and of girls at 18, replacing the hitherto informal colloquies between judge, defendant, and social worker with stricter rules of court procedure and evidence, and strengthening methods for the protection, guidance, care, custody, and guardianship of boys and girls deemed delinquent, neglected, dependent, or in need of supervision. As recently as the early 1970s, however, complaints were rife that the system was imperfect, most markedly in that truants and runaways were locked up with delinquents; and the plaint of Juvenile Court Judge William Sylvester White had a familiar ring to it: "The basic problem is that we haven't supplied the kind of institutions and facilities in sufficient numbers or given them sufficient strength to do the job we know must be done. The court is aware that anti-social behavior of a child often is induced by the poor home in which he lives. But too frequently the judge's choice is between returning the child to that home or incarcerating him."

2.

Two weeks before the Juvenile Court Act was signed into law, in 1899, the Association held its 25th anniversary banquet in the Palmer House, a gala event attended by most of its 700 members. Such past presidents as Benjamin F. Ayer (1875), John N. Jewett (1877), Judge Farlin Quigley Ball (1884), James B. Bradwell (1885), Frederick A. Smith (1890), and Thomas P. Dent (1895) spoke about their terms of office and the Association's accomplishments and the goals still to be attained, but it remained for Edgar A. Bancroft, his own Association presidency six years away, to close the evening by enunciating lofty aims for the future.

He dwelled on the recent past to note Association victories in helping to frame legislation for a new state revenue statute, to create a commission to revise the code of practice and procedure, and as a capstone of the decade, to establish the Juvenile Court. He paid special tribute to the work of Grievance committees that had initiated action to disbar unworthy practitioners—"those who bear the name of lawyer but dishonor it and use it as the plunderers of the poor and ignorant"— and stressed the imperative need for emboldening such activity, for without it the legal profession would degenerate "to a mere branch of business, and to a very selfish and narrow branch of a very selfish business." He urged the Association to be vigilant in matters involving not only lawyers but also judges. He noted the growing rise of the forces of industry and trade that had made of many lawyers administrators and counselors rather than what he termed "forensic fighters." The Association needed to become a real force for good, and he predicted that it would: "With it shall come a keener sense of responsibility for the acts of every member of our profession, a wider influence in the community, an increasing power for good upon the individual members. With this increased social and professional unification will come a greater courage and vigor in attacking abuses that afflict or cloud our name, wherever they appear." He deplored the fact that, for all the Association's efforts, admission standards were still loose enough so that even a convicted felon could gain entry into the ranks. In a resounding finish, he urged upon the members the maintenance and strengthening of public trust: "Trust so large that no surety company has capital adequate to guarantee them. Trust so delicate and priceless that no indemnity is possible if the trust is betrayed. Trust so broad and comprehensive, so penetrating and universal that, if destroyed, the very institutions of modern society, commercial, financial and political, would disintegrate and fall in ruin."

As if in direct response to Bancroft's call for higher standards, the Association embarked on a number of projects. It sought constantly to persuade the state courts to adopt stricter rules on the granting of certificates of good moral character. Periodically, its Committee on Legal Education criticized state Supreme Court rules, which, despite the existence of the State Board of Law Examiners, still had loopholes, such as the fact that sufficient evidence of a high school general education was a passing grade in a test administered by any teacher rather than a local superintendent of schools. The committee also inveighed against inadequate correspondence law courses as far below proper standards and urged nonrecognition of such courses. In an assault on the still-prevalent ranks of bogus attorneys, the 1904 Grievance Committee recommended publication and circulation of a list of persons in illegal practice as had been done in 1899. Within six months, a bill which declared the illegal practice of law a misdemeanor was drawn and passed by the state legislature. Following up on this legislation, the Association obtained the conviction, between 1907 and 1910, of some 100 offenders, most of whom, as recipients of unfavorable publicity, took up other forms of livelihood.

Beyond doubt, the Grievance committees in this period were the most hardworking of them all. No single year from 1901 through 1911 was without a disbarment; the highest numbers were 18 in 1906 and 35 in 1911. These committees met at least once a week to hear complaints and sift evidence and draw up, if merited, essential petitions for official action by the state Supreme Court. In some years, as many as 80 to 100 complaints were dealt with.

In 1909, a dispute arose with Cook County's energetic state's attorney, John E. Wayman, who insisted that the Grievance

Committee turn over to him all its material on pending cases and stop its own investigations and inquiries. Wayman issued his demand through the newspapers before making his formal request to the committee. The Association refused to yield, and the case was presented to the state Supreme Court, where Wayman filed printed arguments intimating that the Association actually employed its power, in disbarment proceedings, to protect its members and to persecute nonmembers. Furnished with evidence to the contrary, the high court's response was to cancel the state's attorney's role in the process of disbarments, holding that the use of his name was a mere formality. Henceforth—until further changes in ensuing years—the state's attorney's office would be bypassed in disciplinary procedures, with full responsibility placed on the Association.

3.

In this decade too came the climax to years of struggle against an inefficient and flagrantly corrupt judicial institution originally designed to be a "poor man's court."

From its very first days, the Association's minutes were filled with criticisms of justices of the peace and police magistrates who heard minor civil cases—so-called clothesline cases—and petty criminal matters. The system had a long history and tradition, for even before Illinois became a state in 1818, justices of the peace were its earliest judicial officers, appointed by territorial governors along with other civil officers in counties and townships for the preservation of peace and good order. As the population increased in the years after statehood, the number of justices of the peace and police magistrates grew in Chicago and elsewhere in Cook County, but the quality of justice grew worse. The state constitution of 1870, in addition to setting up a revised court system, provided that justices of the peace, previously elected, were to be appointed by the governor on recommendation of local higher-court judges. As previously, these officials were not salaried but were paid by fees and costs collected from the litigants who filed suits before them. In far too many cases, the appointees were political hacks of low character and virtually devoid of legal training or ability. Too often, they decided cases arbitrarily in favor of plaintiffs to gain continued patronage from the complainants. The system often worked excessive hardships on those who lived or did business in Chicago because, under existing law that conferred countywide jurisdiction on justices of the peace, many unmeritorious and harassing suits for small sums were filed before justices of the peace in distant sections of Cook County. In many such instances, cases were set for an hour before a defendant's train arrived, and the hapless fellow would find that a judgment had already been entered against him.

Proposals by the Association for reform of the system or its complete abandonment intensified during the late 1880s. Leader in the campaign was Charles E. Pope, who drew up a resolution in 1888 calling for abolition of justices of the peace and the establishment instead of three courts for the main divisions of the city—South, North, and West—each with a competent and trained lawyer as judge, who would be paid by fixed salary and whose decisions were subject to appeal only if the amount in a specific controversy exceeded $50. "We are all cognizant," declared Pope, speaking in support of his resolution, "of the existing evils in the justice courts, especially when the courts have constables of such character as are now seen at them. We propose to abolish the name of justice of the peace. So great is the odium attached to these words that few good men are willing to take the places. The questions as to what power the proposed new courts shall have is left to the discretion of the legislature. As to the question of fees, we all know the difficulties of getting an unprejudiced judgment from justices. The justice depends too much on his fees. If these fees are paid to the city, the city can afford to pay salaries to the justices, thereby removing prejudices from them."

The Association's Committee on Amendment of the Law was directed to prepare a report, and that December 20, its chairman, Harvey B. Hurd, offered a resolution calling for the Association to recommend that the legislature take official action to replace the justices of the peace with what he called "district courts" in all cities of 50,000 or more, with well-qualified judges appointed by the governor or elected to serve four-year terms and paid by designated salaries instead of fees. The resolution to amend the constitution in this way was promptly defeated in the legislature, primarily because of strong opposition from a bloc of legislators representing smaller cities and others who saw personal advantage in retaining the system. "They feared," reported Hurd to the Association in his 1889 year-end report, "that the method that might be adopted would disturb the plan of dividing the offices between the political parties."

But the fight for reform continued throughout the 1890s. Unable to arouse significant action in Springfield, the Association cooperated in civil suits where defendants claimed they had been defrauded by secret deals between justices of the peace and attorneys for plaintiffs. "There is in this justice practice in the city of Chicago," concluded one Grievance Committee report weighing disbarment proceedings against such an attorney, "a crying evil which should be remedied, and against which the hand of every lawyer of standing and every lover of justice should be raised." New resolutions were composed, new bills devised. A significant editorial in the *Chicago Legal News* was headed "REFORM THE JUSTICE OF THE PEACE SYSTEM: THIS IS THE CRY OF THE BAR ASSOCIATION AND OF MANY MEMBERS OF THE BAR AS WELL AS THE GENERAL PUBLIC" and touched upon the core of the problem: "It is mainly the fee system. If the compensation of the judges of our courts of record was derived from fees, it would have substantially the same effect upon those judges. We can remember when John M. Wilson was judge of the Common Pleas Court and George Manierre judge of the Circuit Court, that these judges received a fee of $1.50 in every appeal case, $2.50 in every common law case and $3 in every chancery suit, and although these two judges were as honest and as capable as any two judges that ever sat on the bench in Cook County, they ran a race with each other to see which could obtain the most fees. They held court evenings to clear their dockets and make room for new cases, for parties who brought collection suits would very generally bring them in the court that had the fewest cases upon the docket. The tendency of the fee system, even with these learned jurists, was to make them exceedingly technical and miserly of the time devoted to the hearing of motions and the trial of cases. The fee system was as great an evil then, in our courts of record, as it is today under our justice of the peace system."

Subjected to increasing pressure, the state legislature, in 1904, adopted an amendment to the 1870 constitution that called for the establishment of a municipal court for Chicago. Justices of the peace were to be limited to jurisdiction in the territory outside city limits. At the same time, the Chicago Charter Convention called by the Civic Federation, the activist reform group headed by George "Buzz Saw" Cole, named a committee of three Association members—Circuit Court Judge Murray F. Tuley, John S. Miller, and John P. Wilson—and three laymen—Mayor Carter H. Harrison, Jr., and industrialists Bernard A. Eckhart and Bernard E. Sunny—to secure the drafting and passage of an act to establish a municipal court for Chicago.

The man they chose to create the bill was Hiram T. Gilbert, a legal scholar who had become an authority on ancient German and Roman law before opening a Chicago law office in 1888. Gilbert wanted one court of record in Cook County, with jurisdiction over every sort of case through branches presided over by individual judges. But this was not possible under the state constitution, so he proposed in his bill—along with the sought-for eradication of justices of the peace and constables— the creation of a court with jurisdiction over civil and criminal cases involving no more than $500 and authorization for judges of this court and those of the Superior and Circuit courts to form a manpower pool to be apportioned among the three courts as the burden of litigation required. A chief justice was to preside over the system, with power to set up branch courts, assign judges, prepare and supervise court calendars, and attend to records and accounts of the court's clerk and bailiff. Gilbert also advocated such procedural reforms as oral charges to juries, and, most importantly, nearly unlimited power to judges of the new court to make their own rules, subject only to review by the state Supreme Court.

Gilbert's bill was considered by many to be so novel—even radical—that three weeks after it was presented to the legislature on January 24, 1905, 72 lawyers and judges introduced a substitute measure that, while it retained many of his administrative reforms, considerably weakened Gilbert's concept of the new court. He angrily protested that it would not be much more than a glorified justice of the peace system and argued vigorously against the alternative bill. After many bitter sessions, a compromise bill, adopting some of Gilbert's proposals and some of those in the substitute bill, was drawn; and the long years of effort ended with passage by the legislature that May 18 of "An Act in Relation to a Municipal Court in the City of Chicago" and its adoption by the city's voters on November 17.

Gilbert still maintained that the amended act would impair the usefulness of the court and continued to work for revision, a goal reached with passage of an act in 1907 amending certain features. Whatever his or his opponents' feelings about the final result, the establishment of the Municipal Court was decidedly a judicial innovation and at the time was widely admired as a major improvement over the justice of the peace system. As amended, it called for election of a chief justice and 27 associate judges who would deal with civil actions involving $1,000 or less, all infractions of city ordinances, and all crimes calling for fines or for imprisonment in jail.

For the first election of a chief justice and 27 judges to the new court, the Association joined with the Civic Federation, the Union League Club, the Standard Club, the City Club, and a dozen other civic and businessmen's organizations to form the Chicago League for the Election of Good Municipal Court Judges. Major Edgar B. Tolman, head of a 20-man Association committee—its first on candidates—appeared before both major parties to urge nomination of well-qualified men. To a rather

skeptical Democratic "harmonizing committee" in the Grand
Pacific Hotel, he insisted that the election league wanted to
work with the politicians for the common good and not against
them. "You set the standard this time," he said. "Other nominating bodies are likely to follow. If an inferior bench be
elected, it will be difficult to raise the standard subsequently."

The list of Democratic candidates included nine former
justices of the peace, some with relatively good reputations and
some of lesser standing, and five aldermen. The Republican
slate—submitted to the election league for inspection and
examination before being made public—contained mostly high-
caliber lawyers. Gilbert was the Democrats' candidate for chief
justice, and Harry Olson, who had been a dynamic prosecutor
for ten years under State's Attorneys Deneen and John J.
Healy, was the Republicans' candidate. A group of insurgent
Democrats, backed by the newspapers published by William
Randolph Hearst, entered a ticket under the banner of the
Independence League.

Throughout the 11-week campaign, the Association figured
prominently, issuing, along with the Independence League and
the Lawyers' Association—the latter a fledgling rival group—
sporadic reports on candidates' qualifications. One such report
only three weeks before the November 6 election challenged
the fitness of various candidates on all three tickets and drew
angry rebukes from party managers and the candidates themselves. "STIR OVER BAR REPORT. CLASSIFICATION OF
BENCH CANDIDATES PROVES SENSATION OF THE
HOUR" read a headline in the *Chicago Record-Herald*. The
result was a Republican landslide, with only one Democrat,
Thomas B. Lantry—endorsed by both the Association and the
Independence League—squeezing into the ranks of winners.
Especially gratifying to the Association was the fact that more
than half of the winners carried the Association's endorsement.

It was a welcome victory, and the general mood was optimistic. Olson ascended the chief justice's seat to hold that place for
24 years, longer than any other man in the court's history.
Progressive minded and with an intense interest in the psycho-

logical makeup of criminals, he instituted reforms in that area, culminating in the establishment in 1914 of a laboratory for the study of abnormalities in defendants, and was instrumental in setting up such specific branches as the Domestic Relations, Morals, and Boys courts. As the years progressed, there were periodic complaints from the public, legislators, law enforcement officers, and the Association itself about the poor caliber of some of the judges and excessive political factors in their selection. Yet Olson remained a devout evangelist, inducing some 40 large cities throughout the country to adopt the court plan that he constantly insisted served the mass of citizens to their best advantage.

The future of the Municipal Court would be troubled and turbulent—two decades after its establishment, Gilbert expressed the belief of many that it had more or less fallen into disrepute because of political domination and too many inept judges—but six months after the new court heard its first case, many Chicagoans were quick to agree with the euphoric estimate of Stanley Waterloo that appeared in the *Review of Reviews*: "It has made a clean, wholesome American atmosphere in the judicial strata lying next to the ground in Chicago. Police methods have undergone a vast change for the better. The notorious collection agencies and the shyster lawyers have found business unprofitable. The straw bailer is of the past. The influential alderman has lost his 'pull' in interference with the administration of justice. The poor have found speedy redress for wrongs and the powerful cannot oppress."

4.

The Association in this period was constantly concerned with other matters relating to the judiciary.

Its efforts were not always successful. In his year-end president's report in 1902, Edwin M. Ashcraft found cause for complaint. "Your president is much dissatisfied and finds much to criticize in the work of the Association during the year. Much more could and should have been done. For two years, the Association has urged that certain of the judges be assigned to hear chancery cases. The Association appears to have no influence in the matter. It has no means of making its suggestions effective." Deploring the lack of unified action on recommendations for judges, Ashcraft declared, "If three lawyers were consulted, at least four opinions were obtained as to what was best to do, and the members were equally divided as to at least six different methods of making its influence felt, with the result that it had little influence."

Ashcraft's admonitions appeared to yield results in June 1903, with what was termed a "bar primary"—the first to shift from a citywide vote to one of only Association members—in the upcoming election of 14 Circuit Court judges and one Superior Court judge. Sent to the Association's 830 members were letters giving instructions about the time and manner of casting votes and stating this óbjective: "At every election of judges, the lawyer is appealed to by his clients, friends and neighbors, for information as to the comparative merits of the candidates. It has been deemed best by the Board of Managers for the Bar Association, as a whole, to furnish the public such information by the members expressing their preference for fifteen candidates. All of the political parties desiring to nominate candidates for the bench have done so and they are now all before the public. It is the duty of the Bar Association to register its deliberate conviction on this question and of every member to vote and use his utmost influence to select the very best men for the places. It is presumed that every candidate is personally known or has a reputation that is known to every practicing lawyer. A canvass among the lawyers is therefore unnecessary and you are asked to cast your vote at once."

Association officials considered its primary a relative success —one of the few in these years—because 660 of the total active membership cast votes in a mail ballot and because 11 candidates of the 15 on the bar primary ticket were elected and the remaining four received the most votes among those not elected.

The Association also plumped soundly for more compensation for judges and dealt with other issues that ranged from whether all judges should wear robes during court sessions to such serious matters as charges against Arthur H. Chetlain, a judge of the Superior Court. The judge, who in his youth had served as a messenger between the American legations in Paris and London during the Franco-Prussian War and later was first assistant corporation counsel under Mayor Hempstead Washburne in the early 1890s, had been on the bench since 1894. In May 1906, allegations that he had engaged in various improper activities and unsavory financial transactions appeared in the newspapers. In response, Judge Chetlain requested that the Association conduct an inquiry. "Quite conscious as I am," he wrote, "that there is much in these accusations as to improvidence and lack of proper prudence in incurring considerable pecuniary obligations which now greatly embarrass and distress me, I am equally conscious that never has my judicial conduct been influenced or affected by any consideration which I would not willingly submit to the scrutiny of the profession and the public."

The Association's Judiciary Committee—headed by Lessing Rosenthal, son of the esteemed legal veteran Julius Rosenthal, and comprising Clarence A. Burley, Joseph H. Defrees, a future Association president, and Walter S. Holden—undertook the unpleasant but necessary task. At Judge Chetlain's request, the hearings were open to the public and began on July 2 in the courtroom of United States District Court Judge Peter S. Grosscup and continued throughout that month and in October and November.

Fifty witnesses appeared, and the eventual transcript ran to 2,100 pages. Testimony disclosed that the judge, among other things, had ruled in favor of a Jacob Kruckstein in a mandamus proceeding while Kruckstein held his promissory note; had improperly accepted, without customary investigation, a close friend and creditor, Matthew S. Baldwin, as surety on a defendant's bail bond that was later forfeited; had dismissed charges of forgery of a part of a City Council record against William Loeffler, a friend to whom the judge owed money; and had repeatedly appointed his minute clerk, Edwin J. Zimmer— to whom he owed $1,500—as a receiver, despite complaints of improper conduct against Zimmer. Judge Chetlain, evidence showed, evidently was a sucker for blue-sky ventures. He had served as a director of a highly speculative gold-mining company in Puerto Rico and had induced various attorneys who appeared before him to invest in an equally risky lumber syndicate. Virtually all his investments had soured so that his debts amounted to over $39,000, and even his salary as a judge had been pledged to creditors, some of them lawyers representing clients in his courtroom.

After a thorough investigation, the committee found Judge Chetlain guiltless of actual corruption but certainly guilty of conduct unbecoming a judge, since his reckless actions "seriously impaired his usefulness in that high office." The censure did not prompt Judge Chetlain to resign; he stayed on until 1910, after which he practiced law for many years until his death in 1940 at 92.

Reflecting on Judge Chetlain's hapless investments, the committee sternly advised other jurists similarly inclined: "The person who fills that office must hold himself aloof from such activities as not only require his devotion to a business enterprise, but may sooner or later involve the good faith of his personal assurances. There is in our institutions no room for the judge promoter."

And further: "The ethical plane of a judge must be a high one. It is not enough that a judge is not corrupt—he must be above suspicion. If the fountain from which justice flows is thought to be impure, the stream will be regarded with distrust. Arthur H. Chetlain the judge is quite a different person from Arthur H. Chetlain the individual. The people made the one; they did not make the other."

5.

Throughout most of this period, a man important in the long history of the Association was laying the basis for his many years of valued service.

In 1902, a tall, solemn young man of 23, Clarence Paul Denning, was hired as an assistant to Carlos P. Sawyer, the librarian in charge of the collection of 6,000 volumes in one of the two rooms occupied by the Association in the new Chicago Title and Trust Building at Clark and Washington streets. Denning had graduated two years earlier from Illinois Wesleyan University and had worked as a railroad hand in downstate Normal until a college classmate, John G. Tucker, advised him to go to Chicago. His duties as assistant librarian were menial. He polished tables, dusted books, and filled orders from 9:00 A.M. to 5:00 P.M., with no time off for lunch. The day he went to work was Friday, June 13, and forever after in his 50 years of service to the Association—as he acquired his law degree from John Marshall Law School and as he progressed to other positions until he assumed the vital post of executive secretary in 1923—he reckoned all Fridays that fell on the 13th as lucky days.

A Major Victory

1.

EARLY IN 1910, the Association's president, Joseph H. Defrees, a lawyer keenly interested in public affairs and the founder of a firm that ultimately became one of the city's largest, deplored what he felt was a lack of interest by too many members not merely in Association activities but in its duties to the public and the profession. Earlier in his term, he had asked Emil C. Wetten to organize a membership drive that had increased the ranks to 1,300, but when only a small percentage of these seemed to manifest concern in the Association's varied projects, Wetten urged the creation of a pocket-size monthly publication that would contain news and articles of special interest to lawyers. After a number of conferences with Defrees and Clarence Denning, now serving as the Association's assistant secretary, and cautious approval by the Board of Managers—the initial cost for a four-page magazine was reckoned at only $30, but this was a board diligently concerned about every expenditure—Wetten was named editor, and he produced his first issue of *The Chicago Bar Association Record* on May 9.

In it, Defrees enumerated how the magazine would handily supplement the annual Association yearbook by advising members at shorter intervals what the officers had under consideration and would also afford them a means of enunciating freely their views on matters relating to the profession. The monthly magazine would, among other things, list the names of applicants for membership, along with those of their proposers and

seconders, the applicants' length of practice, and some statement of their general qualifications. Defrees considered that
this method, which he thought far superior to the prevailing
one by which lawyers were notified about potential members
by postal cards, would enable members to express more readily
to the Admissions Committee their approval of or objection
to candidates. "While the policy of the Association should always be to strive for new members," wrote Defrees, "I have
never felt that quality should be sacrificed in the interest of
quantity." The first issue was chock-full of information: changes
in court rules and practice decisions since the first of the year;
a report on actions of the Grievance Committee; a list of the
18 downstate judges holding court in Cook County; a brief
biography by Thomas Maclay Hoyne of the Association's first
president, William C. Goudy; a report on the monthly dinner
meetings addressed by prominent lawyers and judges; data on
28 pending applications for membership; and the names of 155
candidates elected in the previous year. This publishing ven-
ture survived for six more issues, through May 1911—the plan
for monthly publication appears to have been dropped with
the June 1910 issue—and then was abandoned completely for
reasons of economy, not to be resumed full-scale until October
1918 as *The Bar Association Record*. Since then, except for
suspension of publication for a brief time in the 1930s, it has
continued on the precepts enunciated by Defrees—to serve
the members as a medium of information and open expression
of opinions on matters affecting the profession and the public.
Its alterations have reflected the times and the personalities
and tastes, serious or humorous, of its editors. Over the years,
such well-read sections as Charles C. Arado's "Here and There
in the Criminal Courts"; "De Minimis," a column of anecdotes
in a light vein; historical notes by George W. Gale; and "The
Bookshelf," the prevailing librarian's reports on new volumes
of special interest, were introduced and later dropped as editors
changed. Debates-in-print between members—especially on
topics of major disagreement, such as New Deal legislation in
the depression years or aid to Great Britain in pre-World

War II days—regularly appeared in its pages, and always, well into the present as the erudite *Chicago Bar Record,* appeared "The President's Page," with detailed information about important pending or completed projects and even with occasional inspirational messages designed to instill pride in the practice of law.

Another contemporary innovation that endured and also set the pattern for similar ventures was the committee created during the presidency of Edgar B. Tolman in 1912 to help indigent defendants. It was variously called the Committee on Defense of Prisoners and the Committee on Defense of Poor Persons Accused of Crime. In line with provisions of the state's criminal code and state Supreme Court rulings that all accused persons, whether able to pay or not, were entitled to counsel, the committee called for volunteers from among Association members to make up a list that would be submitted to judges sitting in Criminal Court for use in appointing defense counsels. "While previous experience in the practice of criminal law is desirable," read the *Record's* statement seeking such volunteers, "it is in many cases not necessary, and any well informed attorney of good ability is qualified to perform this duty." As did the *Record,* this committee would undergo various changes, not the least among them a considerable expansion and utilization of senior students in Chicago-area law schools as aides to more experienced attorneys. But the basic responsibility remained constant—to guarantee that an indigent defendant received a fair trial, in which all of his legal rights and remedies were observed to the fullest.

2.

With the advent of World War I, the Association faced new challenges and new problems. Even before the United States' entry into the conflict, the Board of Managers made its sentiments known with an especially strong resolution calling on members and nonmembers to unite in making the lawyers' division in the city's gigantic Preparedness Day parade of

June 3, 1916, "an impressive demonstration that lawyers are second to none in love of country and devotion to their duties as citizens." In his inaugural address, the Association's wartime president, Joseph W. Moses, noted the need for lawyers on the home front to serve their country, community, and profession, and soon a War Committee comprising 25 members was formed, and an office opened adjoining the Association's rooms in the old Fort Dearborn Building at Monroe and Clark streets. Henry R. Rathbone, its chairman, went to New York, Washington, and other large eastern cities to study the work of similar committees and returned with a plan to subdivide the committee into four groups that ultimately employed the volunteered services of 500 lawyers.

The first and largest of the groups, with Carl R. Latham as chairman and Frank W. Gordon as secretary, furnished free legal advice to all men in uniform and their dependents and worked without fees on welfare cases referred to it by the American Red Cross and for draft boards in handling appeals and requests for exemption from service. Several attorneys who balked at the Association's resolution decreeing that all war work be done without charge and were taking money for routine services were called before the War Committee and asked firmly to desist. "We are confident that the strong stand taken by your committee in this regard and also by the Chicago Bar Association," reported Rathbone in citing the impressive statistic of 3,000 cases promptly and satisfactorily disposed of in the first year of activity, "has redounded to the honor of the legal profession and has added to the confidence of the community in general in the unselfish and patriotic efforts of the lawyers of our city to aid their country and its government in the war." Another group headed by Silas H. Strawn, the Association's president in 1913 and a partner in a major firm, furnished lawyers to take over unfinished cases of colleagues called to military service. The third group, headed by Levy Mayer, raised funds to alleviate any financial woes of families of lawyers in uniform; Mayer, head of a leading law firm, himself subscribed to $1,500,000 in Liberty Bonds. The fourth,

124

with Mitchell D. Follansbee, the Association's president in 1914, supplied speakers for patriotic rallies and Liberty Loan campaigns.

Unremitting patriotism and war service were the twin themes of the period not only of the Association but also of various individual members. At the 1917 annual meeting ending his two terms as president, former Probate Court Judge Charles S. Cutting, in presenting a service flag inscribed with the names of 143 men in the armed forces, intoned as he reflected on prewar America's isolation and affluence: "We little thought and we had no reason to dream that the time was not far distant when war, not one with an American continental enemy but with the greatest military power the world has ever produced, barring none, should be our fate. The question arose at once as to whether a democracy could rise to meet such an emergency, whether it were possible that a nation, organized wholly along the lines of peace, could suddenly transform itself into an organ of warfare and conduct a successful campaign against a thoroughly organized and long trained force of such an enemy. This would be impossible of accomplishment if it were not for the fact that somewhere lurking in the American character there is the remnant of that old spirit of '76, which fought the British regulars to a standstill, and the same spirit which animated the men of '61, and now finds in their sons and grandsons and descendants, when again the bugle calls to the ranks."

And on one wall of his courtroom, Circuit Court Judge Lockwood Honore, member of a pioneer Chicago family, put up, a few days after the United States entered the war, an elaborately printed document he described as his "war creed" and kept it there for the duration. It read:

When you are sure you are being forced into a fight, not of your own seeking, then, like a man of action, choose your most advantageous battle ground. Don't let the aggressor make his choice.

We are sending an army over to prevent the war from

coming to us, to prevent any war at any time in the future coming over to us.

We must pay in blood the interest on the indebtedness of blood we owe to our forefathers for making this land free.

Those among us who are qualified by youth, vigor and gallantry will spring to the task gladly. Those who are left behind sadly stand at the seashore with consecrated hands and must dedicate to our beloved soldiers all our earthly possessions and fervently send to heaven our hopes and our prayers for their speedy return.

But "The world must be made safe."

As the war neared its close, the new Association president, Amos C. Miller, appealed to all members, in a front-page statement in the revitalized *Record,* to ease what he termed "a critical situation." Because of the enlistment or drafting of a great number of youthful lawyers and young clerks, many law offices had literally been stripped of their clerical forces, creating a situation in which cases would frequently be reached on the trial call when one or the other side might not be represented or in which indispensable witnesses would be absent because of their military service. Because of such developments, Miller asked that in all cases where strict adherence to customary rules of practice would work havoc, leniency should be shown toward opposing counsel and parties and attorneys on either side of litigated cases cooperate to avoid injustice and hardship. This was followed by a meeting of the Association's Committee on Rules of Court with the executive committees of the Circuit and Superior courts and a representative of Chief Justice Harry Olson of the Municipal Court. This meeting resulted in the adoption of a set of emergency rules that provided for cases to be continued until a participant who was absent because of a reduced office staff could make an appearance. These rules were no more than a few weeks in use when the war ended; and within months, as men began to return from military forces or civilian war duties in Washington and other cities, normal procedures prevailed.

But the work of the War Committee was far from over,

although their counterparts all over the country quickly suspended operations. Two young attorneys who did not belong to the Association, David H. Bloom and Raymond Waite, continued to give free legal aid and counsel to returning soldiers and sailors well into 1921, a service for which the Board of Managers voted to elect the pair to honorary membership. In addition, the Association cooperated with the Chicago Association of Commerce in seeking jobs for hordes of unemployed veterans in the city. A typical appeal in the *Record* read: "We have welcomed home the returning heroes. All this is very fine. It is entirely proper that we should honor these fighting men on their return, but our duty is not thereby fully discharged. They are proud and sensitive. They do not deserve charity and few will accept it. None should be compelled to do so. They must be assimilated as speedily as possible into civic industry, from which they were withdrawn for a specific purpose. The job and the man must be co-ordinated and brought together."

3.

Throughout the decade and even in the midst of wartime conditions, the Association did not lessen its surveillance and scrutiny of one of the keystones of the legal apparatus—the judiciary. As in the past, relations with the judges varied with events, although each retiring president avowed that in all the Association did in this regard, the fundamental objective remained—to place the courts and the administration of the law on an even higher plane.

Despite the periodic differences between the Association and the judiciary or the election of men other than the victors in bar primaries, the Association continued the traditional practice of holding banquets for newly chosen judges.

At one banquet in 1911 at the Mid-Day Club, Judge Orrin N. Carter, chief justice of the state Supreme Court, took it upon himself to offer the new men a set of rules designed to heal any breach in friendly lawyer-jurist relations. "Remember, once you were lawyers," he said, "and may be again. Do not forget lawyers are still men. The ideal judge is he who treats all lawyers alike, irrespective of age or station in that profession. Be courteous, patient, and fair. The judge who is not a hard worker cannot be a success. You are to enforce the law in spirit, not the letter. This is a government of law, not of men. Give the devil his dues, whether right or wrong. Regardless of the passions of the hour, you are here to uphold the law. Laws expand with the country—the courts must keep pace with it. There is no better final charge than that given by King John: 'To no one sell delay, to no one deny right, to no one deny justice.' " At a banquet that year honoring Judge Farlin Quigley Ball on his retirement at 73 from the Superior Court bench, the guest of honor, like Judge Carter, offered advice to fellow jurists: "Don't talk, let the lawyers do all the talking. Get all the lawyer has to say that is good before giving a decision. In sixteen years on the bench I have not made one thrust at another judge, nor has any judge taken a thrust at me. Be not only a judge of the Superior Court, but be a Superior Court judge, one of a constituent body, representing more than just an individual."

During a period of agitation for recall of judges by public petition, led mostly by leaders of Theodore Roosevelt's new Progressive Party, the Association took due notice—"Courts have become the targets, not only of demagogues but also of many thoughtful men who have at heart only the welfare of the Republic and of the community in which they live," declared John T. Richards, president in 1913—and conducted innumerable debates on the subject. Most of the members opposed recall, a stand for which speakers had no hesitation in excoriating them as a visiting eastern lawyer, Arthur Eddy, did at a monthly dinner in the Mid-Day Club: "I dare say that nearly every man present this evening is here in an attitude of deep-seated hostility toward the very suggestion of the recall, not because it is utterly devoid of merit but because it is something so new you don't like it. You class it with and as a shade worse than the initiative, the referendum, and woman suffrage. Gentlemen, I hate to be the bearer of depressing news to a festive occasion, but, believe me, all these things are coming. They are at your doors, knocking in a manner that will not be denied, and the sad part of it is that you lawyers, you men who should be alive to rightly help and shape every movement that has to do with the welfare of the people—you sit back in the traces like balky mules and try to block the procession."

Constantly, the eternal subject of how to improve the judiciary concerned the Association. Members applauded the kind of proposal set forth by Sigmund Zeisler for nonpartisan judicial elections and the abolition of all party designations on tickets. They expressed agreement with the classic description of the perfect judge as expressed more than half a century earlier by the great trial lawyer Rufus Choate: "He shall know nothing about the parties, everything about the case. He shall do everything for justice, nothing for himself, nothing for his patron, nothing for his sovereign. If on one side is the executive power and the legislature and the people—the sources of his honors, the givers of his daily bread—and on the other an individual, nameless and odious, his eye is to see neither great nor small, attending only to the trepidations of the balance." Association members pondered the possibility that a way to remedy most of the judicial ills, undue expense, and time in Cook County would be to establish one single court to replace the existing Circuit, Superior, Criminal, County, and Probate courts, with a single administrative head, one clerk, and one chief bailiff. They listened thoughtfully in 1915, when Louis D. Brandeis, the eminent New York attorney and soon-to-be United States Supreme Court justice, noted that while labor unions and leaders of the Socialist and Progressive parties were denouncing judges for adverse rulings in cases stemming from industrialists' challenges to workmen's compensation laws, businessmen were equally irate about court rulings on matters relating to antitrust legislation, recently strengthened by passage of the Clayton Act. They persistently heard reports from assigned observers that too many bailiffs in the various branches of the Municipal

Court were loud and boisterous and showed favoritism in the manner of calling cases and that much time was wasted by lawyers and litigants because of lack of punctuality by judges in opening court.

The Association's concern about judicial behavior and decorum extended even to the issue of whether all judges should wear black robes. There were still some who could recall John Peter Altgeld's sardonic comments in 1891: "No robe ever enlarged a man's brain, ripened his wisdom, cleared his judgment, strengthened his purpose or fortified his honesty. If he is a little man without a robe, he is contemptible in a robe. It is the fawning and the hanging-on element, the element which flatters and seeks a rear-door entrance to the judge, which favors them. In the past, gowns have not prevented judicial murders, wrongs and outrages, the infamy of which reaches to hell. So long as we tolerate this insignia of medieval connections, just so long we must confess that we have not reached a high state of development." The Association's official stand, some distance removed from that harsh evaluation, was that the judicial robe was essential to the establishment of a public image of a judge as an impartial dispenser of justice, the very personification of a dignified tribunal aloof from the influences and thrusts of everyday life. When, in 1919, the judges of the Circuit and Superior courts adopted a rule requiring that they wear gowns during sessions and that their bailiffs don uniforms and a star, the *Record* was quick to comment: "The judges believe that a distinguishing robe will add dignity not to the man but to the office; that thus attired the judicial position will be more respected and its influence will be broadened; that a more formal and solemn administration of the oath to witnesses and others by a person bearing a sign of office and a more orderly regulation of conduct in the courtroom will tend to greater respect of the law and better administration of justice. In these views the Board of Managers of the Bar Association unanimously concurs."

And the Association waited for a new opportunity to oppose political rulers who sought to use the courts to their own advantage and to increase their power and affluence. That opportunity leaped into existence soon after the start of a new and turbulent decade.

4.

In 1920, the powerful political machine built by Mayor William Hale "Big Bill" Thompson, with the counsel and guidance of his political mentor Fred "Poor Swede" Lundin, seemed invincible.

A year earlier, Thompson had been reelected for a second four-year term, and in April 1920, that triumph was enormously enhanced by the national presidential landslide victory of Warren G. Harding. Len Small, the doughty Thompson-Lundin candidate for governor, won over the dapper, bewhiskered orator Sen. J. Hamilton Lewis. Pugnacious Robert E. Crowe, the new state's attorney, was in control of law enforcement machinery, and dour Frank Righeimer, the new county judge, was in command of election machinery. The Thompson-Lundin organization held seats of power in the City Hall, the statehouse, the Board of Education, the library board, the Sanitary District, the state legislature. Governor Frank Lowden, whose hopes for the Republican presidential nomination Thompson had been instrumental in smashing at the party's convention, called it "Thompson's Tammany," and Arthur Evans, the *Tribune's* political expert, wrote: "It has full swing as a city-county-state ring. It is the most powerful machine the state has known." On election night, Thompson bellowed: "We ate 'em alive! We ate 'em alive with their clothes on!" And that week one of his most loyal adherents, Michael J. Faherty, chairman of the Board of Local Improvements, declaimed at a meeting of the American Road Builders Association: "William Hale Thompson is the greatest statesman Illinois has ever had since Abraham Lincoln! As a politician he is without a peer and I believe he will be President in four years!"

While Thompson gloried in his victories and laid out plans for a gigantic $1 million Pageant of Progress at Municipal Pier that would depict the city's past, present, and a Thompsonian future and whose theme would be "Throw Away Your Hammer! Get a Horn! Be a Booster for Chicago!" Lundin quietly parceled out hundreds of political jobs to loyalists and contemplated a new major grab for power. Not even a suit by the *Tribune,* charging that the Thompson-Lundin organization had been involved with various officials in milking the city of nearly $3 million in overpayment of fees, illegal payments, and kickbacks in connection with the building of the Michigan Avenue Bridge and other construction projects, fazed Lundin as he plotted the next step.

Scheduled for June 6, 1921, was an election of 20 Circuit Court judges and one Superior Court judge. Under existing law, the Circuit Court held domain over the South Park Commission, most affluent of the city's three such bodies and on the verge of starting a multimillion-dollar beautification program on the Lake Michigan shore. This meant more jobs and more contracts. Lundin, hungering for both, needed judges he was certain would heed his soft-spoken but firm commands and through whom he and Thompson could control patronage appointments of referees and masters in chancery.

To effect this control, Lundin and Thompson set out to oust all the Circuit Court incumbents except two they considered their allies. Now virtual lords of the Cook County Republican Central Committee because of the smashing victories of 1920, they decreed the selection of judicial candidates they considered "safe." Some of the men on their slate were reputable and might well defy the two political bosses, but Thompson and Lundin felt no qualms. Big Bill was especially pleased that Judge Kickham Scanlan was denied a place because Scanlan, a man of stern probity, had dared to order the return of Charles E. Chadsey to his job as superintendent of schools after Thompson had brusquely fired him.

Response to the announcement of the Thompson-Lundin slate was prompt and vociferous. For the first time since it began citywide bar primaries in 1887, the Association, having been unable through Amos C. Miller, chairman of its Committee on Candidates, to get even a routine response from the

City Hall bosses as to their motives, abandoned its usual practice of recommending the election of individual judges regardless of party ticket and proposed to the Democrats led by George E. Brennan and to such anti-Thompson foes as Charles S. Deneen and Attorney General Edward J. Brundage a coalition ticket made up of men from both parties, mostly the best of the sitting judges.

"LEADERS OF BAR WARN OF CITY HALL BENCH RAID" cried a *Tribune* headline atop a front-page story that quoted Miller as saying: "The public and the bar at this time face a situation unprecedented in this county . . . . Control over the judiciary is of itself a public menace, the baneful effect of which is not destroyed by the character of an individual judge. Regardless of questions of personal preference and party affiliation, we believe that all who appreciate the vital importance of free and independent judges should unite to resist this assault upon the judiciary. The plans of the powerful faction now striving, for their own purposes, to gain control of the bench cannot be defeated except by a unity of purpose and action."

In the Association's primary, the coalition ticket won over City Hall's choices, 1,545 to 177, with three-fourths of the members casting ballots—a percentage larger by far than in any preceding contest. So conclusive was the result that Association President John R. Montgomery authorized appointment of a campaign committee to engage in the coming battle, and for this purpose, a fund, ultimately amounting to $61,000, was set up. In the May 1921 issue of the *Record*, a front-page editorial urged support of the coalition ticket: "When the lawyers of a great city, by an overwhelming vote, have registered their conviction in favor of the coalition nominees, the situation is unanswerable. No argument is possible that partisans, cliques, or group representatives only have spoken. The so-called City Hall faction cannot meet this conclusive evidence. They must of necessity resort to the hackneyed generalities, familiar in all political campaigns, that mean nothing."

Lawyers who stumped for the coalition nominees were joined

by reform organizations, churchmen, and lately enfranchised members of various women's clubs. Montgomery expressed apprehension that if the Thompson-Lundin ticket won the Juvenile Court, "the great social institution it has been since its inception" would fall under the influence of a politically dominated Circuit Court. "The last vestige of the people's liberty is at stake," he told the Woman's Club of Evanston. "Anarchistic conditions are sure to follow if the Thompson ticket wins, for it will take a revolution to liberate Chicago and Cook County if the machine captures the judiciary!"

At first, Lundin scoffed at the furor. "It'll die down. No one stays excited about a judicial election." The total vote, he estimated scornfully, would go no higher than a scant 200,000. But early on Election Day, Lundin grew apprehensive and ordered switches in the locations of polling places in "doubtful areas" so that independent voters were compelled to walk a mile or more to the newly designated polling places to cast their ballots for the coalition ticket.

The outcome underscored the most successful campaign ever participated in by the Association. Instead of 200,000, more than 600,000 voted—a record for a judicial election—and handed Big Bill an astounding defeat. "Thompsonism has been dealt a smashing blow between the eyes," cried the *Daily News,* reporting the victory of the entire coalition ticket by over 100,000 votes. Exultant, the Association reprinted in the *Record* telegrams of congratulation from such eminent New York lawyers as George W. Wickersham ("Splendid demonstration of the spirit of the bar in its jealous resentment against attempted political control of the fountains of justice") and Morgan J. O'Brien ("Your victory is in line with the best traditions of the profession"). In its front-page editorial, headed "A GREAT VICTORY," the *Record* emphasized that the coalition plan had been originated and fostered by the Association's Committee on Candidates: "By its successful fight in the June election, The Chicago Bar Association has advanced far toward the goal of leadership in this branch of its legitimate functions and has won the right to expect the people to look to it for guidance in future judicial elections. It is our hope that the day is not far off when the nominees of The Chicago Bar Association for the judicial office will be without opposition from any quarter, and will be assured of election."

Association efforts in subsequent judicial elections would yield less impressive results, but now the inveterate Thompson-Lundin political foes and all who had joined in the battle for a righteous principle savored the triumph and watched as a host of misfortunes befell Big Bill and Poor Swede and their recently impregnable organization. In the wake of the June 6 defeat, allies became enemies. State's Attorney Crowe squabbled with Thompson's chief of police, Charles C. Fitzmorris, a former city editor of the *American*; and as the break widened, the state's attorney brought before the grand jury charges that the chief Republican machine men had been dipping into school funds. Crowe's action climaxed months of rumors and newspaper reports of graft, fake contracts, favors for friends of the mayor, needlessly expensive purchases, and browbeating of teachers and principals. After six months of hearing hundreds of witnesses, indictments were returned against 23 men, including Lundin, William A. Bither, the school board's attorney, and several school-board members. It would take the combined efforts of four of the city's most talented specialists in criminal law—Clarence Darrow, Ben Short, Charles Erbstein, and Patrick O'Donnell—to gain acquittals for Lundin and the others. At the time of this trial, Bither was already under a one-to-five-year sentence in an earlier case involving fraud in the purchase of school lands; this judgment was later reversed on a technicality, and the Association's strong effort to disbar him was rejected by the state Supreme Court.

Meanwhile, Governor Small was encountering woes in Springfield. Attorney General Brundage won an indictment charging him and others with mishandling $2 million in funds while Small was state treasurer because that sum was kept in private banks owned by one of Small's close friends—and kept there with no interest being paid to the state. After a lengthy trial, Small was acquitted of the charge, although later he was ordered to pay $600,000 to the state treasury in the aftermath of a citizen's accounting suit.

Other misfortunes befell Thompson—indictments of grafting policemen, charges that his appointees had looted the city treasury of $250,000, a rise in the city's bonded indebtedness— and although he had continually vowed to run for a third successive term, he heeded Fred Lundin's advice and decided not to. He was far from through either as a politician or mayor, and he would return later for another tumultuous, scandal-ridden term. But now, reeling from the succession of blows that had begun with his resounding defeat in the 1921 judicial election, he issued a statement denouncing those he called "my enemies" and "the trust press" and went off in pursuit of various untroubled pleasures, including an expedition to the South Seas to hunt for tree-climbing fish; it was a venture as ill-fated as his grab for judicial control and ended long before his cypress yawl, the *Big Bill*—especially constructed and with a full face of Big Bill carved in oak as its figurehead—touched port at New Orleans.

Cook County Courthouse and Chicago City Hall in 1890, at Clark and Randolph streets, the hub of the legal community.

First National Bank of Chicago

Highly decorated downtown street heralding start of the World's Columbian Exposition of 1893.

Author's collection

CIRCUIT COURTS ORDER

TO CLOSE THE WORLD FAIR ON SUNDAY

SUPERSEDEAS

CHIEF JUSTICE FULLER KEEPS THE FAIR OPEN ANOTHER SUNDAY=

Tribune cartoon about Melville Weston Fuller, chief justice of the United States Supreme Court, granting the right to Sunday openings for the World's Columbian Exposition. Association members were prominent in campaign to keep the exposition open on Sundays.

Chicago Tribune

Harvey B. Hurd, a prominent Association member who wrote the bill establishing the Cook County Juvenile Court in 1899, first of its kind anywhere in the world.

At the turn of the century, this private residence on Adams Street was transformed into the first detention home for juveniles.

Mary Margaret Bartelme (right) served first as an aide to the judge of
the Juvenile Court and in 1923 began a ten-year term as Circuit Court
judge in the court. She was the first woman ever elected a judge in
Illinois.

Chicago Daily News

This pictorial report by Frederic Remington is of a scene in the Union
Stock Yards during a labor conflict in 1894, with strikers, according to
Remington's caption in *Harper's Weekly,* yelling "To hell with the gov-
ernment!" as federal troops marched in the streets.

The Canalport station police force in the late 1890s.

Clarence Denning, when he joined the Association in 1902 as an assistant librarian. He served the Association for 50 years, many of them as executive secretary.

Association headquarters at 105 West Monroe Street in 1908.

First of the motorized police patrol wagons was used in 1905 during the
garment workers' strike. *Chicago Daily News*

Interior of police court building in 1900s. Chicago Bar Association

"Keep the Judiciary Out of Politics"

1.

SPURRED BY THE VICTORY over the Thompson forces in the 1921 judicial election, Association spokesmen announced intentions to continue what Frederic Ullmann, Jr., editor of the *Record*, referred to in a front-page editorial at the start of the new year as a "militant policy." Ullmann called for a survey under Association auspices into conditions affecting the criminal law and the criminal courts. It cited increases in such crimes as street robberies, burglaries, and mayhem and the recent escape of Terrible Tommy O'Connor from the county jail almost on the eve of his scheduled hanging for the murder of a policeman, and took special notice of a public statement by Kickham Scanlan, chief justice of the Criminal Court, that Chicago was beyond doubt one of the most lawless communities in the entire country. "It would seem that these matters deserve consideration by people of this community," Ullmann wrote. "Indeed, it need hardly be urged that something is radically wrong. The trouble is that nobody knows much about facts. Nobody knows where the weak spots in our present system lie, nor does anybody know much about the methods of curing them." Ullmann maintained that a survey conducted impartially "and without politics and without fear" could be a first step toward improvement of a system that appeared to be characterized by lax prosecution of criminals and long delays in trials. The new president, Roger Sherman, likewise called on the Association to exert its influence in seeking swifter

145

prosecution of criminal cases and in rooting out of the profession lawyers too closely allied with gangsters. In a letter to all Association members, he called for the disbarment of those who used false affidavits and perjured testimony and then warned against indiscriminate action against lawyers merely because they did appear in behalf of criminal defendants. "The Association owes it to itself and to the profession to see to it that lawyers generally are not charged with offenses of which they are not guilty. To satisfy the public demand, the press too frequently lays the blame for many things at the door of the lawyers, when in fact the lawyers are not in the least to blame."

Whatever crime existed to inspire exhortations for surveys and cleanups was relatively mild compared with what occurred after William E. Dever, a dignified and highly respected jurist, succeeded Big Bill Thompson as mayor in 1923.

For all of Thompson's raucous bragging about how he would drive criminals out of the city, the formidable syndicate—organized in 1920 by John Torrio after the slaying of his overlord and benefactor, Big Jim Colosimo—operated with minimal interference from the City Hall or police authorities. The proud holder of a membership card in the William Hale Thompson Republican Club, Torrio had, with the advent of the prohibition laws, forced himself into partnerships with various owners of breweries. After some early difficulties with other gangsters who were reluctant to join him—problems quickly and bloodily resolved under direction of Al Capone, whom Torrio had imported from Brooklyn early in 1920—he had set up a system for controlling the illicit beer and liquor traffic in Chicago and elsewhere in Cook County. To selected lieutenants, including such erstwhile foes as Dion O'Banion, Polack Joe Saltis, the brutal Frank McErlane, and Ralph Sheldon, Torrio allotted specific areas in which they would be in charge of beer shipments, deliveries, and collections, payoffs to crooked policemen and politicians, and, when necessary, the disposal of recalcitrant underlings. In this alliance, fostered less by mutual admiration than by respect for Torrio's close affiliations with powerful

146

men in the City Hall and his organization acumen, Capone was a district captain on the West Side, sharing varied duties with such worthies as Frankie Pope, "the Millionaire News-boy," and Harry Guzik, a longtime procurer who would be pardoned with his wife, Alma, by Governor Small without serving a day of a sentence for operating a recruiting ring for Torrio brothels.

So successful was this beer and liquor operation that, despite occasional turbulence and flurries of crime of the kind that evoked demands for surveys and disbarments and issuance by the Chicago Crime Commission of its first list of "public enemies" with Capone at its head, the alliance worked as Torrio intended it to, smoothly and affluently and with relative tranquillity. In a single year, his syndicate grossed $9 million in the city—$4 million from beer sales, $3 million from gambling, $2 million from prostitution—and $4 million from such enterprises in the suburbs.

But in the new mayor, the city had a conscientious man who believed that the laws needed to be enforced. He ordered incessant police assaults on speakeasies, all-night cabarets, "alky-cooking" flats, gambling houses, brothels. Torrio's syndicate began to quiver and fall apart. Bereft of highly placed friends in the city government, Torrio went with his wife and mother for a vacation in his native Italy. Capone surged into the suburb of Cicero to set up a string of brothels and gambling establishments and an armored headquarters in the Hawthorne Inn. The district leaders, feeling the pressure of incessant police raids, began to arrange for their own protection and greedily crossed into rival territories to hijack trucks, rob warehouses, kill and pillage, and force customers to handle their beer and liquor. O'Banion was among the first to break the bonds, invading the West Side territory of the murderous Genna clan. A week after the elections of November 1924, in which Robert E. Crowe retained his powerful position as state's attorney, O'Banion was shot to death in his State Street flower shop across from the imposing Holy Name Cathedral. And month by month the carnage continued. Hymie Weiss, an evil-tempered

O'Banion loyalist, tried to assassinate Torrio, wounding the gang chieftain severely and ultimately compelling him to scamper off for Europe, leaving his bloodied domain to Capone. In the offing were the slayings of three of the infamous Genna brothers, who presided over a West Side bootleg empire; the mysterious murder of William McSwiggin, one of Crowe's ablest young assistants; a mad assault on Capone's Cicero headquarters by Weiss and dozens of gun-carrying gang members from an 11-automobile caravan; and the machine-gunning of Weiss 20 days later as he and several friends got out of an automobile near Holy Name Cathedral.

While Capone went about the grisly business of eradicating rivals and consolidating his gains, Crowe constantly promised, "I'll oust gangsterism." To explain the city's soaring crime rate, he offered platitudes—citizens were not religious enough, too many people shirked jury duty, capital punishment needed to be meted out more frequently—and complained of insufficient judges to hear criminal cases and a lack of sufficient and capable prosecutors. In response to the latter, the Association, in July 1925, offered to help Crowe prosecute cases by organizing a cadre of 400 members from whom he could select aides to help speed up preparation of cases. "We realize," said the new president, Russell Whitman, "the seriousness of the crime situation prevailing here. We will do all in our power to assist in the swift punishment of criminals at the bar of justice." Toward that end, its Committee on the Administration of Criminal Justice met with the chief justices of the Superior, Circuit, and Criminal courts and with Crowe, and it was decided that more courtrooms were needed and more judges should be assigned. It was determined that several rooms in the County Building could be converted into temporary courtrooms, but the finance committee of the County Board, then headed by the rising Democratic political aspirant, Anton J. Cermak, refused to appropriate funds needed for the conversion. And the rhetoric echoed throughout the city, and the gangs continued their depredations, and the reputation of Chicago's infamy thrived.

Meanwhile, other Association officials and members prepared for upcoming elections that would test the organization's influence with both the political leaders and the general public.

At the start of his presidential term in the summer of 1926, William C. Boyden called attention to the fact that in the upcoming year 35 judges were to be elected in various courts. Of immediate concern was the November election of one judge to the Probate Court, another to the County Court, and 12 to the Municipal Court. Stressing the need for the members and the Committee on Candidates to render to the voters intelligent guidance devoid of political partisanship, he also invoked the triumph over Thompsonism: "The memory of the judicial election of 1921 and of the proud part of the Chicago Bar Association therein is still fresh in our minds. If occasion requires, we should be prepared to render services of equal importance during the coming year."

It was soon apparent that the occasion did require such services. The April 1926 primary had been fraught with so much violence, mayhem, and chicanery that the Board of Election Commissioners sent to the Association a request for watchers to prevent fraud on Election Day. In quick response, Boyden named a special Committee on Elections, with Urban A. Lavery, an expert on election law, as its chairman. Some 400 members, mostly war veterans, volunteered to serve and were dispatched to polling places in wards where irregularities and flagrant violations had been most rife in the April primary. They served from before dawn until midnight and reported threats, browbeatings, assaults, faulty ballot-counting procedures, and drunkenness. "I apprehend one could die for no worthier cause than for the protection of the ballot box," read one watcher's statement to Lavery. "Nevertheless, if in the future I shall be drafted for this kind of service, would the Association be kind enough to supply me with a sawed-off shotgun, such as seemed to click all about me at that most adorable Goose Island precinct of the Capone preserves?" After plowing through 200 detailed reports, Boyden reported to the membership that the committee had furnished a "living picture" of what occurred on Election Day: "In this picture we see candidates flitting in and out of the polling places, friends and supporters of candidates seeking unfair advantages at the counting of ballots, judges of election imposing upon illiterate voters, tired clerks counting the ballots in the late hours of the morning following election physically unfit to perform their work. In short, we have presented to us a travesty. After the report is read the reader cannot help but be convinced of the futility of choosing judges in this manner. It explains why good judges are sometimes defeated and poor judges are sometimes elected."

Copies of the general report and the 200 individual statements were turned over to Crowe. When the state's attorney refused to take any action, Boyden presented to County Court Judge Edmund K. Jarecki a petition for the appointment of a special state's attorney to investigate frauds. Crowe, the petition charged, had too great a personal and disqualifying interest in the outcome of these elections. As an ally of Homer K. Galpin, Republican county chairman, and once more of Big Bill Thompson, he was again embroiled in intraparty rivalry with the forces of Sen. Charles S. Deneen, an undisputed fact that made it "inexpedient and improper" for him to act as prosecuting officer in connection with any election frauds.

Crowe's initial response was brief and brusque: "It's just politics." But he filed a reply maintaining that the Association's request was unjustified and improper. Judge Jarecki acceded to the Association's petition, however, and named Charles Center Case to the post. Case was given a mandate to inquire into charges of fraud at both elections and make necessary prosecutions. While the city resounded with the cries of Thompson as he assailed such onetime associates and present foes as Dr. John Dill Robertson, his former health commissioner, in the 1927 Republican mayoral primary and after Thompson's victory that April against Dever, Case took diligently to his task. He began to amass evidence that ultimately resulted in 40 convictions, many of them upheld by higher courts. But despite

150

repeated requests to the County Board for payment and
promises by them that appropriations would be made, not one
cent of the $78,000 due him for fees and expenses was paid.
One reason for this was that Crowe furnished the board with
an opinion that such an appropriation would be illegal. More
pragmatic causes for the board's stubbornness were that most of
its members were adherents of the Thompson-Crowe-Galpin
faction of the Republican Party and that Cermak, chafing
under the continuing domination of the longtime Democratic
boss George E. Brennan and yearning to establish a power base
of his own, was receptive to demands of the mercurial Crowe,
a possible ally, despite his avowed Republicanism, in any
future move for political gains.

3.

On another front during these hectic months, the Association
made plans for active participation in the June 6, 1927, election
of Circuit Court judges in another effort to emulate the 1921
victory. For a brief time it appeared that the prospects for such
an eventuality were, if not assured, at least promising.

In advance of conventions to nominate slates of candidates,
Republican and Democratic chieftains and leaders of party
factions seemed amenable to the suggestion of the Committee
on Candidates, then composed of former Association presidents, for a coalition pact that would result in the reelection
of worthy judicial incumbents. "The Democratic party," George
E. Brennan told committee members, "stands now where it
stood in 1921. It again puts good citizenship above partisanship
and prefers to have justice administered by lawyers, not by
precinct committeemen." Galpin issued a statement oozing
with promise of cooperation: "Some weeks back Robert E.
Crowe and myself visited George E. Brennan . . . and stated to
him that we were in favor of the principle of coalition in
judicial elections and that we believed the judges, irrespective
of party affiliations, who had made good records, should be
retained on the bench." Edward J. Brundage, leader of the
Republican faction bitterly opposed to the Thompson-Crowe-

Galpin combine, also supported coalition, emphasizing that any new aspirants should be those approved by the Association.

Lofty promises notwithstanding, it soon became evident that the party bosses, having made a bipartisan pact that involved control of the County Board, Sanitary District, and other offices for patronage purposes, had no intention of heeding the Association's counsel about the retention of capable judges, or, even more important, its suggestions for men to fill vacancies on the ticket. "As a peacemaker," reported Parke Brown, the *Tribune's* political editor, "the Chicago Bar Association Committee on Candidates hasn't found the doors as wide open as usual. It has been unable to obtain what might be considered satisfactory assurances that all the sitting judges whose record it approves will be renominated, and it hasn't any promise that its opinion will be sought concerning new candidates to be seated. . . . Several of those whose names have appeared are beginning to feel that neither the approval of the Chicago Bar Association nor any other influence than that of practical politics is going to cast the decisions when the conventions assemble."

While the Association had no objections to most of the incumbents named on the coalition ticket, it sought to concentrate on support for three judges—Frank Johnston, Jr., a Democrat, and Republicans Charles M. Thomson and Oscar M. Torrison— who showed up far higher in the Association's primary than their designated replacements. Sounding anew the slogan "Keep the judiciary out of politics!" the Association organized a special committee headed by Amos C. Miller and with Silas H. Strawn in charge of finances. In the three brief weeks before Election Day, the committee waged a campaign, but it was a listless one in which only $12,500, about a fifth of the 1921 expenditures, was spent. The time was short and the voters were apathetic, seemingly numbed by Thompson's raucous mayoral campaign based on a platform of "America First!" and promises to cleanse the school system of what he deemed to be insidious British influences. Attendance at rallies sponsored by the Association under the banner of the Independent Judicial Party was sparse; Edward M. Martin, a zealous young political observer who was to write a masterwork on the Association's role over many decades in electing judges, recalled attending one meeting in the University of Chicago's Harper Library that had an audience of 25, including the three candidates and their aides. "There has been little noisemaking," wrote a *Daily News* editorialist two days before the election. "The Chicago Bar Association has used the mails rather than the public platform to rouse the voters. The candidates on the coalition ticket backed by the politicians have made little or no campaign. They are relying on the organization stalwarts to go to the polls and the independent voters to remain at home."

The editorialist was only partially prophetic. The coalition ticket triumphed with 209,700 votes, but the independents did snare 97,000 votes, a result that heartened the Association sufficiently for it to vow future forays against judicial slates devised primarily for political considerations.

4.

In the city's continuing political warfare, battles between Republican factions maintained a far more intense pace than those between rival parties. Early in 1928 a bloody climax was reached, setting off a series of events that would bring further shame upon the city and involve the Association in an effort to cleanse the stain.

Most ardent among the loyal followers of Senator Deneen in his constant and bitter rivalry with the Thompson-Crowe-Galpin forces was Giuseppe Esposito—"Diamond Joe" of the teeming Nineteenth Ward, where for years he commanded affection, allegiance, and tribute of thousands of Italian laborers, shopkeepers, and alcohol cookers employed by the Genna brothers. A man of great charm and benevolence, a giver of gifts to the newly born and the newly wed, and a dispenser of spaghetti and warm bread every Christmas at his Bella Napoli Café, he was also a fixer for gamblers and brothel owners and a longtime protector of the Gennas.

With an important primary in prospect that April 10 in which he was to run for ward committeeman and in which

Deneen offered formidable opponents to those put forward by the Thompson forces, Esposito started his electioneering early. Twice he was warned by Capone gangsters to desist from urging his compatriots to vote for him and for the stolid jurist John A. Swanson for state's attorney instead of Crowe and for Louis L. Emmerson for governor instead of Len Small. On the night of March 21, an automobile bearing three men slowed down near a street on which Diamond Joe strolled, and he was slain with poisoned bullets from sawed-off shotguns. As he lay in a gutter, his $5,000 solitaire diamond ring, his belt buckle with his initials in diamonds, and his diamond pin and shirt studs sparkled in the mud.

In Washington, Deneen issued denunciations and vowed that when Swanson was elected, his first task would be to send the killers of Diamond Joe to the electric chair. Swanson affirmed that goal. Five days later, a bomb hurled from a passing car demolished most of Deneen's three-story home on the South Side, and another was thrown outside Swanson's home. The newspapers dubbed the election contest the "Pineapple Primary," one columnist writing:

> The rockets' red glare,
> the bombs bursting in air,
> Gave proof to the world
> that Chicago's still there.

Nebraska's Sen. George Norris seriously proposed to President Calvin Coolidge that the United States Marines then battling insurgents in Nicaragua be sent to Chicago.

At first, Crowe offered a reward for the arrest of the bombers. But soon, nettled by the uproar and the persistent accusations by Deneen and Swanson of a secret Thompson-Crowe-Galpin alliance with Capone, the short-tempered prosecutor cried: "They did it themselves to get sympathy! I am satisfied that these two bombings are the result of a conspiracy on the part of a few Deneen leaders to win the primary election."

And Big Bill Thompson blithely told visiting newspaper

reporters curious to know about the city's bombings and crime: "Sure, we have crime here. We will always have crime. Chicago is just like any other big city. You can get a man's arm broken for so much, a leg for so much, or beaten up for so much. Just like New York, excepting we print our crime and they don't. Bombings? There'll always be bombings just as long as there is prohibition."

Many, of course, disagreed. Before the bombings, more than 85 percent of the Association members had lent their names informally to Crowe's renomination. Now, in a poll—the first ever taken in a state's attorney's contest—the vote was five to one against him. This tally evoked threats from Crowe, still smarting over the Association's action in securing a special prosecutor in the previous year's vote-fraud inquiry, and he resigned his membership. The Chicago Crime Commission, which had endorsed Crowe earlier, swiftly withdrew its support, its chief and former Association president, Frank J. Loesch, calling him "inefficient and unworthy of his great responsibility to maintain law and order in the city." Business leaders who had praised Crowe when he offered statistics to show an increase in the number of convictions of labor racketeers in his term now issued statements denouncing him. And clergymen cried, "Ours is a government of bombs, of bums, of grafters and crooked politicians."

Everywhere on Election Day, there were sluggings, vote stealing, riotous disturbances, and ballot-box stuffing; and at its end, Thompson's forces had been routed, with Crowe the loser to Swanson by 200,000 votes. In the Bloody Twentieth—the ward ruled by Thompson's city collector, Morris Eller, and his son, Judge Emanuel Eller of the Criminal Court—murder climaxed the awful day. Octavius C. Granady, a black lawyer and Eller's opponent for ward committeeman, was fired on by four men in a moving car as he stood near a polling place. He leaped into his own car and drove off, but he was pursued by another automobile bearing three more men. More shots were fired, and Granady, filled with more than a dozen shotgun slugs, crashed his vehicle into a tree.

At first, the Granady slaying received routine mention in the newspapers; it was just one more incident in the hectic primary. But interest in it and its ramifications and symbolism—as an example of extreme lawlessness in the city—intensified. Francis X. Busch, who had served as Mayor Dever's corporation counsel, and Charles Center Case appeared at the inquest as Association representatives and received permission from Coroner Oscar Wolff to question the jury. They soon determined that the jurors were typical of those chosen for lesser cases: Five had been jobless for months, two had minor criminal records, and several had been active Thompson workers. Busch and Case successfully argued for dismissal of the nondescript group and appointment of a blue-ribbon jury. The new men chosen included a building contractor, a highly respected railroad attorney, and an executive of a large mercantile establishment. Dozens of witnesses were summoned in hearings that lasted many days, but not one could identify Granady's killers. So the verdict affirmed only that Granady "had come to his death by gunshot wounds fired by one or more men who are unknown to this jury" and was accompanied by a statement deploring "conditions of extreme lawlessness" that had existed that April day in the Bloody Twentieth.

Busch and Case promptly prepared a report of the proceedings for Carl R. Latham, the Association's president. In it, they recommended that the inquiry into the Granady slaying not be abandoned and that application be made to the Circuit Court for appointment of a special grand jury and special prosecutor.

On the afternoon of May 8, Latham, flanked by Busch and Case, appeared before Judge Harry B. Miller bearing a 60-page petition that had been prepared by Case and ex-president Russell Whitman. Crowe, the petition stated, was unfit to carry on because of his close relationship with the anti-Deneen faction of the Republican Party. Moreover, the petition charged that Crowe's supporters were directly responsible for the bombings of the Deneen and Swanson homes.

Crowe was present to hear the charges and to protest that his office was capable of making the inquiry and had, indeed, already begun to do so. Latham, however, replied that Crowe had impeded the investigation from the very beginning by having his aides ask desultory questions of witnesses at the inquest. To Crowe's statement that he intended to investigate not only the Granady case but also all crimes committed in the "Pineapple Primary," Latham retorted: "Mr. Crowe is a leading member of the political faction which is to be investigated. He has sat in office for seven years and continuously has refused to prosecute a single offender among the hundreds guilty of vote frauds. He has sought to throw obstacles in the way of those others who have been active in imprisoning election crooks. Chicago needs a housecleaning, and Chicago will get it despite Mr. Crowe."

Despite Crowe's objections, the petition was granted. Attorney General Oscar Carlstrom named Loesch as chief prosecutor, with half-a-dozen aides including former Municipal Court Judge Frederick L. Fake; Edwin J. Rober, a former assistant state's attorney; Ferre C. Watkins, past Illinois commander of the American Legion; and Harold M. Tyler, a prominent black attorney. One of Carlstrom's appointees, Lloyd D. Heth—a future Association president known as "Sure Fire" because of his persistent record of convictions of an assortment of murderers as an ace prosecutor under Crowe—begged off because of the press of civil cases. The drawing of 100 names from which 23 members of the special grand jury would be selected began promptly, and within days, the arduous task of determining responsibility for Granady's murder and the Election Day fraud and terrorism was under way.

5.

While the Granady investigation proceeded, the Association sought anew to play a crucial role in the judicial election of June 4, 1928.

Interest centered primarily on the contest for six Superior Court posts. When, in the Association's primary, Walter Steffen was the sole incumbent seeking reelection to receive a favorable vote of the majority of members, the Board of Managers had agreed to ask for new nominations. From among 33 names proposed, the Association drew up its slate of six candidates and on May 4 announced its intention of filing a coalition non-partisan ticket under its own name. "For many years the Chicago Bar Association has taken its stand for a non-partisan judiciary," its statement read. "Whenever candidates have been nominated for judicial office by the respective political parties, the Bar Association has by a vote of its members recommended the best qualified of the nominees without regard to their political affiliations. . . . It now appears that the Crowe-Thompson-Galpin faction of the Republican party, being still in control of the county convention which nominates candidates for judges, entered into a deal with the Democrats and succeeded in forcing upon the voters a *single* ticket of candidates for Superior Court judgeships. We were powerless to prevent the nomination of such a bi-partisan ticket, but it is the view of an overwhelming number of lawyers that an opportunity should be given voters to choose their own judges instead of permitting political bosses to appoint them."

Interestingly, three of the candidates on the Association ticket were on the slate offered by the political coalition forces. The election laws then prohibited the name of a candidate from appearing on more than one column of the ballot. Pragmatists all, the three so honored chose to be candidates on the Democratic-Republican ticket, which appeared in the Republican columns, but the Association continued its endorsement of them in campaign literature and advertising.

For the first time, the Association was now virtually a political party as it waged a broad advertising campaign, requested 1,000 clergymen to urge their congregations to vote for the Association slate, and sought various civic organizations as allies. One hundred billboards throughout the city asked, "SHALL THE POLITICAL BOSSES APPOINT OR THE PEOPLE ELECT YOUR JUDGES?" George E. Brennan and John R. Montgomery, chairman of the Association's campaign committee, engaged in a notable and lively debate at the City Club. Brennan insisted that he was not a political boss but "the successful head of a successful organization," inveighed against the "Bar Association organization bosses," and denied any alliance with Crowe ("On this coalition there is not a single Crowe man!"). Montgomery asserted that a larger question of public policy was involved: "The election is one of a long series in which the political leaders have sought to control the courts. But for the Bar Association ticket, there would have been no opposition, and the result would have been the appointment of the judges by the party bosses."

As in the previous year, the Election Day turnout was low—only 22.7 percent of the registered voters—and once more the political coalition nominees were victorious, polling 211,200 votes to the Association ticket's 96,700. In a close contest—partisan in nature, as had been the case in 1921—that big a bloc of votes might have been crucially significant; but now, opposed by the joint power of both political parties, the effort, however diligent, was futile.

In the November 1928 election, the results were far more salutary. Swanson, the Association's choice for state's attorney, won by more than 151,000 votes over Superior Court Judge William J. Lindsay. Of 12 judicial candidates recommended by the Association, all but one were elected. Association President Sidney S. Gorham considered this so gratifying that he asked William H. King, Jr., the *Record's* editor, to display prominently a letter from a member, Joseph R. Noel, expressing gratitude to the Association for its efforts and offering a kind of affirmation: "My analysis of the election returns indicates that the voters followed your primary recommendations in a most amazingly satisfactory manner, and this fact in itself seems to disprove the popular impression that the great mass of voters do not vote intelligently. That indictment cannot stand in the face of the fact that at the last election approximately 500,000 voted right."

6.

That November election was remarkable for more than the triumph of the Deneen candidates. In the week before the voting, Frank J. Loesch took time out from the special grand

jury inquiry into the Granady murder and ancillary crimes to
pay an important call. The recipient of his visit, as Loesch disclosed some years later in an address before the Southern
California Academy of Criminology, was no less a citizen than
Al Capone, who, ensconced in his suite in the Hotel Metropole,
greeted Loesch at a massive desk behind which hung oil
portraits of George Washington, Abraham Lincoln, and Big
Bill Thompson. Eager to prevent a duplication of the "Pineapple Primary" and aware that any request by him to Thompson for extra police protection would be fruitless, Loesch had
decided on this highly unorthodox action.

"Look here, Capone," he said, "will you help me by keeping
your damned cutthroats and hoodlums of the North Side from
interfering with the polling place booths?"

Capone replied that he would and offered an amazing
assurance on how rival gangs would be restrained. "I'll have
the cops send over the squad cars the night before the election
and jug all the hoodlums and keep 'em in the cooler until the
polls close."

The election proved to be one of the quietest in many years,
a development for which Loesch was grateful but which did
not deter him from pushing ahead on the Granady inquiry to
the extent that within several months one of those indicted for
involvement in the killing was a steadfast Capone lieutenant,
James Belcastro, dubbed by the newspapers "King of the
Bombers," and along with him a veteran police officer, Lt.
Philip Carroll, and three members of his squad.

The trial before Judge Joseph B. David, a testy and often
eccentric jurist but a stickler for adhering closely to rules of
procedure, turned into a fiasco for the aged prosecutor.
Margaret Welch, who had implicated Belcastro and James
Armando directly in her testimony before the grand jury, was
heralded as one of Loesch's star witnesses. But when she was
called on to testify, she fell to her knees, raised her hands in
supplication to the startled judge, and cried out, "Protect me,
oh, protect me! It isn't true and I can't go on with it! I can't go
on!" Then, after Octave J. Ruffin, a tailor who had implicated

Carroll earlier, recanted his testimony and Helen Madigan, on whom Loesch relied for incriminating testimony, denied she had seen Lieutenant Carroll fire any shots, Judge David told Loesch, "Never in all my long experience have I heard such perjured testimony as the state has presented," and he vowed to free all the defendants even if the jury brought in a verdict against them.

Thwarted, Loesch moved to dismiss the charges. "Your honor," he declared, "has heaped abuse on witnesses and counsel for the state and has made it intolerable to go on." Judge David mumbled an apology to Loesch but granted the motion, and the case came to an abrupt end. Loesch soon resigned as special prosecutor and departed for Washington for a meeting of President Herbert Hoover's National Crime Commission. To the end of his life in 1944 at 92, he would be continually vocal about demanding strictest enforcement of all laws designed to curb organized crime.

As for Judge David, the Association instituted an official inquiry into his conduct of the trial. When a report was issued chiding him for some of his actions ("The judge ... talked too much and participated in the examination of witnesses to an undue extent"), Judge David retorted that the Association might do well to investigate as a matter of public concern the disbursement and expenditure of some $300,000 that had been raised by public subscription for the investigation of the Granady case and the trial. No action was taken on the judge's suggestion, however. The controversy gradually dimmed, and the slaying of Granady remained forever officially unsolved.

Achievements and Amusements

1.

CONSIDERABLY LESS TUMULTUOUS for the Association in this decade of the 1920s were other events ranging from a major move to new quarters to formal institution of one of its most enduring traditions—the rollicking, impudent, and uninhibitedly perceptive annual frolic known as Christmas Spirits.

At the end of 1921 in the presidency of William Tracy Alden, the drive for a new home began with a front-page editorial in the *Record*. Its editor, Frederic Ullmann, Jr., noted that the Association's lease on offices and cramped quarters in the Standard Trust and Savings Bank Building at Monroe and Clark streets would expire on May 1, 1924, and he proposed that action be instituted to celebrate the Association's 50th anniversary on that occasion with erection of a structure devoted entirely to the Association. "What more appropriate monument to our fifty years of service could be erected than a Chicago Bar Association building? An office building for lawyers, members of the Association; club rooms to accommodate all the activities of the Association, including all dinner and luncheon meetings, roomy quarters for the library. Is this too much to hope for?"

Unabashedly, Ullmann ventured to ask if initial financing for such a building might come from "some forward looking member of the Association to whom fortune has come in his professional and business life." Expressing confidence that many members would be able and willing to contribute to the over-

163

all cost, the *Record* called for a man "who will tender to the Association the princely and magic sum which spurs to untiring effort in achieving the goal."

Prospective donors were reminded: "The fame of our greatest lawyers too often passes with their generation. There can be no more fitting, no more lasting monument to the genius and success of the Chicago Bar than a Bar Association building erected through the generosity of its leaders of the present generation."

Evidently no such benefactor nor the largess sufficient to the needs of the project resulted from these efforts at persuasion. A year later, buttressed by the critical information that the annual rent would be raised from $4,620 a year to $15,000 if the Association decided to stay in its existing quarters, Ullmann tried again, with another front-page editorial, to arouse interest. Commenting on explorations into the problem by a special 25-man Committee on a Permanent Home appointed by President Roger Sherman, the editorial asked all members to give serious thought to the plan for a building—"As we are brought to a realization of the direct benefit that would come to every member of the Association from such a program, there comes a conviction that the enthusiasm which such a project is capable of arousing, combined with the pressing necessity that now confronts us, is capable of making this building a reality"—and implored each member to pass on his views.

The outcome of this request and further study by the Committee on a Permanent Home was abandonment of the idea of a Chicago Bar Association building. In its stead, they proposed to lease for 15 years the top floor of the 20-story Burnham Building, at the northwest corner of La Salle and Randolph streets diagonally across from the massive edifice that housed the City Hall, the County Building, the Circuit and Superior courts, and the civil branch of the Municipal Court. To help finance the move and subsequent rental, the Board of Managers submitted a resolution to increase annual membership dues, a proposal overwhelmingly adopted—1,251 to 76—late in 1923 and supplemented by a drive under auspices of a special Finance Committee on Equipment for a $50,000 fund to pay for furnishings and varied accoutrements. Increases were on a sliding scale, with the highest—$22—assessed against members in practice for more than ten years. Of that amount, according to the reckoning in yet another front-page article in the *Record,* the actual net increase came to $16, since a boost of $6 would have been necessarily imposed on members in that category if the Association remained in the bank building. Ullmann then meticulously broke down the elements of the increase: "Is it not worth twenty-five cents a month to a member to enjoy the pleasing surroundings afforded by a modern building such as the Burnham Building, when he visits the rooms of the Association, rather than to find himself in the older and less attractive quarters now in use? If so, an increase of that amount, or $3 a year, is to his advantage. Again, is it not worth fifty cents a month to him to enjoy the privileges of a new luncheon club, with its comfortable lounge, besides the new conference rooms, in close proximity to the Court House, where every effort will be made to serve a tasty meal? If so, an increase of $6 a year is to his advantage." As for the remaining $7, it would go for maintenance of conference rooms to be used primarily by those groups, ranging from the Grievance Committee to the Committee on Candidates, whose functions "include a public service which is necessary for every practicing lawyer, as well as for the public itself."

On June 4, 1924, only a few weeks after the Association's official golden anniversary, there was a buoyant housewarming in the Burnham Building quarters—consisting of offices, a library, general clubroom and lounge, consultation rooms, a main restaurant, and several smaller private dining rooms— attended by 1,000 of the 3,000 members. Two weeks later, for the first time in the Association's history, its annual meeting and dinner was held in its own rooms. The *Record* was pleased to report that only 15 members had resigned because of the increase in dues as against the receipt of 321 applications for membership and requests for reinstatement from 18 former members whose interest in the Association had been revived by all the activity. There would be another major move in the future, but now the *Record* hailed the event as one signalizing "the close of an epochal year" as the Association "enters upon its second half century of service."

2.

In two other areas, the Association took progressive action amid its periodic conflicts with political bosses and assorted foes.

For a decade and more, the Association had attempted to furnish adequate legal assistance to indigent persons. Its Committee on Defense of Prisoners submitted lists of volunteer members to Criminal Court judges. The task was rather formidable, inasmuch as nearly half those arrested for crimes could not afford counsel. Consequently, volunteer attorneys had to be found annually for more than 600 cases. The ranks of such volunteers were hardly sufficient to serve the full needs of defendants; moreover, many of these attorneys were equipped neither by training nor by experience to handle criminal cases, and others indulged a natural tendency to put off work on cases without fees, especially with other matters pressing for their time. Periodically, Association presidents issued appeals for more volunteers, but without the guarantee of some form of compensation, the response was rather meager. State statutes provided for compensation, not to exceed $250, for indigent representation only in murder cases; and in such instances and others as complex, expenses for a volunteer could run to many hundreds of dollars more, to say nothing of extra hours expended in investigations and in preparing briefs.

This system was in a faltering condition when, late in 1926, at the urging of John H. Wigmore, dean of the Northwestern University Law School, and Joel D. Hunter, superintendent of the United Charities of Chicago, a plan was developed by which a member of the Association's Committee on the Defense of Prisoners would serve alongside representatives of the university and the charitable organization in a united effort. The Association would continue to furnish attorneys to give advice to accused persons and to appear at trials if necessary, but the burden of making investigations would fall on the

United Charities' Legal Aid Bureau and that of conducting a legal clinic and providing lawyers' assistance—primarily by law school students and graduates—to the university through its James and Anna Raymond Foundation for Legal Aid to the Poor. Thomas S. Fitzgerald, an Association member long involved in social-service work, was named managing attorney to supervise and coordinate these three main phases. His salary was to be paid by the Raymond Foundation, which would also contribute funds for clerical expenses. The new system proved to be far superior to the old, with the Association supplementing its participation by continuing the activities of the Committee on Defense of Prisoners in criminal cases, and in later years, by instituting an effective and well-acclaimed Lawyers' Reference Plan. In addition, members contributed part of the annual cost of what came to be known as the "poor man's law office."

The second of these positive steps involved a change in educational requirements for admission to the bar. In the 1890s, the Association had ended a long and rather bitter battle by gaining the Illinois Supreme Court's adoption of Rule 39, which raised the existing standards. Now, throughout 1923, members of the Committee on Legal Education made painstaking investigations and held scores of conferences with the deans of every law school, large and small, in Chicago. As a result, amendments to Rule 39 were proposed. One was the requirement of at least two years of general college, or its equivalent, in addition to the four-year high school course previously required before entering law school. Another major change was that the time an applicant pursued his legal studies in a law office was increased from three to four years; such applicants, in addition, would now be required to submit to an examination annually during the first three years of such study. Those attending an accredited law school were required to show at least 1,200 classroom hours, with credit in any one year limited to 432 hours. The committee's recommendations were duly presented to the Illinois State Bar Association and embodied in a resolution that was adopted and submitted to the state Supreme Court. Despite some grumbling—although infinitesimal compared with the general uproar over adoption of Rule 39 in 1897—the high court granted its approval that October, and the *Record* was quick with apt commendation: "It is a source of gratification that the Association, through its Committee on Legal Education, has thus been permitted to contribute to the raising of the standards of legal education in Illinois."

3.

Among the Association's accomplishments in this period, and certainly one of its most pleasurable, was the inauguration in 1924 of Christmas Spirits, a show that poked fun—sometimes good-naturedly and sometimes savagely but invariably with wit—at the high, the mighty, and the politically powerful; gibed at all aspects of the very profession that afforded its lyricists, composers, performers, musicians, and stagehands their daily livelihoods; and hurled social, professional, and civic criticism not even the most diligent and daring Association official or committee, after months of inquiry and conferences, might ever dare to utter.

For at least 20 years, some form of entertainment, usually a few songs by a glee club comprising a dozen members singing topical songs, had been offered at the Association's annual dinners. Starting in 1919, the Law Club of Chicago presented annual Christmas-season shows in a spirit of considerable joy and some mockery. Typical of the tone of these revues was the ditty that had been written in 1915 by no less a legal personage than the celebrated Dean John H. Wigmore. It was titled "Nunc Pro Bunk," and its lyrics, sung to the tune of "Love's Old Sweet Song," went:

> All the law we ever saw,
>   We've banished from our sight!
> Nunc Pro bunk, the law is junk,
>   We've scrapped it for tonight!
> Judgments, trials, writs, denials,
>   Motions, all taboo!
> Every kid in this club is bid
>   Be gay clear through!

No red tape or prosy paper,
    Full of highbrow worth,
Shall destroy our giddy joy
    Or curb our schoolless mirth!
Any judge can go to fudge
    For all we care tonight;
Once a year we reverse our gear—
    Our hearts are light!

Among those most active in producing Law Club shows and starring in them was John D. Black, son of John C. Black and nephew of William Perkins Black and a future president of both the Chicago and Illinois State bar associations. A superb trial lawyer, his keenness and strategy were matched by his sharp and freewheeling sense of humor outside a courtroom. From producing Law Club shows to leading glee clubs in song at Association dinners to organizing the Association's first Christmas Spirits revue was a natural progression for Black. He also starred in the second show on December 17, 1925, along with such other regulars from Law Club extravaganzas as former president Russell Whitman; Edwin C. Austin; Homer H. Cooper, who had written the books of all the Law Club shows; and Richard Bentley, one of the best of the group's actors, singers, and writers. Set in a courtroom, the one-act skit dealt mainly with prevailing complaints about delays in the trial of lawsuits, with Whitman as presiding judge trilling:

The judge I am, the judge I am.
For the law I do not care a damn!

And the chorus responding:

The judge he are, the judge he are—
They ought to can him from the bar!

As the action proceeded, characters named Charlie Curbstone, Clarence Harrow, and Sen. J. Ham Lovus—rather heavily obvious parodies of Charles Erbstein, Clarence Darrow, and Sen. J. Hamilton Lewis—became involved in ludicrous and long-winded arguments before the judge. Various songs dealing with contemporary matters were sung. The most well-received song, sung to the tune of the drinking song from *The Student Prince,* stemmed from the recent capture of Martin Durkin, a young desperado who, while free on bond in connection with a robbery case, had shot a policeman:

> Bail! Bail! Bail! For all of the yeggs,
> Don't keep 'em locked up in the coop.
> Bail! Bail! Bail! For gunmen and thugs,
> Why keep 'em on biscuit and soup?
> Fix a bond that will give 'em the air,
> Why should we fill their brave hearts with despair?
> Why detain 'em without consent,
> If they're free they may repent.
> Bail! Bail! Don't treat 'em rough,
> They're young, what if they're tough?
> Bail! Bail! Bail!
> Just sign a recognizance, that is enough,
> For bail!
>
> Bail! Bail! Bail! For drunkards and bums
> A copper picked up on his beat.
> Bail! Bail! Bail! For pickpockets, too,
> Caught plying their trade on the street.
> They're the victims of brutal police,
> Tenderly, trustfully grant their release.
> Don't compel 'em to stay in jail,
> If confined they may grow stale.
> Bail! Bail! Please have a heart,
> They're young, give 'em a start.
> Bail! Bail! Bail!
> Let ev'ry old crook have a chance to depart
> On bail!

The 1926 show, set in a country law office, satirically contrasted the allegedly simple and uncomplicated rural practice with the activities of a high-powered urban firm ("MacChesney, Choate, Marshall, Kirkland and Rosenthal, Ltd."). The songs re-

170

ferred to Terry Druggan and Frankie Lake, two bootleggers who
had been given lavish privileges while ensconced in the county
jail awaiting trial, and to Rumania's imperious Queen Marie,
whose recent visit to the United States had been festooned with
tons of newspaper publicity. In the 1927 show, there was many
an assault on William Hale Thompson, based on his election that
April to his third term as mayor. The climax of the show was a
poem, "The Burning of Rome"—recited by Charles O. Rundall
as William Hale Nero—that was based on the threats of Big
Bill to rid the schools of "British influence" and the vow of one
of his minions, Urban J. "Sport" Hermann, to rid the libraries of
all "subversive books" in a bonfire; its closing lines were:

> For centuries I've been the goat
> Of every bum that ever wrote
> A history of ancient times
> In verse, or prose, or silly rhymes.
> Foul charges on my name they've tossed
> As author of this holocaust.
> But you can see that my intent
> Was really but to circumvent
> The wicked purpose of those men,
> Who sought by word and deed and pen,
> To make of Rome a colony
> Of that cursed nation 'cross the sea.
> But Rome was burned that Rome might live,
> And I to you this tip will give:
> 'Tis better that a city perish
> Than that those ideals which we cherish,
> Should be destroyed or undermined
> By propaganda of that kind.
> Another thing I might confess,
> It's safe to tell it now.
> This fire gave all our boys a chance
> Their private fortunes to enhance.
> The city being burned to ash
> They made a pretty piece of cash
> By the big building that we did.
> You get "Big Billding," don't you, kid?

This ode was composed by George Swain, an inveterate lyricist for both the Law Club and Association shows, whose major triumph was to come in the 1929 production with "The Junior Partners," a number that achieved the status of a Christmas Spirits classic, to be repeated again and again as encores in subsequent extravaganzas. It evoked considerable applause from younger Association members, among whom it struck especially responsive chords. Typical of the many verses, sung to the tune of "Mister Dooley," were these:

> A bankrupt client wants to save a
> few bonds and stocks,
> He wants you to preserve them in
> your safe deposit box.
> When on this base proposal you
> have properly enlarged,
> In whose box do you keep the
> stocks until he is discharged?
>
> The junior partners! The junior partners!
> They're the ones who bring in all the fees!
> They are the aces, they win the cases—
> They change the appellants to appellees!
>
> A steno had a baby although she'd
> not been wed,
> The senior's hair was auburn and
> the baby's hair was red!
> Who was it that came forward and
> shouldered all the blame?
> Who made the girl his blushing bride
> and gave the child a name?
>
> The junior partners! The junior partners!
> They're the ones who bring in all the fees!
> They are the aces, they win the cases—
> They change the appellants to appellees!

Another 1929 hit poked considerable fun at the Committee on Candidates' annual reports on judicial nominees. At this time, many nominees had been judged "qualified" whom the membership considered to be less than ideal for the bench, and much criticism had often been expressed about the indiscriminate use of the label. The puckish creators of that year's production offered wicked commentary. Portraying the committee, Swain, Archibald Cattell, Herbert M. Lautmann, and Richard Hayes ridiculed the ease with which the "qualified" ranking was achieved:

> Suppose a lawyer takes a little bribe
> Or to a padded payroll does subscribe.
> You might expect from us a diatribe,
> But we're not so mean,
>   We just wash him clean.
> He's qualified, yes he's qualified.
> Qualified to be judge.
> Our OK is the sesame
> To whiten any smudge
> If he'll promise us he will give back
> To the people all the stolen jack
> We will sing him this elegiac,
> "We deem him qualified."

> Some judges from a trifling incident
> Fly into a wild spell of temp'rument.
> They rave and swear and get quite violent,
> But still their rage does cool,
>   When they hear us drool.
> He's qualified, yes he's qualified.
> Qualified to be a judge.
> Our OK is the sesame
> To whiten any smudge.
> Though he knows not any law at all,
> He has friends down in the City Hall
> So from our lips these magic words still fall,
> "We deem him qualified."

Accurately, the *Record's* critic, George Packard, in writing about the 1930 production that derided the police, the press, the crime-fighting organization known as the "Secret Six," lawyers specializing in criminal cases, mayoral aspirants, and the state's attorney's office, commented: "Bootleg liquor and Christmas Spirits grow deadlier every year, but the stouter they are the better their patrons seem to enjoy them." And, prophetically, he noted, "The perpetuation of Christmas Spirits as a yearly event seems assured."

The "street of lawyers"—La Salle Street—as it looked in 1917, north from Jackson Boulevard.

Chicago Today

Association members not only served in all branches of the armed forces in World War I but also were active in Preparedness Day parades. This is a photograph of one such parade in 1916.   *Chicago Tribune*

The "Black Sox" trial of 1920, in which members of the White Sox baseball team were tried—and acquitted—on charges of fixing the 1919 World Series, was held in this courtroom of the Criminal Courts Building. The same building housed the pressroom that was the setting for the famous Ben Hecht-Charles MacArthur play, *The Front Page*.   *Chicago Today*

A powerful triumvirate in 1920: Governor Len Small (left) and Mayor William Hale "Big Bill" Thompson flank their master political strategist, Fred "Poor Swede" Lundin. *Chicago Today*

THE CHICAGO BAR ASSOCIATION

RECORD

PUBLISHED MONTHLY

Vol. 4   CHICAGO, JUNE, 1921   No. 9

A GREAT VICTORY

A FITTING CLOSE to the year's activities of the Association was the judicial election on June sixth. Never in recent years have its leadership and influence been manifested in the selection of judges to the extent accomplished in the recent campaign. While this result could not have been obtained without the support and co-operation of the party and other organizations and the newspapers, yet it must not be lost sight of that the coalition plan was originated and fostered by The Chicago Bar Association through its Committee on Candidates, under the Chairmanship of Mr. Amos C. Miller.

The Association has long aspired to leadership in the selection of our judges, for it is the lawyers of the Community who know best the qualifications of the candidates, and it is in their hands that the selection should be reposed.

By its successful fight in the June election, The Chicago Bar Association has advanced far toward the goal of leadership in this branch of its legitimate functions, and has won the right to expect the people to look to it for guidance in future judicial elections.

It is our hope that the day is not far off when the nominees of The Chicago Bar Association for the judicial office will be without opposition from any quarter, and will be assured of election.

George E. Brennan, chairman of the Cook County Democratic Central Committee, who joined the Association in working for a notable defeat of the Thompson-Lundin machine in 1921.

Chicago Daily News

When the Association triumphed over the Thompson-Lundin organization in the June 1921 judicial election, this was the *Record's* front-page statement.

Chicago Bar Association

178

In the aftermath of the Thompson-Lundin defeat in 1921 and various scandals, Fred Lundin was among several of Big Bill Thompson's adherents tried for fraud in connection with the misappropriation of school funds. It took a corps of lawyers headed by Clarence Darrow (right), seen here with Lundin, to win acquittal.

An aggressive Republican office-holder with whom the Association contended on various issues during the 1920s and later was Robert E. Crowe, posing here for photographers when, as Cook County state's attorney, he directed the prosecution of Nathan Leopold and Richard Loeb for the murder of Bobby Franks.

After the murder and mayhem of the April 1928 election primary, Frank J. Loesch, a former Association president and veteran crime fighter, made a bold move by asking Al Capone to help curb Election Day violence in November. Here, Loesch and his wife cast their ballots in what turned out to be one of the quietest elections in the city's history.

Chicago Daily News

Prominent in investigating vote frauds and scandals in the Chicago Sanitary District toward the end of the 1920s was an Association leader and author of many legal books, Francis X. Busch.

Author's collection

180

Recommendations
of the Chicago Bar Association

The Chicago Bar Association recommends for nomination for the office of State's Attorney the candidates whose names are marked below with a cross.

For State's Attorney

Republican	Bar Ass'n Votes	Democratic	Bar Ass'n Votes
☐ Robert E. Crowe	463	☒ William J. Lindsay	1837
☐ Maxwell Landis	16	☐ Daniel F Murphy	132
☒ John A. Swanson	2191		

The Association also by vote of its members recommends the candidates for nomination for the office of Judge of the Municipal Court whose names are marked below with a cross.

For Judge of the Municipal Court

Republican

- ☐ Henry E. Ayers
- ☐ Louis N. Blumenthal
- ☐ James B. Cashin
- ☐ Joseph F. Cervinka
- ☒ George E. Dierssen
- ☐ Thomas L. Donnelly
- ☐ Alfar M Eberhardt
- ☒ Theodore F. Ehler
- ☒ Frederick W. Elliott
- ☒ Alfred O. Erickson
- ☒ William B. Gemmill
- ☒ John F. Haas
- ☐ Harry Hamill
- ☒ Howard W. Hayes
- ☒ William E. Helander
- ☐ Marion G. Kudlick
- ☐ James C. Leaton
- ☐ Joseph J. Nagle
- ☐ John R. Newcomer
- ☒ John R. Philp
- ☐ Henry M. Porter
- ☐ John Richardson
- ☒ William H. A. Rust
- ☐ George J. Spatuzza
- ☐ Charles L. Swanson
- ☐ Stephen A. Thieda
- ☐ Leonard J. Wissman

Democratic

- ☒ Francis B. Allegretti
- ☒ Frank C. Bicek
- ☒ Francis Borrelli
- ☒ Edward M. Burke
- ☐ John B. Devine
- ☒ Cassius M. Doty
- ☒ Philip J. Finnegan
- ☐ Thomas A. Green
- ☒ Matthew D. Hartigan
- ☐ N. A. Lawrence
- ☒ James B. McKeon
- ☒ Donald S. McKinlay
- ☒ Frank M. Padden
- ☐ Abdon M. Pallasch
- ☒ Jay A. Schiller
- ☐ Thomas J. Sheehan

> **NOTE**
>
> The names of Municipal Court candidates have alphabetical arrangement on the official ballot, but *rotate* as to position in different precincts.

For Judge of the Municipal Court
(To Fill Vacancy)

Republican

- ☒ Donald H. McGilvray
- ☐ Robert E. McMillan

The Chicago Bar Association
160 North La Salle Street

CARL R. LATHAM, President   HERBERT M. LAUTMANN, Secretary

Cut This Out and Take It With You to the Polls
(This advertisement paid for by The Chicago Bar Association)

In the November 1928 election, the Association took full-page advertisements in the newspapers to offer its recommendations to the voters.

Chicago Bar Association

For most of the decade starting in 1924, the Association's headquarters were in the Burnham Building at La Salle and Randolph streets.

Lounge of the Burnham Building.

More Jousts with Judges

1.

THE SPECIAL grand jury that had been picked to investigate the slaying of Octavius C. Granady concerned itself with other matters, particularly reports of profligacy at the Sanitary District of Chicago. This vast engineering system had been created by the state legislature in 1889 to furnish cleaner water by breaking up sewage, to reduce the possibility of flooding, and to afford other boons to the populace. In subsequent years, as the project—labeled by civic publicists "the eighth wonder of the world"—grew and vast amounts of money were expended to construct the Sanitary Canal, the district's main channel, and ancillary enterprises, a board of trustees was elected to administer its manifold activities. Almost constantly, complaints were heard about excessive spending, but none matched in breadth or intensity the ones sounded during the presidency of Timothy D. Crowe. From a rough-and-tumble boyhood in the city's steel-mill neighborhood, Crowe had risen steadily in Democratic Party ranks to win election as a Sanitary District trustee in 1922 and its president in 1926, the year the district began to construct a series of sewage treatment plants. Crowe was defeated for reelection in 1928 not long after the convening of the special grand jury to probe the Granady case, and Frank J. Loesch broadened the jury's scope to include investigation of what the newspapers soon came to call the "Whoopee Era" because various trustees were disclosed to have held raucous parties in New York while there presumably on business. On one such pleasure jaunt a number of celebrants and their hired lady companions, after consuming much prohibition liquor, had hurled some $7,000 worth of furniture out of the windows of the old Waldorf-Astoria Hotel. A charge by an auto livery company of $120,000 in a single year was shown to include expenditures not only for cars but also for women entertainers, liquor, powder puffs, and silk underwear. Loesch's inquiry also revealed that the Crowe trustees had approved contracts for construction of a bridle path along the north shore of the Sanitary District's main channel; the total cost was $1,068,000, but no horseback riders were ever seen using it. In addition, certain favored contractors, already paid to haul cinders away from the Sanitary District's plants, had been paid again for the cinders that were spread on the bridle path. In all, it was estimated, some $5 million had been wildly and carelessly spent.

Of greatest concern to the Association was the revelation that among scores of men and women added to the district payrolls in the "Whoopee Era" were lawyers who did little or no work. On November 22, 1928, the Association's Board of Managers voted to establish a special Committee on Public Law Offices to look into the matter and make appropriate recommendations. Headed by Edgar B. Tolman, this group sent to every member of the Sanitary District's law department an incisive questionnaire asking everything from how much time was spent on district duties and the precise nature of those duties to rates of compensation and whether "conscientious and full service" had been rendered for that compensation. Meeting three times a week, Tolman's committee also invited each of these lawyers to appear before it for further examination and elucidation and scrupulously examined thousands of work sheets and employment records.

By the next April, even though he emphasized that the investigation was not finished, Tolman had heard and probed enough to issue an interim report. This detailed document that listed the kinds of work done by the Sanitary District's law department—including litigation that evolved from a United States Supreme Court decision ordering the raising of Lake Michigan water levels and preparation of opinions, ordinances, contracts, leases, and other documents relating to real estate transactions—traced the history and development of the district. Most pertinently, the report enumerated the diverse payrolls, singling out the one termed "Miscellaneous" as that which served to conceal employment of lawyers far in excess of the number needed to handle all the district's legal affairs. An indication of what was soon to come was Tolman's description of the district as a "dumping ground" used to reward job recipients for political service or to grant favors to politicians who had sponsored trustees' appointments. "Political debauchery in the Sanitary District has of late gone to unprecedented lengths. . . . Information furnished the Committee disclosed the closest kind of a working alliance between the bosses of the different political parties and factions. Democratic bosses procured from Republican trustees numerous jobs for Democratic workers, and Republican workers from Democratic trustees. Apparently no thought was given to the public interest, no attempt was made to protect the public treasury, in this wild scramble for spoils. It is a striking example of the evils of political manipulation of public office for personal ends, and well illustrates the betrayal of public trust which invariably occurs when the people elect spoilsmen to office."

As Tolman's committee continued its diligent examination into the new year and the time approached for its final report, some of the lawyers who had appeared before it, aware of the direction in which the committee was heading, offered to repay whatever salaries they had received, and close to $18,000 was thereby recovered. As for the others, on June 15, 1930, the Association filed a petition before the Illinois Supreme Court charging 55 lawyers with unprofessional conduct and asking that punishment be meted out as the court deemed fit to uphold the standards of the legal profession. Fees paid to lawyers on the "Miscellaneous payroll" ranged from $1,000 to $23,000 and those who had accepted them, the petition asserted, "were guilty of dishonorable conduct, denoting a lack of good moral character."

Most prominent among those so accused was the head of the Sanitary District's law department in the "Whoopee Era," Maclay Hoyne, scion of one of the city's foremost legal families —grandson of an Association founder, Thomas Hoyne, and son of the estimable Thomas Maclay Hoyne—and a highly effective state's attorney from 1912 to 1919, when he had made an unsuccessful race for the mayoralty as an independent candidate. His most successful assistant during his service as state's attorney, James C. O'Brien—nicknamed "Ropes" because of his success in sending killers to the gallows—also was listed in the petition, as was William Scott Stewart, famous among lawyers specializing in criminal cases.

Hoyne promptly accused the Association of "placing itself above the law." Stewart called its action "tyrannical." But the state Supreme Court directed that a formal hearing be held before Circuit Court Judge Thomas Taylor, Jr., a jurist of impeccable reputation. It was another six months before these hearings began, with Walter F. Dodd and Willard Matheny representing the Association and a battery of six men, including Grover Niemeyer and J. Hamilton Lewis, appearing for Hoyne.

Those named in the petition testified, many admitting to doing, at most, cursory research in the Association's library for an hour a day one week each month. But primary attention centered on Hoyne. Under Niemeyer's questioning, Hoyne, dignified and articulate, testified that lawyers had been hired for his department, temporarily or permanently, on Crowe's mandate and that he himself had never recommended anyone for employment and had no authority to discharge anyone.

On July 8, 1931, Judge Taylor issued a 175,000-word report for consideration by the high court at its October session. The first 150 of 700 pages narrated the history of the Sanitary District; another 150 pages traced the quick growth of the law department under Hoyne; and the rest presented summaries of work records and testimony of 55 of the men, Hoyne's assertions and defense as department head, and finally, the judge's recommendations of a two-year suspension for Hoyne and 10 others, one-year suspensions for 27, permanent disbarment for 9, a continuance for one, and dismissal of charges against the remaining 7. (Crowe and five trustees were tried later that year for their participation in the depredations of the "Whoopee Era." Sentenced to one to five years, Crowe vowed he would not serve a single day in jail—a prediction borne out when he died of a heart attack in the summer of 1933 while his appeal was pending. The five trustees were either acquitted or given light sentences.)

Virtually all the penalties recommended by Judge Taylor were initially reduced by the Supreme Court, and, after appeals, were lightened further early in 1933. The suspensions of Hoyne and 12 others were reduced to 90 days, another man was barred from practice for two years, and 21 were censured for dereliction of professional duty. Only one, Frank Brewbaker, was disbarred; and the rest, including Stewart, were exonerated.

The eventual outcome of disciplinary action instigated by the Association was obviously far below original expectations. But its role in the proceedings had well displayed the Association's concern for rectitude in a public agency. Some inspiration and instruction could be found in that portion of Judge Taylor's decision that replied to Hoyne's claim that he was not responsible for what had occurred because he was subordinate to the trustees and could not countermand their orders: "A lawyer's duty to his client is subservient to that which is ethical. His relations with the taxpayers, collectively, of the district were more important than those with the trustees. They may have been ignorant or inefficient or criminal; he, as a lawyer, was assumed to be skilled in his profession, expected and required to act only in the highest of good faith for the best interests of the Sanitary District. It did not call for any great heroism or saintly virtue to quit, but a mere recognition of the fact that he could not be reasonably and honorably useful, and could not, as a lawyer of good moral character, go on and ostensibly sanction what was being done, that he must give up his client, suppress his motive, his desire for position and salary in the interests of his professional duty and honor.... The practicing lawyer must be more than a law-abiding citizen. He should be in his professional conduct a sociologically con- scientious one, and that because the final goal of our juris- prudence, generally considered, is identical with morality, and the lawyer is its especial sworn and licensed practitioner and especially so when employed by a public corporation...."

2.

This period was marked once again by the Association's deep involvement in judicial campaigns and in jousts with judges.

Efforts in the June 5, 1933, Circuit Court election were de- cidedly intense, almost equaling in zeal and activity—if not in expenditure of funds—the triumphant contest of 1921 that con- tinued to serve as an example the Association sought to emulate. The motivation now was to prevent the reelection of sitting judges who were considered unfit by age or temperament, or, more specifically, of those sitting judges who had been accused in preceding months of political favoritism in naming receivers for millions of dollars' worth of foreclosed properties. When its regular poll in February gave low scores to six of these jurists, President Charles P. Megan issued a statement directed at the political chieftains who were reportedly planning a coali- tion ticket: "It is the duty of the party organizations to name for judicial office only those candidates who possess the highest qualifications. The press and good citizens in general are con- tinually urging the Association to take the leadership in securing the election of good judges."

At a brief conference with George E. Brennan's successor, Patrick A. Nash, and two of the Democratic central committee's powerful members, Jacob M. Arvey and Moe Rosenberg—the latter recently indicted for income-tax evasion—Megan pre- sented the results of the Association's poll. He also furnished copies of the vote to the various factions of the Republican Party, in general disarray since the defeat of Mayor Big Bill

Thompson by Anton J. Cermak in 1931 and the accession to the mayoralty by Edward J. Kelly, Nash's close compatriot, after the fatal shooting of Cermak earlier that year in Miami by an assassin allegedly aiming at President-elect Franklin D. Roosevelt. But Megan's efforts were fruitless. As leader of one of these factions, Robert E. Crowe, in a typical bipartisan deal with his political rivals, was receptive to the idea of a combined ticket, and a coalition slate—promptly dubbed by rival Republicans the "Moe and Crowe ticket"—was soon announced. In it were included all incumbents except one among those rejected in the Association's poll. The regular Republican list, almost certainly doomed to defeat, excluded three of the judges who had failed to win Association approval. Faced with this situation, the Association polled its membership again and was authorized by a five-to-one vote to submit an independent "Bar ticket" with six new candidates to supplant the ones turned down. The Association then began an offensive, under the direction of Henry A. Gardner, in which over $26,000 would be spent in a few brief months. Throughout the city billboards urged: "Keep Politics Off the Bench! Elect Judges Endorsed by the Chicago Bar Association." Thousands of automobile stickers bearing that message were distributed. Over a million sample ballots were sent out by many dozens of cooperating groups ranging from the Alliance of Business and Professional Women to a complex of civic organizations organized under the cumbersome title of Joint Committee for the Co-operation with the Chicago Bar Association for the Election of Qualified Judges. In the 24 hours before the election, sound trucks coursed through the streets rasping pleas for support of the Association ticket.

Despite these and such other efforts as frequent statements on radio by Association spokesmen, nearly 100 speeches to clubs, and newspaper advertisements, the "Moe and Crowe ticket" won handily, snaring 74 percent of the vote. The reasons for the Association's defeat, beyond the undoubted vote-getting strength of the Democratic organization, were varied. The Association had publicly condemned the receivership scandal but had made no move against members involved in it, a failure that undoubtedly contributed to apathy among voters hopeful for aggressive action against those who had been accused of favoritism and receipt of abnormally high fees. Moreover, the Democrats were more formidable than they had been in many years; not only did the local organization control most of the city, county, state, and federal offices—and patronage—but also it was riding high on the crest of Roosevelt's tremendous presidential victory and his inauguration of the New Deal, aimed at the country's economic recovery. Equally decisive was the fact that even with espousal of "moral issues" and earnest endeavor, tremendous obstacles to duplicating the 1921 triumph were faced by an aggregation of volunteers battling the experts of a solid and impregnable political organization.

Although the Kelly-Nash organization maintained—and indeed strengthened—its power and control, the Association made new attempts in 1934 and 1935 to influence judicial elections. In each instance, it met with defeat, mainly for the same reasons that prevailed in 1933.

After the election in 1934 of a slate of Municipal Court judges mostly held by the Association to be without merit— perpetuating the system in which nominees invariably were chosen more for political reward than ability—disappointment was epitomized in the *Record* along with a tentative proposal for reform: "Unfortunately a judge in Chicago rises or falls by no rule of merit, logic or public welfare. He is nominated solely on a basis of political expediency. His election and continuation in office are ruled by the fortunes of politics. . . . The Chicago Bar Association has fought vigorously through bar primaries and campaigns for the nomination and election of better qualified candidates to the bench. Its efforts have had some effect, but not enough to be very encouraging. The energy that has gone into such activities seems to us largely wasted. The boys in charge of the Democratic and Republican machines (The G.O.P. used to have one) are still the judge-makers and won't surrender that strategic power until they are pried loose from it. This can only be accomplished by statutory changes in the system of electing judges and constant vigilance over the administration of it."

The idea of responsible judicial selection by alternative methods had been proposed in previous years—notably in a 1920–22 state constitutional convention—but had not won voter approval, and the matter of judicial reform would continue to maintain high priority on the agendas of future Association presidents. Reflecting sadly on the results of these elections, the Association meanwhile continued to condemn coalition tickets picked solely by political bosses who refused to hearken to proposals from any source, and it cited with approval the postelection statement of a *Daily News* editorialist: "Hidden beneath a legal elective system we have a non-legal appointive system of the most vicious kind. The balloting merely screens the operations of the party machines. Yesterday the screen was scant enough for all to see under it. The wise thing would be to take it down completely and establish legally an appointive system that would be non-political and openly responsible." And Clarence Denning, in the wake of the 1935 Superior Court election, offered perceptive commentary before the Law Club of Chicago on reasons for the dilemma and a firm promise of sustained movement for change: "It is a situation traceable directly to the method of selecting judges adopted in a slower age for use in smaller communities and not adaptable to a great cosmopolitan city where racial groups demand and secure representation in return for votes for the party ticket, where political thugs do likewise in return for votes for thousands upon thousands of stolen votes, where party leaders lack the moral courage to insist on good candidates, where 'Put in the fix, fix, fix' is a marching song from job to job. The only way out is to arouse intelligent people to the necessity of adopting a method of selecting judges which fixes responsibility for selection within a very narrow compass and holds the responsible officer to a high degree of selection. To bring this about will be no easy political struggle, but the bar association has accepted the responsibility. It will produce a sound plan. The day will come when good judges will have longer periods of service, will be judges in every sense of the word, and the percentage of those who debase the bench will be very small!"

3.

Steadfast in its criticism of a judiciary it considered beholden to political influences, the Association soon became embroiled in controversy with most of the 48 judges of the Superior and Circuit courts.

Early in March 1936, in the midst of a general election primary, every city, county, and federal judge in Cook County received from the Board of Managers a copy of this canon of the American Bar Association: "While entitled to entertain his personal views of political questions, and while not required to surrender his rights or opinions as a citizen, it is inevitable that suspicion of being warped by political bias will attach to a judge who becomes the active promoter of the interests of one political party as against another. He should avoid making political speeches, making or soliciting payment of assessments or contributions to party funds, the public endorsement of candidates for political office and participation in party conventions. He should neither accept nor retain a place on any party committee nor act as party leader, nor engage generally in partisan activities."

Accompanying the statement was another criticizing those jurists who were making speeches in behalf of candidates on local and national tickets. During the primary, young Association members kept notes on which judges orated at ward meetings or on radio or made public endorsements of candidates in newspaper stories.

These notes formed the basis for complaints against 22 judges, and in May, the Board of Managers announced that these judges would be invited to appear at hearings on the complaints. The move, President Herbert M. Lautmann emphasized, was not meant to put any judge on trial: "The Association has no power to try judges except in disbarment cases.

The Association is merely holding hearings on the conduct of members of the Association with respect to their conformity or non-conformity with the canons of ethics."

Two judges appeared, but four others—Harry M. Fisher of the Circuit Court and James J. Kelly, John J. Sullivan, and Oscar F. Nelson of the Superior Court—sent a letter to Lautmann stating their refusal to answer the charges or come before the board. Moreover, they and 39 other judges gathered in the courtroom of Judge Kelly, drew up a tartly worded resolution condemning the board's inquiry—"The judges of these courts," stated the resolution, "support the position taken by the judges who refuse to answer alleged charges against them, deeming it incompatible with the proper performance of their judicial duties for judges to be subservient to any group of lawyers practicing in their respective courts"—and announced they were resigning from the Association.

Taking no notice of their withdrawal from membership, Lautmann asserted, "It is to be regretted that the resentment of a few judges who are charged with having engaged in political activities, and who object to being questioned thereon, should have obscured the real issue in which the public is interested, which is whether judges should be permitted to indulge in political activity in violation of the canon of judicial ethics," and he affirmed the intention of continuing the investigation.

By mid-June, the Association was ready to report the expulsion of all four objecting judges from the Association and the censuring of nine others. Judge Nelson responded with a laugh and the comment, "The Association wants to mislead people into thinking we judges are still members." Judge Sullivan insisted that the core of the case was not violation of judicial ethics but his support in the primary of the unsuccessful candidacy of the regular Democratic gubernatorial candidate, Dr. Herman N. Bundesen, against Henry Horner, who had defied the Kelly-Nash organization by seeking a second term.

The wits of the Christmas Spirits show could not, of course, refrain from comment. One of the hit songs of the 1936 production—which also gibed at easy paroles, at the *Literary Digest's* enormous gaffe when its poll predicted Alfred M. Landon the winner over President Roosevelt, and at such New Deal luminaries as James L. Farley and Harold L. Ickes—was "Judicial Independence," sung by a sextet of jurists labeled Svenson, Tardy, Turmoil, I'llbuy, Fissure, and Skinloose and offering such pertinent—and impertinent, in the view of some—verses as these:

> In us you see a Superior Court.
> We're far above the Bar.
> No big guns and no canons can
> Our reputations jar.
> We love to deal in politics
> Our jobs to make secure.
> Despite the hubbub we remain
> Complacent and demure.
>
> Rah for the Superior Court,
> Tra la la la la la.
> Politics is still our forte,
> Tra la la la la la.
> You may summon us, you sons-of-guns,
> Our actions to explain.
> Your nerve defies description,
> And you give us all a pain.

The stalemate prevailed until well into 1937 when Mayor Kelly's highly astute corporation counsel, Barnet Hodes, undertook to effect a reconciliation, aided by his predecessor and former Association president, William H. Sexton. In a series of informal meetings in the chambers of state Supreme Court Justice Francis Wilson, Hodes brought together for the Association its new president, Hayes McKinney, and Henry P. Chandler its first vice-president, and for the jurists Judge Sullivan, risen to the Appellate Court, his colleague, John O'Connor, and Judge Fisher. Ultimately, the conferees formulated a resolution that participation of judges in political campaigns should be reduced to a minimum and that judges and lawyers should work within the Association toward that end instead of engaging in acrimonious debate. Shortly after the start of the new year, the Board of Managers formally invited all 43 judges to resume their membership, and although four rejected the invitation, the clamor was stilled for the time being, and the more optimistic among both sets of adversaries looked forward to tranquillity and cooperation.

4.

In the midst of rancorous disputes came calmer and more gratifying events.

Chief among them was passage of constructive legislation long sought by the Association, notably the Business Corporation Act and the Civil Practice Act.

The latter was long overdue. Among the nation's populous states, Illinois had been the most backward in effecting reforms in statutes governing civil litigation. Headed by Harry N. Gottlieb, a future Association president, a committee working in conjunction with an Illinois State Bar Association counterpart drafted, after nearly three years of toil, an act for consideration by the legislature in 1933. Designed to modernize civil practice thoroughly, including abridgment of the governing statutes from four volumes to 100 pages, the act provided for the replacement of antiquated forms of pleadings and excessive use of stilted legal verbiage with plain, concise statements of fact, for summary judgments to expedite action in the courts and relieve the dockets of cases lacking merit, for declaratory judgments and pretrial discovery measures to expedite disposition of cases, for simpler appellate procedures, and for improved methods of selecting and instructing jurors. The new Civil Practice Act, repealing procedural provisions of the old Chancery Act of 1872 and of the Law Practice Act of 1907, became effective early in 1934, and although other factors would cause sporadic court congestion in the future, the new act was then adjudged a notable advance in eliminating legal red tape and laggard disposition of litigation. One outgrowth was the scrapping in 1940 of 310 complex rules of procedure for the Municipal Court and their replacement with 80 simple ones, as well as the establishment of a pretrial branch of the court where issues might be clarified, technical motions disposed of, and equitable settlements reached.

Another heartening move in the decade was the formation of the Younger Members Committee. This came about as the result of complaints that Association members in their 30s were constantly being overlooked as candidates for important committees. Forty years earlier, similar grumblings had led to the creation by Eugene Prussing of the Law Club of Chicago. In Los Angeles, more recently, a group of youthful lawyers had organized the Young Barristers as a rival to the established association. To forestall a similar situation, Charles P. Megan and Clarence Denning proposed to the more vociferous young men that they establish a Younger Members Committee on a two-year trial basis. Edward J. Fleming became the new committee's chairman, George W. Gale its vice-chairman, and Donald B. Hatmaker its secretary. Among their most active colleagues were such lawyers of future fame and accomplishment as George Ball, Albert E. Jenner, Alex Elson, Leon M. Despres, and George F. Barrett and such later Association presidents as Jerome S. Weiss and James A. Velde.

The young lawyers agitated for variegated goals, from lower dues for Association members under 30 to serving slices of cheese with apple pie in the dining room. Many worked arduously in the period's judicial contests, and it was because of evidence collected by them that the more conservative-minded on the Board of Managers were persuaded to support action against judges who were politically involved in the 1936 primaries. They acted as observers in various branches of the Municipal Court, and some of them managed to land on several influential committees; Elson and Jenner were especially active on those committees seeking further reforms in court rules and procedures. Rebuffed by the elders of Christmas Spirits, the youthful upstarts—including a talented young woman member,

Kay Barasa—organized their own revue in 1935 and presented it a month before the established annual frolic. The most satirical of their skits, "Alice Bond in Foreclosure Land," highlighted receivership scandals. So popular was this show that the entire cast—sans Miss Barasa, for no woman had yet appeared in Christmas Spirits—was invited to participate in the 1936 production, with Weiss portraying Senator McGlook in a sharp thrust at the state's lax parole system.

And although the activities of the Younger Members Committee as a unit languished and remained primarily social in subsequent years until its strong resuscitation nearly four decades later, this initial phase of its existence did have the positive effect of injecting able and energetic young lawyers into the mainstream of some Association affairs. In 1943, a rule that 20 percent of all committee members had to be under 36 years old was established.

Another important step for the Association was the acquisition of new quarters. In the years it had occupied space in the Burnham Building at La Salle and Randolph streets, hopes had prevailed that with removal of the nearby South Water Street market and the completion of Wacker Drive, there would be a northward trend in the location of law offices. But the expected movement did not occur. When the two top floors in a 13-story building at 29 South La Salle Street, in the heart of a district containing hundreds of law offices, were vacated by the National Life Insurance Company early in 1936, steps were instituted to lease them.

A special committee was appointed to consider all aspects of the possible shift—including the offer of the building's owners to spend as much as $100,000 for remodeling and refurbishing —and alternative locations. Once the committee decided on the La Salle Street location, President Charles M. Thomson advised the members in that December's issue of the *Record* that suggestions to submit the proposed change to a vote had been deemed impractical. First, the decision was up to the Board of Managers, said Thomson, and second, its many angles and ramifications made it virtually impossible to obtain intelligent and satisfactory action through a referendum. "The Board," he wrote, "has endeavored to meet what it considers its responsibility with the most careful thought and with an eye single to the best interest of the Bar Association."

In the next three months, the move to the two designated floors and a portion of the eleventh floor was carried out, and ever since early in 1937 the Association's headquarters—with executive and administrative offices, meeting rooms, a dining room, a lounge, and a well-stocked library that most members consider among the Association's vital assets—have remained there.

Changes for the Better

1.

PERSISTENT EFFORTS in the 1940s to upgrade the methods of selecting judicial candidates were sometimes successful, often fruitless. Echoes of an earlier squabble were heard in 1947 when the Association declared an old adversary, Robert E. Crowe, unfit for reslating as chief justice of the Superior Court on a coalition ticket. In the Association poll, Crowe, who had been elected in 1942, received only 42 percent of the members' votes, nearly 30 percent below the "qualified" mark.

At once, the feisty Crowe accused the Association of harboring old grudges against him and of being dominated by Henry A. Gardner, a former president whom he assailed as an "internationalist" because Gardner had been active in Wendell Willkie's presidential campaign back in 1940. "I'm for America first, last and always!" declared the aging jurist. "And that vote was not at all representative. It included less than 20 percent of all Chicago Bar Association members and only 15 percent of all lawyers. Who watched the counting of the ballots?"

Despite his clamor, Crowe was dropped from the ticket, a move that prompted him to send a letter of resignation to the Association. His tempestuous judicial career was at an end, and in the years until his death in 1958 at 78, he practiced law and made occasional speeches espousing ultranationalistic causes.

Paralleling this and lesser conflicts were significant developments that many in and out of the Association considered long overdue.

Never since its founding in 1874 had the Association admitted a black lawyer to membership, and midway in this decade, a concerted move began to right this wrong.

There had been black lawyers in Chicago since the late 1860s. The first of them was Lloyd G. Wheeler, admitted to practice April 20, 1869, with James B. Bradwell, then a county judge, attesting to his good moral character and welcoming him to the profession with a brief statement in the *Chicago Legal News*: "Mr. Wheeler is an intelligent and worthy gentleman, an honor to his race and no disgrace to the bar of Illinois. He is the first Negro ever admitted to the bar in this state. We wish him success." A year later, Richard A. Dawson, a recent graduate of the old University of Chicago Law School, was granted his license, with B. W. Ellis, formerly a slaveholder in Arkansas, as a sponsor. From that time until near the end of the century, 29 other blacks became lawyers. Among these were Ferdinand L. Barnett, Jr., a journalist and schoolteacher, who later married the energetic Ida B. Wells, outstanding among reformers and advocates of antilynching legislation; Louis Washington, a former slave who had fled his native Alabama to walk to Vicksburg, Mississippi, where he had joined an Illinois Volunteers regiment in the Civil War; Edward H. Morris, also a former slave, who was so poor at the time of his examination before the Appellate Court in 1879 that he wore a long overcoat to cover his tattered clothes but who ultimately became an affluent practitioner and real estate investor; John G. Jones, who became especially expert in criminal law; S. Laing Williams, an educator, skilled writer, and husband of Fannie Barrier Williams, first black woman ever admitted to the Chicago Woman's Club. The sole woman was Ida Platt, a native Chicagoan who switched from a musical career to legal studies at the Chicago College of Law. Upon her admission to the bar in 1894, one of the Illinois Supreme Court justices commented, as he signed his name to her license: "We have done today what we never did before—admitted a colored woman to the bar. And it may now truly be said that persons are admitted to the Illinois bar without regard to race, sex, or color."

Such was obviously not the case with admission to membership in the Association. Periodically, Judge Bradwell recommended for membership various practicing black attorneys, but in each instance, the applicants were rejected without comment, and none preferred to press his cause. Some lawyers on the various membership committees might well agree with the sentiments expressed by the good judge in a long article in his journal in October 1896: "Considering the fact that less than forty years ago a large majority of the race in this country to which these colored lawyers belong were slaves, and that several of the lawyers themselves had been slaves, the race prejudice they had to overcome and the difficulties they had to encounter, with no rich or influential friends to give them a helping hand, the record they have made at the bar is an honor to the colored race and may well be held up to the colored men and women of their cities as worthy of imitation." But accepting them into the Association was another matter; racial lines not only here but also in virtually all professional associations as well as in the social and business sectors of the city—and indeed, the nation—were strictly drawn, and few dared then to call for their elimination. As the years passed and the rebuffs mounted, two dozen black lawyers formed, in 1914, the Cook County Bar Association along the lines of the organization from which they were barred but with special emphasis on cooperating with civic groups to attempt to improve living and working conditions in the South Side neighborhoods in which most of the city's blacks were herded. Although its Grievance Committee occasionally conferred and cooperated with its Association counterpart in specific disciplinary cases, the gap was deep and wide. Sometimes anger at the Association's rigidity burst forcefully into the open, as in the reply of the Chicago chapter of the National Association for the Advancement of Colored People to the Association's plea for support of its candidates in the 1933 judicial election:

"We feel that the axiom—'He who comes into equity must come with clean hands'—obtains in this case. We have advised all churches and their pastors of the attitude of your Association toward Negro members of the Illinois Bar, and while we feel that some of your recommendations may be good, we also feel that you should not place your recommendations on the high ground of 'social justice and purity' when you are so obviously unfair, un-American and devoid of social purity in the matter of admission of Negroes to your organization."

In the 1940s, amidst action to break down racial segregation and discrimination in many segments of society locally and nationally, considerable agitation was stirred—especially by young Association members such as Charles Liebman, Elmer Gertz, Robert T. Drake, Frank McCulloch, and Leon M. Despres— for an end to refusal of membership to blacks. Each year highly regarded black attorneys applied, and occasionally an application or two was accepted by the Committee on Membership, only to be rejected by a majority vote of the Board of Managers, from whose decision there was no appeal.

Late in 1943, four of the city's best-known black attorneys forwarded applications: Archibald J. Carey, Jr., in addition to his legal career the pastor of the Woodlawn African Methodist Episcopal Church and son of a bishop of that church; Earl B. Dickerson, former alderman, onetime assistant state's attorney, veteran of World War I, and recent candidate for Congress; Rufus Sampson, Jr.; and William Sylvester White, who had recently resigned as an assistant United States attorney to become a naval ensign and whose application bore the sponsorship of United States District Court Judges William J. Campbell and Michael L. Igoe. After nearly six months, all four applications were rejected, as others had so often been in previous years.

But now the decision was not to stand unchallenged. Superior Court Judge John P. McGoorty led a committee—including McCulloch, Herbert Bebb, and Mitchell Dawson, for several years the *Record's* bright and witty editor—in drafting a letter to the Board of Managers asking for a reconsideration

of the ruling. When that letter went unanswered, it was dupli-
cated and sent to every member of the Association. Russell
Whitman, former president and one of Dickerson's sponsors,
termed the denial of membership "ghastly" and added: "This
white supremacy stuff is exactly the kind of thing we are
fighting against in Germany. I've been fighting racial discrimination for 50 years and I'm going to keep everlastingly
at it. I never get mad because it doesn't do any good, but this
matter should be inquired into and the Admissions Committee
should be made to explain why it rejected these attorneys."
Liebman followed with a suit in Circuit Court to compel the
opening of Association records relating to the rejection of the
blacks and asked that the issue be put to a vote of the full
membership. Charles Leviton, the Association's general counsel, countered with a motion to dismiss Liebman's suit because
the internal affairs of the Association, as a voluntary and not-
for-profit organization, were not subject to review by the
courts.

Before Circuit Court Judge John Prystalski could issue a
ruling, Liebman and his associates gained an unexpected but
vital ally in J. Francis Dammann, a corporation attorney whose
sister was the outspoken, progressive president of New York's
Manhattanville College of the Sacred Heart, the fashionable
Catholic girls' school where Elmer Gertz's ward, Muriel Reno,
was a student. Shortly after Dammann succeeded Stephen E.
Hurley as Association president in mid-1945, Mother Dammann
died. Gertz knew Dammann only by his formidable reputation
in corporate legal circles, but he was moved to write a letter to
him. In it he told of his affection and respect for Dammann's
sister and related how she had stolidly maintained non-
discriminatory policies at her school in the face of protests from
wealthy alumnae, parents, and some students.

"I hope you will forgive me," Gertz wrote, "if I tell you that
the greatest memorial to your sister in our community will be
the admission of Negroes to membership in the Chicago Bar
Association during your term as president."

In his reply, Dammann wrote that Gertz's letter had touched

him deeply. "Be patient with me," he wrote, "and I promise you that while I am president of our Association Negroes will be admitted to membership on the same terms as whites."

Dammann fulfilled his promise by giving the issue top priority, and at every opportunity pressed forcefully for a reversal of the Association's stand. In November, Dickerson was admitted to membership, as were Irvin C. Mollison, a Phi Beta Kappa graduate of the University of Chicago and a recent appointee to the United States Customs Court of New York, Sidney A. Jones, Jr., and Loring B. Moore; and in their wake came Carey, White, and others. The number of blacks increased gradually, and many who assumed active roles in Association affairs served on committees and on various Boards of Managers. And while an occasional grumble might be heard from members who considered the Association a kind of elitist organization with no need to maintain a racially and professionally balanced constituency, the reform long sought had been effected, and a baneful barrier forever destroyed.

2.

In this period, which saw an end to one outworn tradition, a concerted drive against another antique—the Illinois Constitution—was undertaken, with the Association in the forefront of what would be a complex, prolonged struggle.

When Illinois became a state in 1818, the simple constitution adopted by 33 delegates in an 18-day convention at Bennett's Tavern in Kaskaskia was obviously sufficient for the needs of the citizens. It had a strong rural basis, and a predominant feature was the bestowal of powers to the state legislature, including selection of two United States senators, four state Supreme Court justices—also required for their annual $1,000 stipends to hold Circuit Court sessions—secondary state officials, and a variety of local officers, including justices of the peace. For 30 years, while the state grew in population from some 50,000 to over 700,000 and during which time several propositions for new constitutional conventions were rejected by voters, the constitution remained largely unaltered. In 1848, after persistent demands for change ranging from those of Jacksonian Democrats who wanted the governor to have more authority, principally the right of veto, to those of Whigs who sought to end voting by aliens freshly arrived in the area, a new and considerably expanded constitution, devised during a three-month convention, was overwhelmingly approved by the populace. The new constitution curbed legislative powers somewhat and provided, among other things, for popular referendums on policy issues and for popular elections of all state officials, three state Supreme Court judges at a salary only $200 higher than before, nine Circuit Court judges, County Court judges, and a larger number of justices of the peace.

Before long, this constitution, also designed for a predominantly agricultural society, proved woefully inadequate, what with rapidly burgeoning industrialism, the rise of cities with a host of accompanying problems, and an immense influx of newcomers from the East and South—the former settling mostly in the northern area, the latter primarily in the southern section, thereby establishing an upstate-downstate division in politics, culture, and social outlook that would persist for years to come—and immigrants from Europe, mostly Germans after the quelling of the Revolution of 1848 and Irishmen fleeing potato famines and the British rule. Again, there was evident need for modernization. A revised constitution produced in an 1862 convention failed to win voter approval, but seven years later, with the state's population now at over 2,500,000, a strong campaign led by Gov. Richard J. Oglesby and many big-city newspapers resulted in another convention call. Eighty-five delegates—56 of them lawyers, mostly young—gathered in the Springfield statehouse to debate, argue, and dispute for five months before hammering out a new constitution that was duly ratified in 1870.

Destined to be the state's basic set of laws for the next 100 years, it was still chiefly agrarian in nature, although some provisions were considered advanced for their time. A judicial article increased the number of Supreme Court justices to seven, authorized the creation of an intermediate Appellate Court, and laid the basis for establishment of a Probate Court in populous counties. Blacks were given the right to vote, although women were not; many delegates during convention sessions inveighed against advocates of suffrage as "long-haired men and short-haired women."

But as in the past, needs systematically outstripped the constitutional tenets. Deploring the static legal instrument unsuited to a constantly developing industrial state, the state Senate passed a resolution in 1893 declaring that "weighty social and economic issues persistently pressing upon us and demanding solution cannot be squarely met and intelligently solved with the present constitution in any way." In 1902, a committee of the Illinois State Bar Association singled out for special criticism the procedure for amending the constitution as impractical and cumbersome because any alteration needed approval by two-thirds of the state legislature before submission to voters at a general election in which a majority of all votes cast was necessary for adoption as law. Typical of demands for reform was that of a *Chicago Tribune* editorialist: "The constitution has outlived its usefulness. It is not the ark of the covenant. It has no sacred qualities. We may touch it without dropping dead."

Not until 1918 were the cries heeded, with the endorsement of another constitutional convention, which was convened in 1920. After two years of acrimonious debate and inevitable conflicts between urban and rural interests, a new constitution was drafted that showed some progress by granting a slight measure of home rule for Chicago and providing for the abolition of cumulative voting and the further revision of the judicial system and procedures. For three months, foes and friends of the proposed constitution, comprising 233 separate sections, sought to present their views to the public. The Association urged approval, exhorting members in the *Record* not only to vote in favor of adoption but also to propagandize among friends and neighbors: "The consolidation and efficient organization of Cook County's courts in one is in itself a sufficient reason for adopting the new constitution." Such support, buttressed by statements of approval from leading railroad and utility lawyers, furnished fuel for opponents' claims that this was a "lawyer's constitution," devised primarily for the benefit of large corporations rather than the public. Foremost among the constitution's controversial articles was one authorizing a general income tax on all net incomes, prompting widespread negative reaction from labor unions, World War I veterans, teachers, major leaders of both political parties, and an assortment of civic groups banded together as the People's Protective League, with Harold L. Ickes as president and Clarence Darrow and former Gov. Edward F. Dunne as prominent members. Because the convention delegates had made the fateful decision to submit their product to the voters for acceptance or rejection as a complete package, virulent opposition to this specific revenue article foreshadowed its doom, and on December 12, 1922, it suffered a crushing 8-to-1 defeat, with voters in Cook County turning in a negative response of almost 20 to 1.

For the next two decades, advocates of constitutional change persisted, mostly with campaigns for adoption of the Gateway Amendment, so-called because it sought to liberalize revision procedures by freeing the legislature from the rigid prohibition against proposing amendments to more than one article in the same session or to the same article more often than once in four years. Such an amendment had failed to win voter approval twice in previous years. Thrice more in these next 20 years it was offered in general elections, and thrice more it was turned down, mainly because too many voters simply neglected to vote on the separate ballots provided with those for a multitude of offices in the general elections.

The defeat of the fifth Gateway Amendment proposal in 1946 did nothing to stem the movement. Indeed, younger advocates of reform took up the fight anew, spurred by constant reminders from Kenneth C. Sears, a constitutional authority on the University of Chicago Law School faculty, in speeches and articles reprinted in the *Record*: "The greatest long-range governmental need in Illinois is a new constitution" and "Illinois, everything considered, is in the worst position of any state in the Union." One such Association member was Samuel W. Witwer, who earlier had come under the influence of an especially ardent reform proponent, George B. McKibbin, a fellow Republican and state revenue director. Witwer had been named by President James F. Oates, Jr., to work alongside Austin L. Wyman on a special Association committee in behalf of the 1946 Gateway Amendment campaign and had derived from the defeat the lesson that far more was needed than occasional newspaper editorials favoring constitutional revision or sporadic meetings of civic groups. He spoke often and volubly on strategies and techniques of sustained public education on the issue and stressed the importance of obtaining strong support from both major political parties.

Before long, a delegation including Walter V. Schaefer, an equally articulate adherent of reform and a devout Democrat, and Katherine Fischer, of the League of Women Voters, approached Witwer with the suggestion that he head a new Association committee that would concentrate on working for constitutional revision. They had already conferred, they assured Witwer, with Oates' successor, Erwin W. Roemer, and he had given ardent approval. Witwer agreed, with this proviso: "Our effort must be nonpartisan and the people we have on this committee will be politically astute and even have the likelihood of being active politically in the years ahead." The committee was so constituted. Called first the Committee on the Constitutional Convention and Amendment and later the Committee on Constitutional Revision, its roster was especially remarkable for a mingling of philosophical idealists and political pragmatists. With Witwer and Schaefer were Adlai E. Stevenson, little more than a year away from election as governor; Barnet Hodes, the city's former corporation counsel, as sagacious as ever in political matters and a law partner of Jacob M. Arvey, chairman of the Cook County Democratic Central Committee; Stephen A. Mitchell, who would soon serve as Stevenson's campaign adviser; and Otto Kerner, Walter Cummings, Jr., and Wayland B. Cedarquist.

After an Association poll indicated that two-thirds of those voting favored yet another convention call, Witwer and Schae-

fer sought to plead their case in Springfield before the Senate
Executive Committee. Senator Abraham L. Marovitz arranged
for their appearance. As Senate spokesman at an Association
dinner earlier that year for Cook County members of the legislature, Marovitz, a protégé of Arvey's, had made an especially
strong impression by urging broader Association interest not
only in general legislative matters but also in social issues,
housing problems, the rise in juvenile delinquency, and constitutional revision; and he had evoked considerably favorable response from the Board of Managers when he elaborated
on this theme in a private session. As it developed, Marovitz
was virtually the only member of the Senate group to give re-
spectful attention to Witwer and Schaefer. After a long wait in
the corridor outside the committee's meeting room, during which
Witwer and Schaefer and the several accompanying members
of the League of Women Voters could hear loud and raucous
discussion about such a weighty topic as the forthcoming
annual baseball game between the House and Senate, Marovitz
was able to prevail on the committee's chairman, Charles
Carpentier, a powerful downstate politician, to let the delegation enter. But when Witwer began to read the statement he
and Schaefer had put together in an all-night session, Carpentier turned his back on him, and most of his colleagues
mumbled to each other or riffled through papers.

The discourteous reaction and consequent rejection of the
convention proposal spurred Witwer and his committee to
greater efforts. Witwer proposed a systematic barrage of
articles by committee members on varied aspects of the problem. He wrote one for the *University of Chicago Law Review*
titled "The Illinois Constitution and the Courts," which was
later reprinted and sent at Roemer's direction to all 6,500
Association members. Hodes wrote treatises on how the creaky
1870 constitution hampered home rule for Chicago and other
cities ("They find themselves hopelessly shackled by their
infantile status"), and, at every opportunity, propagandized
among powerful Democrats for change. Cedarquist was the
authority on the responsibility of political parties for constitutional revision; Cummings wrote on the necessity for reappor-

tionment. Most of these articles appeared in the *Record*, and some were reprinted under Association auspices and sent, with accompanying letters from Witwer, to every newspaper in the state.

Hopes ran high among the constitutional reformers after Stevenson was inaugurated in 1949 and promptly gave high priority in his legislative program to constitutional modernization. Witwer, who had helped in preparing the section of Stevenson's inaugural address that related to the convention call, was invited to Springfield to speak in support of a proposed resolution and did so in the House chamber before a full audience, half of it hostile to the whole idea. One crusty House member later denounced Witwer as a "Communist" for making such a daring proposal, and several letters were received by the heads of Witwer's law firm demanding that he be fired.

After Stevenson's proposal lost by only two votes, he was prepared to accept a resolution by Senate Republicans for another Gateway Amendment that would alter the requirement for passage of individual constitutional changes from a majority of all voters in a general election to two-thirds of those voting on the specific amendment and would increase the number of amendments that could be submitted to the legislature on a single occasion from one to three. Witwer and Louis A. Kohn, a Stevenson confidant and an especially evangelistic member of Witwer's committee, urged Stevenson to reject the proposition and hold out for a straight majority or 60 percent approval vote. But Stevenson was reluctant to do so, saying, "My whole legislative program has been held up for months. I'm getting no place and if I insist on changing the Republican proposal, they'll say I'm petulant, and then I'll be in real trouble. We can't wait forever for urgent constitutional reforms. It's better to have something than nothing."

Loyally, Witwer and Kohn assumed command of the campaign for popular sanction of the Gateway Amendment in the general election of November 1950. Kohn and George B. McKibbin became cochairmen of the Association's Committee on Constitutional Revision when Witwer assumed the chairmanship of the newly formed statewide Illinois Committee for Constitutional Revision, popularly known as ICCR and encompassing some three-dozen varied agencies from the Illinois State Federation of Labor and the Illinois State Industrial League to the Chicago Association of Commerce and Industry and the Illinois Agricultural Association. In a close relationship with ICCR, the Chicago Bar Association furnished speakers for meetings and helped prepare leaflets and pamphlets. Stevenson joined in the speechmaking, characterizing the constitution as "peculiarly the people's document" and declaring: "The wider acceptance of the democratic process throughout the world appears to be a condition of our survival as a nation. We can make of constitutional revision a vivid reaffirmation of our faith in our system of government in Illinois. It can be an example for all to see." Campaign committees were created in all but 18 of the state's 102 counties. The legislature revised election laws so that the ballot for the Gateway Amendment would be more discernible. It was colored blue, and on its outside was a reminder: "The failure to vote this ballot is the equivalent of a negative vote." And in the November election, the amendment won massive approval, with an affirmative vote from 67 percent of the voters.

For the first time in the century, constitutional modification had been facilitated, if in a piecemeal fashion. Witwer was sanguine enough to realize that the ultimate triumph—a new constitution—was far from attainment. But at the moment, he savored this victory and lauded his Association colleagues who had originated the battle and had helped to build political support and public opinion—and who gave promise of sustaining and strengthening their aid and cooperation in the undeniable effort that still lay ahead.

3.

Other constructive events in this decade included participation in an impressive antivote-fraud campaign and institution of programs designed to give improved service to the public and to aid Association members.

In 1940, the Association joined with the League of Women

Voters, the Union League Club, and some ten other organizations to form the nonpartisan Joint Civic Committee on Elections. More than 5,000 workers were recruited, mostly from law offices and large business firms, to work first as official registration canvassers, with the approval of County Court Judge Edmund K. Jarecki, in a small number of Chicago wards. This canvass was successful in removing over 100,000 names of ineligible voters—deceased, nonexistent, or moved—from registration rolls. Then, through lectures, pamphlets, movies, and other educational means, the volunteers were instructed on how to detect fraudulent voting. On Election Day that November the force of poll watchers constituted one of the largest of its kind in the city's history.

Indigent citizens had long been able to obtain advice and assistance through the Legal Aid Bureau of the United Charities of Chicago, or, in the case of those charged with crimes, the Association's Defense of Prisoners Committee. But those of moderate means were ineligible for either or simply did not know how to go about getting a lawyer. Surveys indicated that a great many transactions involving points of law were carried out without any legal advice, leading too often to complications and distress. For years, anyone calling on the Association for aid in locating a lawyer had to be advised to look in the telephone book or a legal directory. In 1939, a special committee headed by Walter T. Fisher set out to seek remedies, and it quickly became apparent that a strong need existed for a low-cost service that would help such people select an attorney for particular problems or business matters involving questions of law instead of choosing one at random or receiving advice from a well-meaning but unqualified layman.

Fisher put out a call to Association members, and for six months, he and his associates studied applications and interviewed some 400 persons who indicated their desire to participate in the project. Each applicant was judged on training and experience as general practitioners or specialists in such varied fields as real estate, probate, wills and trusts, and personal injury. From these, an initial roster of 100 was selected, none an Association officer or a committee member, and a

212

system was established in which no charge would be made for referral but a fee would be set at $3 per half hour and $5 per hour for a consultation with a designated lawyer. When the matter could not be disposed of initially, further fees were to be arranged between lawyer and client, with the Association's Committee on Professional Fees as arbiter in case of any dispute. "It is hoped," wrote Fisher in the *Record* upon the inauguration of the program in January 1940, "that the Lawyer Reference Plan will in the long run benefit both the public and the bar by creating a more general attitude among laymen of consulting lawyers before they get into trouble. While lawyers know that there are plenty of competent practitioners available at moderate rates, a large part of the public is not aware of this fact. When it becomes more widely known that the services of a qualified lawyer may be procured at a reasonable price, it is anticipated that there will be an increased use of lawyers' services which will save many persons from the unnecessary losses and expense likely to result from ignorance of their rights and liabilities."

The Los Angeles Bar Association had been the first in the nation to propose such a program, but Fisher's detailed plan not only was the first to be put into practical operation but also served as the model for scores of similar offices ultimately set up under auspices of the American Bar Association in cities of over 100,000 population. Charles J. Lind, a young Association staff member, was its first secretary, and he set a pattern of courteous and diligent service to those seeking its services that has endured. From the 345 cases handled by volunteers on Fisher's committee, the number has grown to an annual average of 7,000 referred to specific lawyers from among a corps of 1,700, and the Lawyer Referral Service, as it is now called, has continued to be one of the Association's undoubted assets not only because it provides a qualified lawyer to those who need one, and especially to those who have never consulted one previously, but also because, as Franklin B. McCarty, Jr., one of Fisher's successors as chairman, stated, it "fulfills a serious obligation the legal profession owes the public."

At the end of World War II, the Association emulated the

example set after the previous world conflict by establishing facilities to place lawyers—members and nonmembers alike—in jobs. (During the war, over 1,000 members unable to serve in the armed forces responded to a call from Association President Harry N. Gottlieb for volunteers to work on four-to-midnight production lines in the city's war plants, and as many or more served on draft boards and in other essential capacities.) Morris I. Liebman was secretary of a new Committee on Placement, assisted by a former army major, Keith I. Parsons, representing the Younger Members Committee. Notices were placed each month in the *Record,* under the heading "Our Duty to Servicemen" and requesting all firms with available positions to notify the committee. Members were granted free stenographic help in preparing résumés and letters, and specific hours were set aside for them to use telephones in the Association offices without charge. In addition, a series of refresher courses was devised, with authorities in virtually every field of law bringing returning servicemen up-to-date on changes that had gone into effect during their absence. These courses proved so beneficial and popular that, at Clarence Denning's suggestion, the practice became institutionalized at the end of 1946 with appointment by the Board of Managers of a Committee on Post-Admission Education to coordinate and direct instructional meetings designed not only to keep interested members abreast of developments in the law but also literally to teach and instruct in all subjects from irrevocable trusts to organization of family businesses. Ultimately, this became the Committee for Continuing Legal Education, its manifold activities acknowledged by even the least ardent of Association members as valuable and essential.

In 1948, the Association's Chicago Bar Foundation came into being. One of its many avowed objectives was "to promote the study of the law and research therein, the diffusion of knowledge thereof and the continuing education of lawyers." The very first contributor was Floyd E. Thompson, Association president in 1943, and the initial project financed from its funds was the distribution to all judges in Cook County of the 80 standardized jury instructions approved by the Association. Since that time, the foundation has endured as an all-purpose institution not only to carry on its stated educational aims but also to pay for publication of speeches, reports, and treatises; to maintain the Association's well-stocked library; to acquire and preserve works of art, rare books, and documents that have historical legal significance or deal with the administration of justice; and to assist aged, ill, or needy members. As bequests and voluntary contributions mounted through the years, grants were made for a multitude of projects that ranged extensively from binding United States Supreme Court briefs for the Association library and preparation of a criminal practice manual to an annual award to a young lawyer who performs outstanding service to the profession and development of a group term life insurance program for Association members.

4.

Then, as for most of the nearly five previous decades, whatever the changes and innovations and whoever were their moving spirits, detractors, or abettors, always involved was Clarence Denning.

Presidents—forceful or mild, assertive or gentle—came and went. Committees were appointed and dismantled, conflicts with political lords or judges and recalcitrant members rose and subsided, and daring ideas were proposed, some to become integral elements of the Association and others to die aborning. Through it all, Denning, his austere ways and solemn dress much like those of his Methodist minister father, was acknowledged as "Mr. Bar Association."

Not everything that happened in the years since 1902 had been to his liking; he did not always look with pleasure at the growing trend in the Association toward more active involvement in social problems and increased democratization in its membership and attempts by various presidents to strive for ethnic balance. Yet, once a progressive move was instituted, Denning was an efficient administrator, an able executive secretary, fulfilling mandates, helping to administer agreed-upon programs, maintaining the Association's continuity. He supervised the activities of an always growing corps of Association employees down to the smallest detail; his insistence that all the men wear suit coats and ties and the women never use gaudy nail polish and that everyone show extreme politeness to all callers was invariably accompanied by the injunction, "Remember that you represent the Association in the eyes of the public. The impression you make will be the one they carry with them." He was capable of adapting himself to the varying personalities of Association presidents and officials with whom he dealt; somewhat prudish, he nevertheless could join comfortably in laughter at an off-color joke in a dining-room gathering.

The Association seemed always to be his sole interest; he had a family and a home life, but few among his professional associates knew details of either. He was well aware of the varying abilities, motives, and interests of officers and members, but he hoped that all felt, as he did and often stated, that the Association afforded lawyers "an opportunity for greater service in the administration of justice, in the maintenance and dignity of his profession and in the advancement of the interests of his community, his state and his country." More of a scholar than seemed evident even to those who admired his managerial efficiency, he was given to quoting aphorisms of legal notables, one of his favorites that of Edward Coke's: "The knowledge of the law is like a deep well, out of which each man draweth according to the strength of his understanding."

He worked hard and intensely in these years, even after he asked Richard H. Cain, who had come to the Association in 1936 as a page boy and had progressively been given greater responsibilities under Denning's direction, to move his desk into his own rather somber office and serve as his assistant. Denning was especially interested in the mechanics of the Lawyer Referral Service and the growing interest in the details of the continuing legal education classes he had been instrumental in expanding from the postwar refresher courses. But the long years began to take their toll. He seemed to age unusually fast and to lose track of events, and on February 1, 1952—a Friday, the day he had always considered lucky because on a Friday, he had gone to work for the Association exactly half a century earlier and because on a Friday two decades later, he had been appointed executive secretary—he was stricken at his desk with a heart attack. His secretary, Mary Lindemann, summoned a fire department inhalator squad, but it was unable to revive him. To the end, he had concerned himself, as ever, with the minutiae of administration, for on his desk atop a sheaf of papers was a note intended for Mae Johnson, manager of the dining room: "Why should the finnan haddie be so tough as to be very hard to chew? Usually ours is so very good. Could it be that the cook failed to steam it long enough today?"

A *Daily News* editorialist characterized the Association as Denning's "lengthened shadow," and Cain, named his successor, vowed to extend that shadow. In the *Record*, half of which its editor, Hugo Sonnenschein, Jr., devoted to tributes from past presidents and biographical sketches, the resolution of the Association's Board of Managers offered this estimate: "His deepest persuasion was that to practice law was not to indulge in a mere money-getting trade but to function in an honored profession in the Temple of Justice. His feet were on the ground but his head reached high over the clouds into the sunshine."

In the mid-1920s, many of the old-style police motorcycles were replaced by "high-speed flivvers."

Chicago Bar Association

In 1930, a new Criminal Courts Building was opened at 26th Street and California Avenue, far from the center of the city's legal community. Since then, the Association has offered—without success—various proposals for transferring criminal trials and related proceedings to a structure closer to the Loop.

Chicago Sun-Times

219

In the judicial election campaign of early 1933, the Association made
use of billboards, among many devices.   Chicago Bar Association

Chieftains of the Cook County Democratic organization in the 1930s
were Patrick A. Nash (left) and Edward J. Kelly, who rebuffed Association proposals for higher-grade judicial candidates.   Author's collection

Headquarters of the Association were moved in 1937 to 29 South La Salle Street.

1   2

An unusual father-son combination in Association history: Stephen Strong Gregory (1) was president in 1900–1901 and later served as president of the Illinois State Bar Association and the American Bar Association. His son, Tappan Gregory (2), the Association's president in 1939–40, also later headed the state and national organizations.

Chicago Tribune

In 1965, the Chicago Civic Center (3) was completed in an area bounded by Randolph, Washington, Clark, and La Salle streets. It houses all levels of courts—Circuit, Appellate, Supreme—in addition to a small number of city and county offices and the Cook County Law Library.

Chicago Sun-Times

Demolition of the ornate, old Federal Building, housing the United States District Court, was started in 1961, and its courtrooms and diverse federal offices were moved to the gleaming new building across the street (4). Parts of the old structure, a landmark since 1904, can be seen in the foreground.

Chicago Daily News

Judge John S. Boyle confers with judges and associate judges of the Circuit Court, newly elected in 1968 (5). In foreground (right) is Judge Philip J. Romiti, who later presided at trial of State's Attorney Edward V. Hanrahan and codefendants on charges growing out of the fatal shooting of two Black Panther leaders, Fred Hampton and Mark Clark.

Chicago Today

3

4

5

Mass arrests were made in Chicago following riots in the wake of the assassination of Martin Luther King in April 1968. This is a typical scene in one of the courtrooms jammed to excess.

Chicago Sun-Times

Volunteer lawyers were recruited, many of them by the Association, to facilitate the release on bond of scores of those arrested in the rioting that erupted after Martin Luther King's assassination in 1968.

Chicago Sun-Times

The "Chicago Seven" hold a press conference in October 1969 during their tumultuous trial before United States District Court Judge Julius J. Hoffman. At the table is Jerry Rubin and behind him (left to right) are Abbie Hoffman, John Froines, Lee Weiner, David T. Dellinger, Rennie Davis, and Thomas Hayden.

Chicago Sun-Times

Crowds and pickets gather outside the Federal Building in February 1970 to protest sentences imposed on the "Chicago Seven." A jury acquitted them of conspiracy charges but found all except John Froines and Lee Weiner guilty of crossing state lines to incite a riot and making inflammatory speeches to achieve that end. This verdict was reversed in November 1972 by the United States Court of Appeals.

Chicago Daily News

Samuel W. Witwer, president of the Constitutional Convention, presides at introductory session of chairmen and vice-chairmen of convention committees. He is flanked by Elbert S. Smith (left), a vice-president; Odas Nicholson, convention secretary; and Thomas G. Lyons, another vice-president. Calling of the convention climaxed years of effort in which the Association was a leading participant.

Chicago Sun-Times

After nine months of work and discussion, the convention delegates conclude the drafting of Illinois' first constitution in a century, and, on September 13, they vote happily to adjourn.

Chicago Sun-Times

Deeds and Discord

1.

THE DECADE of the 1950s followed a familiar pattern of accomplishments and progress and inevitable conflicts and controversies.

Early in the period, the Association involved itself in a city-wide probe of crime. Cushman B. Bissell, president in 1951, was an incorporator of Citizens of Greater Chicago, an organization aimed at fighting widespread depredation and political-underworld alliances. After Charles A. Bane, chief counsel of a City Council investigating committee, charged that some 800 of the 8,000 men on the police force were receiving illicit payoffs, Bissell's successor, Andrew J. Dallstream, offered an Association-sponsored resolution to the City Council demanding that policemen be required to disclose information about their incomes. "If a police officer refuses to answer relevant questions or furnish pertinent financial data," the resolution stated, "he breaches his duty as a police officer." Although no official action resulted, the seeds were planted for stronger recommendations by the Association in ensuing years in connection with police department irregularities, and these efforts were a factor—along with the continuing fight for judicial change and assistance in revising state Supreme Court rules—in winning a coveted merit award in 1952 from the American Bar Association for outstanding and constructive public service. Dallstream's resolution had received universal editorial support, and upon its rejection by a majority of the aldermen, the

Chicago Sun-Times spoke for many after noting that 10 of the 39 who voted against it were Association members: "They do not deserve the respect of their fellow lawyers."

There were others who, the Association believed, also did not deserve such respect. Disbarment proceedings increased, but the pace continued to be slow, what with the long-established practice of having a section of the Committee on Inquiry make an initial investigation, and, if merited, refer the case to the full committee, from which it was passed on to the Grievance Committee for further action and to the Board of Managers for review before submission to the state Supreme Court for a final decision. Annually, as much as $100,000 was being spent for such procedures, most of which rarely took less than two years. Most lawyers against whom proceedings had started continued to practice during the interim, and often—too often, many thought—the Supreme Court did not follow the specific recommendations of the Association, usually reducing or eliminating the proposed penalties. Indeed, when runners for certain lawyers specializing in personal injury suits descended on victims of an elevated train crash, the *Daily News,* among others, criticized a majority of the high court's members: "The court has handed down some remarkably feeble opinions in disciplinary cases brought before it by the bar . . . (and) has brought consolation and protection to too many scalawags pursued with righteous indignation by the bar." All this had long vexed the press and citizens who had instituted complaints and anticipated swifter imposition of disciplinary measures, and neither could be appeased by periodic official explanations that investigations had to be thorough and that the Association was bound by Supreme Court rules to adhere to intensive methods before making its recommendations.

Much of 1953 and 1954 was spent in a concentrated effort by the Committee on Personal Injury Practice to draft and procure legislation to curb ambulance chasing and to heighten disciplinary action against members and nonmembers accused of flagrant solicitation of personal injury cases. Superior Court Judge Arthur J. Murphy, the committee's chairman, called the practice "a growing evil which has led to a general loss of confidence by the public in lawyers." And the Committee on Public Service prepared a pamphlet for public distribution that warned: "Beware of the stranger who urges you to retain a particular lawyer to handle your case. Persons soliciting may be representatives of hospitals primarily interested in payment of bills or one of a small group of doctors or surgeons primarily interested in fees, a policeman, a hospital orderly or X-ray technician, who will receive kickbacks from the lawyers." The proposed legislation—two of whose chief elements were to change the act of repeated solicitation from a misdemeanor to a felony and to make lawyers as well as their aides subject to formal prosecution—failed to pass.

Late in 1954, a petition for the disbarment of Bruneau E. Heirich was filed with the state Supreme Court. Complaints against him had been received during four preceding years. With 1,891 pages of testimony from 18 witnesses, the Grievance Committee recommended Heirich's removal from the rolls of practicing attorneys because of "a general pattern of misconduct which proved and which indicate beyond any doubt that the respondent has been guilty of conduct involving moral turpitude and because of innumerable instances of soliciting himself or through emissaries many clients, especially those involved in railroad accidents." Nearly two years passed before the high court rendered a decision that not only rejected the Association's recommendation and upheld Heirich's countercharge that seven railroads had organized and financed a Railroad Claims Research Bureau whose special investigator amassed evidence against him through "subornation, trickery, entrapment and false impersonation," but also went on to commend Heirich for "pursuing the personal injury business successfully and aggressively."

2.

In another area involving lawyers—or, more precisely, prospective lawyers—the Association was technically involved in an interesting case that attracted much attention and discussion. Some 20 years after the Association had been instrumental in the institution of the state Supreme Court's Rule 39, relating to higher standards for admission to practice, it had memorialized the tribunal to appoint a Committee on Character and Fitness in each Appellate Court district. Such a court-appointed committee was created in 1917, and in subsequent years Association facilities were used to question those who had recently passed their state bar examinations as to political beliefs and attendant matters.

Late in 1950, George Anastaplo appeared before a two-man committee, composed of Stephen A. Mitchell and John E. Baker, Jr., for the routine fitness interview. A brilliant student then in his last months at the University of Chicago Law School after 38 months' service as an air force navigator in World War II, Anastaplo startled his interrogators by refusing to answer questions about whether he had ever been a member of the Communist Party or of such other organizations as the Ku Klux Klan and the Silver Shirts of America, or, for that matter, the Democratic or Republican parties. He maintained that such a refusal constituted not defiance but high respect for the law. Basing his stand on the Declaration of Independence, Anastaplo maintained—and continued to maintain after the committee recommended he be denied admission and he carried his fight to the courts—the right of revolution and resistance to court decrees at a specific time as a matter of principle.

After the rejection of his application, Anastaplo filed an appeal with the Illinois Supreme Court. Friends and associates of his attested to his solid character, his nonaffiliation with any group, political or social, and his deep scholarship in history and legal lore. A brief in his support signed by Leon M. Despres, Abner J. Mikva, Alexander Polikoff, and Bernard Weisberg—all Association members active in liberal causes— asserted, "Admission to the practice of law should not be denied on the grounds that an applicant holds unorthodox political or philosophical beliefs." The court disagreed, declaring in a four-to-three decision that the practice of law "is a privilege, not a right" and adding, "In granting that privilege we may impose any reasonable conditions within our control, and if an applicant does not choose to abide by such conditions he is free to retain his beliefs and go elsewhere."

By 1960, the case was before the United States Supreme Court, where Anastaplo told the justices that he could not promise always to obey them: "If at some time the members of the court were to become so corrupted, so perverted that the Constitution was destroyed, then one would be obliged to resist. A court which, say, a Hitler dominated would deserve no respect. That is what the Declaration of Independence means, and I have always believed it." The court's five-to-four ruling went against Anastaplo. The state had the legitimate right to bar him from practice, stated Justice John M. Harlan in a majority opinion, because Anastaplo's refusal to answer blocked the committee's proper study of his qualifications. "Were it otherwise," wrote Harlan, "a bar examining committee such as this, having no resources of its own for independent investigation, might be placed in the untenable position of having to certify an applicant without assurance as to a significant aspect of his qualifications which the applicant is best circumstanced to supply." For the minority, Justice Hugo L. Black wrote an opinion many considered one of his most impressive. Anastaplo, he stated, was an outstanding man whose rights had been "balanced out of existence" by application of what he termed "the balancing doctrine," and he added, "Men like these are the kind the American bar needs, men who do stand up."

With this decision, Anastaplo gave up his battle to become a practicing lawyer but went on to teach at the University of Chicago and Rosary College and to produce a powerful book, *The Constitutionalist: Notes on the First Amendment,* in which he reaffirmed his philosophies about the Constitution and its fullest meanings, detailed in a 400-page appendix the events of his ten-year fight, and concluded with "We must not be afraid to be free," a statement from Justice Black's opinion.

3.

A controversy of a much different sort that directly involved the Association occupied officials, committees, and individual members for a full three years and more.

Over the decades, the most heated public disputes had been with Cook County state's attorneys, notably John E. Wayman in 1909 over the handling of disbarment cases and Robert E. Crowe over investigation of vote frauds and Election Day violence in the late 1920s. But neither matched in rancor or acrimony the strife with Benjamin S. Adamowski that started late in October 1957.

Adamowski was an energetic and politically experienced state's attorney who had become a Republican after unsuccessfully contesting Richard J. Daley for the 1955 Democratic mayoral nomination. He began the stormy controversy with a denunciation of Superior Court Judge Henry W. Dieringer after the latter's dismissal of charges against Charles J. Fleck, who had been accused of conspiring to defraud the heirs to a $50,000 estate while serving as Cook County public administrator. Especially angered because the judge had ruled that Fleck's records were private and not admissible as evidence, Adamowski declared, "Judge Dieringer did everything in his power from the very first day to destroy the case against the defendant and to prevent the people from seeing just punishment meted out."

When President E. Douglas Schwantes announced that the Association would investigate Adamowski's accusation and the propriety of his remarks, Adamowski expressed satisfaction, while Judge Dieringer said, "Adamowski's statement is so ridiculous that I will not dignify it with a reply." Two hundred members of the Defense Lawyers Association joined the fray by demanding that the Association castigate Adamowski for his accusation: "It is a breach of professional ethics on its face and it is unworthy of an officer of the court." Unperturbed, Adamowski replied: "That's not news. When the defense lawyers start praising the state's attorney's office, that will be news and I'll have some comment."

After nearly a year, in which 2,700 pages of testimony were amassed, the Board of Managers issued a decision criticizing Adamowski. Nothing in the record indicated that Judge Dieringer had acted improperly, the board found, and although it conceded that Adamowski had acted in good faith, its report asserted that he was not justified in his attack on the judge's character and integrity. Emphasizing that judges and their decisions were not beyond criticism, the board pointedly noted that complaints against them should follow established grievance procedures.

For a time, quiet prevailed, but in June 1959, a new uproar was stirred when Adamowski lashed out at other judges. Now the objects of his ire were Abraham L. Marovitz, the Criminal Court's chief justice and a former colleague in the state legislature, whom he accused of granting probation too frequently, and Criminal Court Judge Harold P. O'Connell, who Adamowski claimed had illegally vacated a 1957 bond forfeiture and was consequently ineligible to preside at the forthcoming trial of Raymond P. Drymalski, chief justice of the Municipal Court, and seven others on a similar charge.

Jerome S. Weiss, nearing the end of his year as Association president, responded that the state's attorney had assailed not only individual judges but also the integrity of an entire court: "Unrestrained comment on pending cases interferes with the conduct of fair trials. It is imperative, if our system of justice is to be maintained, that trials should take place only in a courtroom." Avowing no intention of interfering with the public duties of the state's attorney, Weiss went on to say, "The matter of his conduct, as well as his charges against individual judges and his blanket charges against the court, will be referred to our Judiciary Committee for investigation."

To this, Adamowski affirmed his determination to make public criticism: "I don't intend to withhold any statements concerning the affairs of the people. When I have something to say, I'll say it. Some of the Bar Association members would speak out even more than I do if they were sitting in my chair." The Association's action, he contended, was improper because no signed complaint had been made against him, nor had he been furnished with a list of specific charges. Moreover, he added two other Criminal Court jurists, Joseph A. Pope and Robert E. English, to his list of those he alleged had not imposed heavy enough sentences in certain cases. Prompt reply came from Judge English, who had established a solid reputation for legal knowledge and trial temperament since assuming his post in 1953 after a judicial election noteworthy for bringing out over one million voters to the polls and for being a remarkable upset—spurred by unanimous newspaper support—of the powerful Democratic organization, with victory for him and seven other Republican candidates: "It is the duty of a judge to impose the sentence which he believes is proper for the case, even though he knows, because of the state's attorney's threats, that adverse publicity will follow."

In August, the Association's report was ready. It characterized as "reckless and inflammatory" Adamowski's statements about the Criminal Court jurists and adjudged him guilty of professional impropriety, contending that a state's attorney was bound by the same standards governing other attorneys. Adamowski's pronouncements, it declared, tended to undermine public confidence in the judiciary and "could only be construed as an attempt to exert improper pressure upon the judges in connection with the performance of their duties in office." Once more, emphasis was laid on the public's right to know about any judicial shortcomings and on the method of procedure other than public statements on such alleged defects. In this respect, the report quoted from a United States Supreme Court decision: "Legal trials are not like elections to be won through the use of the meeting hall, the radio and the newspaper."

Adamowski's reaction was characteristically angry: The Association's report he called a "whitewash," an effort to prevent him from telling the truth. "One of the reasons lawyers stand in such ill repute with the public," he declaimed to reporters, "is that every time someone in their profession does something wrong they don't remove the cancer, they try to cover it up. It is in poor grace for the organized bar to protect these men, to imply that they are so holy they cannot be criticized. That includes protection of judges with their preconceived notions about cases, these men who hold nothing more than a kangaroo court." In a 17-page letter to Willis D. Nance, Weiss' successor, he wrote, "I do not intend to sit idly by and let your organization strike at me illegally and unfairly." The Association, he claimed, was limited to investigating him for immorality or criminality and had no right to subject him to discipline.

Nance refused comment on the latest blast, and Adamowski continued his barrage. He held press conferences in which, among many things, he called on Judges Marovitz and Pope to resign, charged that a small group of lawyers received favored treatment in criminal cases, and declared he would petition the Illinois Supreme Court not only to expunge the Association's rebuke but also to appoint a downstate judge to preside at the Drymalski case because, in his view, no Cook County jurist could be counted on to be other than prejudiced in Drymalski's favor. He cited a recent Chicago Crime Commission report that was critical of some Criminal Court judges and challenged the Association to follow up on those criticisms. Adamowski claimed that many Association members and even judges had expressed to him their approval of his bold stand. Partial support for him came from Milburn P. Akers, the *Sun-Times*' editor who had been an Associated Press correspondent in the state capital when Adamowski, Marovitz, and Mayor Daley were young legislators; an editorial conceded "that Adamowski is quick on the verbal trigger and that his conduct as state's attorney has been as unorthodox as his conduct in other public offices" but strongly suggested that the Association not disregard Adamowski's charges against judges and lawyers in the Criminal Court. "This is certainly not forbidden territory to inquiry. This line of investigation is as pertinent as an investigation of the state's attorney because he has sounded off about judges."

The Association's response was to assign the case to a special Committee on Inquiry, headed by Len Young Smith. As this latest investigation got under way, Adamowski presented his petition, 38 pages long with 50 pages of related exhibits, to the state's high court, calling the censure report a "scurrilous document" and accusing the Association of circumventing Supreme Court rules by issuing it. Within a week, the court rejected the petition and also his request for a downstate judge for the Drymalski case, which shortly thereafter came up before the Criminal Court's sole woman jurist—B. Fain Tucker, another Republican winner in the 1953 contest—and she quashed malfeasance charges on Drymalski's plea that he had acted honestly and in good faith and according to precedent in vacating some $250,000 in bail bond forfeitures.

As the year ended, Adamowski was in the headlines again, this time with demands for the ouster of Judge Marovitz's successor, Judge Charles S. Dougherty, and with criticisms of other Criminal Court judges, Fred W. Slater, Thomas E. Klu-czynski, and Harold C. Woodward. In June 1960, with Daniel P. Ward, dean of the De Paul University Law School, slated to oppose Adamowski's bid for reelection, the Association announced its rejection of Adamowski's charges: "The state's attorney's letters contain no allegations that any of the named lawyers used methods which were contrary to practices and procedures under existing law in the trial of cases to which reference was made, no statements that the lawyers used improper influence upon the judges and no declarations that the judges issued their findings of orders as a result of improper influence exerted upon them." Neither the letters nor any subsequent communications provided sufficient information to justify an inquiry into the conduct of the lawyers and judges. As for the exchange of charges in the preceding months, the report commented: "Such statements, however strong and intemperate, are not charges of unethical conduct and hence do not afford a basis for disciplinary proceedings."

The sound and fury generated by the state's attorney was characterized by a *Sun-Times* editorialist as "mostly hot air," but both he and a *Daily News* writer agreed that Adamowski, who hailed the report "a sweeping victory," had reason for satisfaction because the Association did recommend various

Criminal Court reforms that he—and many before him—had proposed. These reforms included assignment of cases by lot rather than by the chief justice, reduction in the number of continuances, and enlargement of the state's attorney's staff.

Temporarily at peace with the Association, Adamowski concentrated on his campaign against Ward and the man whom he continually denounced as Ward's overlord, Mayor Daley. But late in September, the conflict flourished anew when a report of the Association's Committee on Candidates declared him no longer qualified and Ward well qualified. Recalling the Association's support of Adamowski four years earlier—at which time Harold A. Smith, Association president in 1949, had headed an influential pro-Adamowski group—the committee report stated: "However, since that time, his reckless and indiscriminate attacks generally upon members of the judiciary, impugning the integrity of judges who rule against him, have tended to undermine the confidence of the public in the courts and have greatly prejudiced his effectiveness in the office to which he was elected."

Adamowski denounced the report as proof that the Association was protecting judges he considered unfit and continued to allege, even after the membership poll endorsed Ward, that a substantial segment of the legal community supported him. Cranston Spray, a member of the Board of Managers who had voted against the committee's finding, wrote a letter to President William H. Alexander decrying Ward's close connection with the Daley organization and offering to have copies of his letter reproduced at his own expense if it could be sent to all members. Although Alexander made Spray's letter public, he refused to sanction its distribution: "We can't permit one member that privilege unless we afford it to others." A group of seven members, including Smith and such other former presidents as James P. Carey, Jr., and Werner Schroeder, protested Ward's soliciting members to join a lawyers' committee in his behalf. And so the campaign steamed to a finish, with Adamowski calling Ward "the hand-picked tool of the gentleman on the fifth floor at City Hall" and Ward labeling

Adamowski "Bungling Ben" because of a low record of convictions, with proponents and opponents of both inundating newspapers with letters, and with charges and countercharges filling the autumn air. After Ward emerged the victor in one of the closest elections for the office in the county's history, so much bitterness still prevailed that Adamowski failed to appear for the customary meeting with his successor to facilitate turning over myriad details of pending matters and Adamowski's chief aide, Frank Ferlic, and prime investigator, Paul Newey, resigned almost at once after the day of election.

The battle was far from over. Adamowski demanded a recount, and although the ultimate result was even closer than the first tally, Ward proceeded with his new duties. One of his first acts was to appoint a Republican lawyer, Kevin J. Gillogly, as special assistant to investigate reports that a large number of canceled checks and records dealing with Adamowski's contingency fund of $833,000 were missing. Adamowski asserted that much of the money spent went to informers whose names he kept on slips of paper and later burned because a public record would lay them open to reprisal. When President Walter H. Moses declared early in 1963 the Association's intention to study laws governing such contingency funds, the former state's attorney accused him of waging a political vendetta. Adamowski repeated the charge later in the year—after he had been roundly defeated in the mayoral race by Daley— when the Association recommended payment of a $35,000 fee to Gillogly for his ten-month probe; but Moses, a dignified, firm-minded man, refused to reply in kind. Adamowski subsequently ran unsuccessfully for other offices and then settled into a prosperous legal practice, his name and belligerent style to be invoked from time to time by still politically powerful foes whenever a new challenger arose to confront them with loud and irritating accusations.

4.

In another area, at a time when charges of radicalism and communism were being hurled by Sen. Joseph McCarthy at a wide assortment of targets, the Association took a strong position.

Back in 1939, Adlai E. Stevenson, then chairman of the Committee on Civil Rights, had prepared a significant report stressing the Association's responsibility in the maintenance of civil liberties and urging a persistent educational program to keep the public aware of their value: "People tend to favor free speech for themselves but not for the other fellow, without realizing their own free speech is unsafe unless it is assured to others." Liberal members agreed, conservatives found fault, but the Association's official position grew increasingly adamant against so-called antisubversive laws. During Stevenson's term as governor, he received strong support from the Association, among other groups, in his veto of a bill compelling state employees to take loyalty oaths; and when similar legislation was proposed later, the Association's reaction was equally assertive. New bills in 1953 and 1955 were publicly attacked by the Association "as a serious threat to the basic concepts of civil rights," and doubts were expressed as to their constitutionality. After they were passed—they endured until the mid-1960s, by which time various rulings by United States District courts prompted their repeal—the Association found occasion to speak out against what it deemed to be repressive legislation; a report in 1955 denounced various provisions of the Jenner-Butler bill before Congress that would infringe on constitutional guarantees of free speech and jeopardize the independence of the United States Supreme Court as "the ultimate guardian of constitutional liberties of individuals against arbitrary government."

Other basic rights needed reaffirmation. A joint resolution in 1954 with the Illinois State Bar Association, after complaints from some editorialists and conservative organizations against lawyers who represented persons reputed to be Communists or gangsters, asserted the right of everyone to have the assistance of a lawyer and the duty of every lawyer to provide counsel even to the most unpopular and most criticized. In that same year, the inherent evils of wiretapping were brought into focus by an Association report opposing pending congressional legislation that would permit evidence secured in that way to be used in the courts: "In general, Americans should have an enforceable right to speak freely over the telephone. Although the right to be secure from the introduction of wiretap evidence in court is directly valuable only to those whom the government may prosecute, the right not to be spied on is valuable to all. No government, however benign, should invade the right to privacy which is one of the factors making American citizenship so valuable." A longtime Association member and relatively new United States District Court judge, Julius J. Hoffman, reflected this view in an article in the *American Bar Association Journal.* "Even if we are in imminent danger," he wrote, "we could find some better defense than the abandonment of our rights. To give them up in order to make it easier to catch those who threaten them would be like robbing a man of his valuables today in order to prevent a possible thief from stealing them at a later time." (A similar position was taken a decade later but was modified in partial approval of a bill for a two-year test of wiretapping against members of organized crime syndicates.)

5.

The Association took other constructive positions and actions, including drafting of a new act to curb illegal adoptions and a study of abuses by loan sharks, but undoubtedly the most significant development in which it assumed a vital role was in the sector of judicial reform.

Passage of the 1950 Gateway Amendment had spurred Association advocates of constitutional change to place major emphasis on a campaign for a new article that would cut through the judicial thicket that had grown to unmanageable and cumbersome size over the years. The innumerable defects of the state's judicial system, originally designed to serve a population of 2½ million, included a plethora of courts with conflicting jurisdictions and lack of proper supervision, an imbalance between courts submerged under heavy case loads and courts with little business, and political domination of selection of judicial candidates.

After Cushman B. Bissell became Association president in 1951, he gave top priority to what he described to Clarence Denning as "a clean judiciary," and upon his incessant urging, there was soon created, in conjunction with the Illinois State Bar Association, a Joint Committee on the Judicial Article. The long, arduous, and detailed task of effecting a change began, with the overall objective to obtain an amendment providing for appointment of judges at every level by a high-grade commission, thereby eliminating the system of nomination by political parties on partisan or coalition tickets. After continual day and night sessions, drafts and redrafts, and many appearances before unheeding and listless legislative committees, one such article was submitted in 1953 and another in 1955—and each was rejected by the legislature, the primary opposition emanating from representatives of the Chicago Democratic organization and downstate legislators.

Undaunted, the Joint Committee tried again in 1957 with a somewhat modified amendment providing for general reorganization of the entire court system, with administrative powers bestowed on the Supreme Court. Once more, the main foes were Chicago Democrats, avowedly because the new article contemplated including the Municipal Court into a reconstituted Circuit Court. Noting that no Republican had been elected to this court in years, the *Sun-Times*' politically sophisticated Milburn P. Akers wrote: "It is common knowledge that some would-be candidates on the Democratic ticket have had to contribute generously to the coffers of unscrupulous ward committeemen to achieve a spot on the ballot. Naturally, the venal committeemen who work this racket are loath to give it up.... The grim determination of the Democratic bosses to hang on to the Municipal Court without change leaves the unmistakable impression that they regard it as a convenient political instrument for conferring favors on the rank and file."

Amid debate and discussion, the Association injected a note

of confusion. In February, it endorsed 20 sitting Circuit and Superior Court judges, including two—Circuit Court Judges Harry M. Fisher and Thomas J. Courtney—who had fallen below the 70 percent mark required for approval in the Association primary. When newspaper criticism was sounded over this and the fact that several other approved judges would be over 75 years old at the end of their six-year terms, the Board of Managers convened again and reversed its decision on Courtney and Fisher, buttressing its shift with results of a new poll on a single question—"Should he be renominated?"—that showed decidedly negative reactions to both men.

"Rank injustice!" cried Courtney. He intimated that the rejection was motivated in part by Association members whose enmity he may have incurred during his service as Cook County state's attorney in the 1940s and displayed a recent letter from Richard H. Cain that stated: "The records of our association indicate there have been no complaints filed against you that would reflect on your conduct as a lawyer or as a judge." Fisher, long active in Association activities since the days he had helped to amend the Juvenile Court Act in 1907, declined comment.

When, at the June election, both men ran ahead of all their colleagues, the Association's prestige quite naturally was dealt a blow, and political experts predicted that the campaign for the judicial article would suffer because of what many considered inept politicking. "If judicial reform loses this time because of the Courtney-Fisher episode," wrote Charles Cleveland, the *Daily News'* political editor, "the Bar Association will be technically guilty of infanticide—at least they will be partly responsible for killing their legislative child." Cleveland was proved partially correct in ensuing months when the two associations accepted a half-measure compromise that lacked their most ardently sought provision for nonpolitical selection of judges, but contained others considered less than adequate for genuine improvement.

Yet, the next year's campaign preceding submission of the judicial article to a popular vote was a vigorous one under

direction of a Committee for Modern Courts, a new statewide
organization. "Vote Yes on the Blue Ballot" was the theme, and
Mayor Daley, having obtained a clause in the article that left
the matter of judicial selection and tenure up to the legislature
before voter approval, joined Gov. William Stratton in nonpartisan support. In the election of 1958, the watered-down
amendment was approved by the electorate despite some downstate opposition. But the triumph was short-lived. The state
electoral board refused to ratify the result because certain
affirmative ballots were defective, and a suit to overturn this
ruling was defeated.

Once more judicial reform had been thwarted, this time by
a technicality. But the issue would not die. Because of constitutional barriers to submission of amendments to the same article
no more often than once each four years, a further attempt had
to wait until 1962. The amendment was almost a duplication of
its predecessor. It provided for a streamlined system to be
administered by the state Supreme Court, with justices of the
peace and innumerable police magistrate courts and county,
probate, and criminal courts to be incorporated into a unified
Circuit Court. Initially, judges would be nominated and elected
but afterward would be reelected on their records, their names
to appear on retention ballots with no party labels. The Supreme Court districts would be redistributed so that Cook
County would have three judges instead of one and downstate
four instead of six. Other changes were for a full-time Appellate
Court, thus discarding the practice of having trial judges hear
appeals, and for the supplanting of court-appointed masters in
chancery—objects of considerable criticism over the years because of alleged favoritism and excessive charges to litigants—
with salaried magistrates appointed by judges of the Circuit
Court. Important, too, was a provision long sought by the Association for an Illinois Courts Commission empowered to discipline judges for cause or order retirement because of disability.
Again, in a concession to the harsh realities of politics, no
mention was made of a merit system of picking judicial candidates, but Association members, of whom William Trumbull

and Peter Tomei were representative, plunged into the effort to gain passage of the amendment in the legislature, and, afterward, to persuade the electorate to vote for it.

Hardly a month passed without an article in the *Record* on the need for the amendment and exhortations for support from Association President R. Newton Rooks early in 1962 and his successor, Walter H. Moses. Other proponents were joined in a multitude of projects: organizing committees to raise some $125,000 to finance the campaign; staffing speakers' bureaus; setting up interviews with reporters; preparing legal articles, pamphlets, and booklets of questions and answers; engaging in debates with foes of the judicial article; holding dinners for political leaders and ward and township committeemen of both parties.

At one such "harmony dinner" in the Association's headquarters only three weeks before the November election at which the amendment was to be voted on, a momentary jolt was administered by Mayor Daley after Hayes Robertson— Cook County Republican chairman and one of several speakers including Gov. Otto Kerner and William G. Lynch, the mayor's former law partner—made a reference to "political bosses" and left hurriedly, presumably to avoid being photographed with Daley. Called on to speak, Daley assailed Robertson as a "faker" and added, "All you fakers can leave together!" When five men left, Daley cried, "Certainly it's easy for these fakers to leave, because none of them are sincere about judicial reform!" He concluded by chiding the assemblage: "This meeting tonight shocks me. Half-filled, less than a hundred people. The fellow in the shop, he'll be for judicial reforms. And you lawyers, I wonder what you'll do, except attend this meeting?"

Although the incident was glaringly reported in the next day's newspapers, Daley did not withdraw his support of the amendment, and it passed handily, with approval by 57 percent of those voting in the general election. A victory of sorts had been achieved, and there was reason for some exultation. Jerome S. Weiss, in whose administration four years earlier the campaign had intensified, called the event "the most important accomplishment of the Association since its organization," and Louis A. Kohn was named by the Chicago Junior Association of Commerce and Industry as its "Chicagoan of the Year" for his sustained efforts over ten years to achieve judicial reform. But there was still ample reason to maintain vigilance and give close attention to implementation of the judicial article when it went into effect in 1964 and not to lose sight of renewed opportunities to obtain legislative and public approval of a merit plan for choosing judges.

Earnest Efforts

1.

ALTHOUGH for the rest of the 1960s the Association's participation in the quest for a new state constitution remained paramount, a score of other events—ranging widely from the first contested election of officers and other challenges to officialdom to heightened involvement in the thorniest kind of public issues—occupied time and attention.

Over the many years since its founding, the Association had only rarely been confronted with a situation in which a member or two, by securing 100 or more signatures to a nominating petition, sought a specific office or a seat on the Board of Managers. Virtually no such effort had ever succeeded, and the prevailing procedure remained: The Nominating Committee, as in many other such professional organizations, designated a slate of candidates each year, and the two vice-presidents moved forward in successive years to the presidency. But early in 1961, with R. Newton Rooks scheduled to become president in July, rumblings were heard that a dissident group planned to present a full opposition ticket. Prime movers were two well-known lawyers specializing in personal injury suits, John Joseph Sullivan and John J. Kennelly; both had long felt, as did other members, that trial lawyers had been neglected as potential officer material and that the Association's hierarchy had been unduly dominated by representatives of big law firms. Beyond this, there was growing dissatisfaction among some members practicing in neighborhood offices and a belief that not enough was being done in behalf of individual practition-ers. Whatever the validity of such beliefs, they were persistent enough to persuade some members to frame a slate opposing the regular candidates for 6 top elective offices and 7 of 14 seats on the Board of Managers; and soon the contest was on, with Harold T. Halfpenny in the spot against Rooks.

Letters over Halfpenny's signature went out to the 7,000 members. Among the charges were that the Association was generally unresponsive to the needs of a majority of the membership, that it had not taken a firm enough stand against proposed legislation to permit hiring of additional referees to assist judges—a move, according to the "loyal opposition," that could well abrogate the right to trial by jury—and that it had failed to oppose increased Municipal Court civil jury fees, to take positive action to reduce the backlog of civil cases in Cook County courts, to secure a more unified Association, to reduce dues and cut costs, and to act forcefully against unauthorized legal practitioners. The outgoing president, William H. Alex-ander, undertook a point-by-point reply, emphasizing that the Association's management supported most of the rebels' aims and denied that it had ignored or opposed them. On the matter of action against unauthorized practitioners, he could point to steps taken to enjoin one of the community's major real estate firms, Quinlan and Tyson, Inc., from handling legal matters in property sales and purchases. In 1957, based on many months of study and toil by William S. Kaplan and Richard L. Kahn and co-workers on the Committee on Unauthorized Practice, litigation had been initiated and had already led to a favorable court ruling in behalf of the Association's position. (It would be another four years before an Illinois Supreme Court decision would result in a partial victory for the Association by holding that a real estate agent could prepare a purchase-sale contract but that a lawyer would have to be retained for the closing of the transaction.)

The results were in favor of the official candidates but close enough so that Rooks, on assuming office, was strengthened in a move, already considered by him, to enlist greater participation of members in Association activities, principally committee work. He dispatched letters to all members, asking on which committees they wanted to serve. In his term, membership on some committees doubled, sometimes over the protests of older members who thought of their specific committee membership as an eternal right not to be disturbed by an influx of newcomers. Rooks even appeared at meetings of the Plaintiffs' Lawyers Association, to which nearly all personal injury specialists belonged, and spoke candidly, informing the lawyers that some of them were under investigation and urging them to cease unethical practices.

As the decade progressed, internal peace prevailed, despite occasional complaints from members discontented with administration procedures. Not until 1969 was there another major challenge, this time not in an electoral sense but by formation of a group whose members had often felt dissatisfaction with some of the Association's stands and what they considered the slowness of the organization to take firmer positions not only on matters related to the profession but also on vital events of public interest. That June, 350 lawyers formed the Chicago Council of Lawyers. A separate code of responsibility was drawn up for consideration by the American Bar Association, and the new group announced its intention to involve itself deeply in reform movements. A keynote at an initial meeting was struck by Alexander Polikoff, an expert in civil rights cases, who charged that the country's—and the city's—legal system was "order-oriented" rather than "justice-oriented" and that lawyers had to deal more strenuously with injustices inside the legal profession and in society at large. The majority of those who joined the new organization were—like its first president, Judson H. Miner, son of a veteran jurist, Julius H. Miner— members of the Association. Since its founding, the council has increased its membership persistently, has been given official recognition by the American Bar Association, has been quick to speak out on varied issues, and has maintained a high level of irritation for many Association officials and members while evoking the interest and occasionally the admiration of others

who see it—however impulsive its acts and public statements
sometimes may appear to be—as a necessary component of the
legal community.

2.

Actually, the Association was already involved in activities
growing out of the prevailing ferment in an angry and protest-
filled society, and many of its members, as social-minded as
those who formed the Chicago Council of Lawyers, had been
drawn into them.

The days following the assassination of Martin Luther King,
Jr., in Memphis, Tennessee, on April 4, 1968, were full of out-
breaks of racial violence in major cities in the nation. In
Washington, Baltimore, and Kansas City, there were vandalism
and looting and battles between policemen and crowds of
bitter men; and in Chicago, 11 blacks were killed, 500 persons
were injured, and vast stretches of the city were set aflame. A
curfew was declared by Mayor Daley, and 5,000 federal troops
patrolled the South and West Sides. Even after the curfew
ended on April 10, several hundred of the 3,000 persons
arrested, mostly blacks, still languished in jail cells. Charges resounded that due process of law had virtually been suspended
in the Circuit Court—whose chief judge was John S. Boyle, a
former state's attorney—because no preliminary hearings had
been held and excessive bonds had been set, from up to $1,000
for disorderly conduct charges to $120,000 for arson and con-
spiracy charges. The Association's president, Justin A. Stanley,
informed officials that a corps of 150 volunteers was prepared
to give any assistance but was informed that no such help was
needed. The Cook County Bar Association assailed what it
termed "a deplorable breakdown in judicial processes," and this
organization of black lawyers was joined in protest by the
American Civil Liberties Union and the Legal Aid Bureau of
the United Charities of Chicago.

As public passions grew, and with Stanley in New York at
an important meeting of the American Bar Association, John

Joseph Sullivan—who had helped organize the rebel slate of 1961 and was now first vice-president of the Chicago Bar Association—drew up an emergency plan to help alleviate the problem. He persuaded Judge Boyle that tensions in the strife-torn city would be considerably eased if prisoners' releases could be more rapidly effected, and, with the jurist's sanction, he spent hours on the evening before Easter Sunday rounding up by telephone volunteers among members, magistrates, and court clerks for an extraordinary night session in the Criminal Courts Building at which bonds were reduced and hearings held to free over 200 prisoners.

As a result of this action, Stanley directed formation of the Association's Committee on Civil Disorders under chairmanship of Morris J. Wexler, and it set out to develop procedures that would insure fair and expeditious handling of those arrested in widespread civil disorders. By mid-June, Stanley was able to announce details of a plan that would guarantee more prompt bail hearings, recruit volunteer Association members on a permanent basis to help the public defender, and enlist nonlegal volunteers to aid lawyers in verifying statements of defendants. Judge Boyle gave full cooperation to the idea, and Stanley conferred frequently with him, Sheriff Joseph Woods, and various law enforcement officials to make all fully aware of every aspect of the plan. After Sullivan assumed the presidency, weekly meetings were held by Wexler's committee to work out further details. Letters sent by the Association to members and other practicing Cook County lawyers asking for volunteers to serve without compensation in various legal capacities resulted in a sturdy, reliable force of some 400 people. A training system was set up. Volunteers were organized into trial teams and observer teams, with members of the Board of Managers and the Committee on Civil Disorders as coordinators. Regular sessions were held in the Association offices and in the Criminal Courts Building in the early summer months of 1968. Each volunteer was given a kit of informational materials and directives on his role in mass arrests. Tours for the volunteers were conducted of the courtrooms, the

251

county jail, and the House of Correction, and the Association even staged bail bond hearings.

This well-devised mass-arrest volunteer program not only was a model for other cities similarly disturbed but also served notably in the turbulence that shook Chicago during the Democratic convention that August. Frequent clashes between policemen and vast numbers of youthful protesters were climaxed by full-scale violence in Grant Park and in front of the Conrad Hilton Hotel and the arrests of thousands. This time there was little of the clamor over legal procedures that had been raised after mass arrests earlier that year. The prime reason for this was the quick activation of the Association's program. Teams of lawyers were on hand to act as defense counsel in bail hearings from 4:00 P.M. to 8:00 A.M. for three days in a row until all those arrested were processed. In the following weeks, Association volunteers appeared on behalf of defendants, and, in all, nearly 200 lawyers served so ably that the *Daily News* was moved to praise and make pertinent comment: "The involvement of the CBA in such matters is a new departure, although individual members have rendered similar service in the past. In an era of mass protest—as regrettable as it may be—simple justice requires mass defense by the bar. We congratulate the Bar Association on its initiative in this instance and its readiness to act again if it becomes necessary."

3.

The disorders during the week of the Democratic convention not only aroused vociferous nationwide comment—some in support of the city administration, some critical of police over-reaction—and investigations and interparty strife but also had varied repercussions, several evoking Association action or comment.

Four months later, a flock of indictments were returned by a federal grand jury. Some were against policemen accused of beating demonstrators or reporters. Others were against eight men, the first ever to be indicted under provisions of the

1968 Civil Rights Act, which made it a federal crime to cross state lines to incite a riot or teach the use of riot weapons. The group, promptly labeled the "Conspiracy Eight" because all were also charged with conspiring with intent to incite acts of violence, consisted of David T. Dellinger, chairman of the National Mobilization Committee to End the War in Vietnam; Rennie Davis and Thomas Hayden, leaders of Students for a Democratic Society; Abbie Hoffman and Jerry Rubin, leaders of the Youth International Party popularly known as "Yippies"; Bobby Seale, a founder of the Black Panthers; Lee Weiner, a Northwestern University research assistant in sociology; and John Froines, an assistant professor of chemistry at the University of Oregon.

Their subsequent trial, before United States District Court Judge Julius J. Hoffman, attracted worldwide attention. Almost from the outset, turmoil and strife prevailed, with innumerable clashes over legal points between Judge Hoffman and the defendants' lawyers, William Kunstler and Leonard Weinglass, and frequent outbursts from some of the defendants. Seale was the most persistent, protesting the stern-minded judge's refusal to delay proceedings until his lawyer, Charles Garry—recovering from a gall bladder operation—could appear or to permit him to act as his own attorney. A climactic point was reached on October 29 when Judge Hoffman responded to the latest of Seale's loud interruptions by ordering bailiffs to gag and shackle him. For four days, Seale sat thus in the courtroom, while opinions along a wide spectrum were expressed. Some lawyers charged that Judge Hoffman's action was cruel and inhuman. Others spoke out in support of the jurist, basing arguments on precedents established in previous cases where trials had been disrupted.

By this time, the Association's president was Frank Greenberg, a man rarely averse to speaking out on crucial issues. When Lu Palmer, a black *Daily News* columnist, wrote bitterly that the action against Seale was a manifestation of racism, Greenberg addressed a long letter to the newspaper, charging Palmer with "an intolerable distortion of the facts ... and a wholly unwarranted attack on Judge Hoffman's motivation in resorting to this extreme and distasteful method of maintaining at least a minimal semblance of order and decorum in the courtroom." No defendant, Greenberg maintained, had the inherent right to judge for himself the righteousness of laws and disobey them with impunity. Then he called a press conference in which he emphasized again the need for strict courtroom decorum and criticized defendants and lawyers for unruly behavior. "The question here," he said, "is whether the defendants can be afforded a fair trial in the face of their own determination to make a shambles of the proceedings. The name of that game is disruption and anarchy. It is time for our bar to help the public understand the dilemma that forces a court to the extreme and distasteful necessity of shackling and gagging a defendant." Due process of law and the objective of fair and impartial trials, Greenberg emphasized, could not tolerate disruptive conduct and chaos in a courtroom: "It is no good being told that Judge Hoffman should address himself to the social evils that have produced Bobby Seale. That is not the court's responsibility in this case. We cannot suspend the processes of law and government until we have corrected all of the injustices in our society. The eradication of these injustices and the protection of our society against violence are both equal imperatives, but they do not cancel each other out." He was aware, he added, that the shackling and gagging of Seale was "an unholy spectacle" that would undoubtedly be self-defeating in terms of its public impact. "And yet the court seems today to have no other option when the defendants will not behave in a normal way."

After Seale's restraints were removed on November 3, Judge Hoffman, calling him "a dangerous man" whose behavior "was a major threat to the continued existence of our democratic system," found him guilty on 16 counts of contempt of court and sentenced him to four years in prison. He also severed Seale from the other defendants and set a date for a new trial for the Black Panther leader. (Later, the jury, after deliberating 40 hours, acquitted the defendants—who became known as the "Chicago Seven"—of conspiracy charges but found all except Froines and Weiner guilty of crossing state lines to incite a riot and making inflammatory speeches to achieve that end. This verdict was overturned in November 1972 by the United States Court of Appeals, which also criticized Judge Hoffman for making prejudicial remarks and the chief prosecutor, United States District Attorney Thomas A. Foran, for inflammatory statements. Subsequently, Kunstler, Dellinger, Hoffman, and Rubin were adjudged guilty of contempt of court. All charges against Seale were dropped by the government late in 1970.)

The shackling of Seale—given sanction later in a United States Supreme Court ruling on a similar case, with Justice Hugo L. Black's majority opinion affirming a judge's right to deal in this way with "disruptive, contumacious, stubbornly defiant defendants"—and the rambunctious trial itself led to reverberations within the Association.

4.

Year after year, the creators of the annual Christmas Spirits shows had continued impertinent and hilarious satirical assaults on important local, national, and international figures. The list of victims, long and varied, included satraps of the major political parties, gangsters, legislators in Springfield and Washington, judges on all levels, Franklin and Eleanor Roosevelt and New Deal figures, such foreign autocrats as Adolf Hitler, Benito Mussolini, and Joseph Stalin, ambulance-chasing lawyers, the *Tribune's* Col. Robert R. McCormick and other publishers, Thomas L. Dewey, Illinois governors, industrialists, labor union chieftains, police commissioners, diplomats, army generals, baseball managers, university presidents, members of Congress, entertainers, society leaders, scientists, newspaper columnists, and other presidents from Harry S. Truman through Richard M. Nixon. The gibes at Nixon started early. In the 1952 production, "Knee Plus Ultra"—like most of those in the preceding decade written mainly by two brothers, Charles and

James Sprowl—charges against Nixon of fund-raising irregularities in his vice-presidential campaign and his subsequent denial on television in what became known as his "Checkers speech" were duly noted in a song, one of whose verses, to the tune of "Cry," went:

> When into your secret fund they
>   start to pry,
> Makes no difference what you
>   tell them, if you cry.
> When all your lame excuses flop and fail,
> You can still escape by learning how to wail,
> If you can weep, they'll make you Veep.

And to mark President Truman's departure from the White House, the chorus opened the show by singing, to the tune of "So Long, Mary":

> So long, Harry!
> Gee, it's nice to see you go.
> So long, Harry!
> Soon you're gonna miss us so.
> And you'll soon be longing for us, Harry,
> While you roam.
> So long, Harry!
> Don't forget to stay down home.

But the greatest concentration had always been on local personalities and events. In the 1930s and 1940s, no year passed without songs and skits directed at Mayor Kelly and his powerful political organization, its army of payrollers, and its periodic scandals, and after 1955 at Mayor Daley and his equally potent forces. A typical assault on Kelly in 1937, to the tune of the rangers' song from "Rio Rita," went:

> While Benito Mussolini
>   Down in sunny Italy
> Has his Fascisti
>   And Haile Selassie
> Up in Moscow Joseph Stalin
>   Tells his Soviets to fall in

256

The five-year plan,
  And doesn't give a damn.
In der Vaterland the Nazis
  Adolf Hitler do salute.
In Chicago our Ed Kelly
  Makes the boys jump through the hoop.

All hail to dictators,
  Comrades, democracy haters,
Red Shirt here, Black Shirt there,
  Brown Shirt here, Stuffed Shirt there,
Strong arms stop traitors,
  Real propaganda
All now do hand ya
  Do as you're told, pay when told,
Be shot cold, for the bold
  Dictatorship is here!

Few of the local objects of the often-savage wit protested—
at least not publicly. Indeed, Kelly always attended, chortled
manfully, and, on one occasion, mounted the stage at the end of
the revue to thank the company and do an imitation of
President Roosevelt. Others who had been subjected to lyrical
assault had shown forbearance and a sense of humor. In the
1951 production, "Seizin's Greetings," Municipal Court Judge
Joseph Drucker—having been nominated by President Truman
for appointment to the United States District Court but not
confirmed due to the opposition of Sen. Paul H. Douglas because the President had not consulted him in advance—participated in a number in which he played "I Dreamt I Dwelt in
Marble Halls" on his violin. In the same show, former Circuit
Court Judge Julius H. Miner, defeated the previous June by
Walter V. Schaefer for a seat on the Illinois Supreme Court,
appeared as a policeman in a uniform of the 1890s to lament,
"To think that only a year ago I was known as Julius the Just
and now I'm just Julius."

But in the late 1960s, a time of tension and strife, tolerance
for unrestrained jollity dimmed. The pre-Christmas 1969 show,
titled "Heir," offered sketches in which butts of humor in-

cluded President Nixon; Mayor Daley and his son, Richard; Gov. Richard Ogilvie; and Vice-president Spiro Agnew. The laughter was expectedly loud and buoyant. One skit, "Alice in Wonderland," was set in a courtroom with a character bound and gagged, with lawyers shouting and jumping about, and with John C. Tucker, one of its authors, playing a judge resembling Judge Hoffman and repeatedly shouting, "Off with his head! Off with his head!"

Judge Hoffman, justifiably unamused, was in the opening night audience at the Conrad Hilton Hotel but uttered no complaint. Others, however, did. Some members decried the skit as "a shocking lampoon" and "a breach of taste" in unfairly making fun of a crucial and difficult trial. At first, the Board of Managers, after hearing from Tucker and Royce Rowe, chairman of the Entertainment Committee, decided against taking action. But the protests continued. A letter from a group of ten members, including such former presidents as R. Newton Rooks, Norman H. Nachman, and Gordon R. Close, demanded a public apology: "The depicting of the conspiracy trial was clearly unethical since it involved a pending case, and to this must be added criticism for the inexcusable manner in which Judge Hoffman was lampooned." Then the United States District Court's chief judge, William J. Campbell, added his rebuke in a letter to the Board of Managers in which he also stressed the unethical nature of comment, however much in jest, on a pending case—"This is the very type of conduct which both bar and bench so properly and frequently condemn when committed by the communications media"—and suggested that assurances be given him that future productions would be "responsibly edited."

A week after receipt of both letters, the Board of Managers reversed its earlier stand on the basis that although nothing derogatory to the court had been intended, it recognized the validity of Judge Campbell's assertion that the depiction of the conspiracy trial was not proper because it involved a case still being adjudicated. An official apology was rendered, the first ever offered in the 45 years since the birth of the rollicking

shows, but Frank Greenberg could not resist further comment.
On the *Record's* "President's Page," he expressed additional
regret that any offense was given to Judge Hoffman or to any
of his colleagues on the bench but denied that the skit constituted editorial comment on the pending trial. "Surely editorial comments are made of sterner stuff than this excursion
into the extravagances of the Queen of Hearts in 'Alice in
Wonderland'. The authors may have been misguided, the skit
may have misfired, but it seems to me quite clear that nobody
harbored any malicious or even serious intention to make a
comment on the conduct of the trial." As for censoring future
productions, Greenberg spoke for many in the Association—and
certainly for those who had hewed to the steadfast Christmas
Spirits traditions—when he wrote: "The show is either worth
keeping as a free expression by the Entertainment Committee
without censorship by the Board of Managers, or it is not worth
keeping at all. We have seen the risks. But it seems to me that
you either take the risk of the kind of reaction we have just
had or you take an even less acceptable risk of reducing the
show to a level of cautious banality, guaranteed to offend
nobody and to interest few."

To the Association's credit, no system of censorship was
applied then or later, and the shows continued their irreverent
way, offending a few at times but never failing to interest and
delight many inside and outside the Association.

5.

If this was a decade disturbed periodically by disputes, it
was also, like many of its predecessors, one marked by accomplishment.

Legislation was drafted, often in union with the Illinois State
Bar Association, to curtail garnishment of wages by lending
companies, to reform laws regulating the sale of tax-delinquent
property, to strengthen fair-housing regulations, to eliminate
reprehensible renting practices, and to aid victims of unscrupulous real estate brokers. Codes were revised and modern-

ized. After five years of work, a joint committee headed by United States District Court Judge Richard B. Austin produced the Criminal Code of 1961, a codification of substantive Illinois criminal law. This was followed by the Code of Criminal Procedure of 1963, prepared by the same committee. With few changes, the committee's drafts were enacted into law, thereby giving Illinois the first genuine penal code in its history. In their major provisions, the codes infused into Illinois criminal jurisprudence the best products of modern scholarship; with their enactment, a person on probation had the right to appeal, review of judgments in criminal cases was simplified, a substitute for professional bondsmen was provided for, and the procedure in criminal cases was clarified. Another joint project, of which Jerome S. Weiss, a former Association president, was chairman, resulted in a recommendation, subsequently adopted, that the Illinois Supreme Court establish the Illinois Courts Commission, provided for in the 1962 judicial article, as a permanent body to examine complaints against judges and assess their capability for continuing service.

Closer ties were established with the United Charities' Legal Aid Bureau. For many years, the bureau had sought some steady form of contributions from a larger percentage of the membership, and in 1964, the Board of Managers approved the addition of $1 to quarter-annual dues bills, a practice that has been successfully continued. In 1968, during John Joseph Sullivan's presidency, more black lawyers became involved in Association activities and committees, especially a newly organized Urban Affairs Committee, the eventual catalyst in creating remedial legislation on consumer credit and landlord-tenant relations; for his efforts, Sullivan won the Cook County Bar Association's 1969 Award of Merit and Honor. To give further aid to persons unable to pay legal fees, an Interns at Law project was instituted to utilize law students as aides to lawyers assigned by the long-standing Committee on Defense of Prisoners in criminal cases on federal and state levels; and a Committee of Matrimonial Lawyers for Indigents was formed, handling over 200 cases in its initial year.

Meanwhile, in the heightened campaign for constitutional revision, the Association continued its sustained participation.

The need for intensifying that campaign, especially as it related to judicial improvements, was increasingly apparent. In January 1964, when changes required by the new judicial article went into effect, disagreement arose over appointment by Circuit Court judges of 33 former referees, Probate Court assistants, and Torrens land-title examiners to new posts as salaried magistrates. The Association, through President Norman H. Nachman, criticized the naming of five of them to the $16,000-a-year jobs because they lacked qualifications (one, in addition, was a relative of a leading crime syndicate figure), a stand supported by a *Daily News* editorial, headed "Reformed Court Muffs a Chance," that noted sharply, "The slogan on which the judicial amendment was passed, 'Get the judges out of politics,' already proves illusory." Not only did the judges disregard the Association's "unqualified" ruling on the quintet, but a former Association president, Augustine J. Bowe, now a presiding judge of the Municipal Court, chastised the Association for even undertaking to screen the group.

The Association's methods of evaluating candidates had been often criticized ever since institution of its primaries in its earliest years. The criticism came not only from rejected candidates but also from editorialists who, on the contrary, held that approval was too easily achieved or who maintained on other occasions that the Association should be required to give explanations for rejections. Over the decades, the Association had sought to meet such objections by changing its methods of assessment with the aim of improving them, but its officers and especially the members of its various Candidates committees were realistically aware that widespread satisfaction by whatever system was not easily attainable.

In September, new complaints were heard when the Association's poll rejected 8 of 38 sitting judges for reelection. Since the eight had all been endorsed by the Cook County Democratic Central Committee, Mayor Daley called a special press conference to attack the poll. He especially pointed out that little more than a third of the Association's 7,200 members had returned questionnaires, which allotted points to judges on integrity, legal ability, judicial temperament, and diligence. A score of 70 was needed for approval. Daley noted that a "Yes" vote on integrity gave a judge a score of 50, as many as the points for the other three combined. The *Sun-Times* editorialized strongly that the Association should disclose detailed reasons for rejections. The *Tribune*, lamenting lack of support for Republican candidates, asserted that the poll was unjust because of a preponderance of "Democratic officeholders" among the Association membership; a check of all the ballots against lists of lawyers in the offices of the state's attorney, corporation counsel, United States district attorney, and Illinois attorney general disclosed that only 90 ballots were marked by such members.

In reply to varied critics, President Gordon R. Close defended the polling system as one that had served well for a long time. "This poll," he said, "is not a disciplinary procedure. We are saying merely that, based on the judgment of the people appearing before them, some judges have met minimum standards and others haven't." He was not disturbed, he added, that only 2,645 of the members had cast ballots since this indicated that only those with valid opinions cast ballots.

Reassessment of the existing method was instituted, however, and early in 1966, President Thomas J. Boodell announced that although members would still be asked four key questions relating to candidates' diligence, integrity, legal ability, and judicial temperament, the point system would be abandoned. The Committee on Candidates and Board of Managers would, however, be guided by replies to the extent that they could recommend whether sitting judges should be retained in office, such recommendation contingent on whether a candidate received a vote of 50 percent or more in reply to the single question of whether a particular judge should be retained. This, he said, would fulfill the requirement of the judicial amendment that judges run in an uncontested election. Boodell also reaffirmed the Association's intention to help guide all concerned in the matter, from party leaders to candidates to voters: "We believe the electorate is entitled to have the best available, unprejudiced information as to the qualifications and performance of the judges made available to it. The Chicago Bar Association considers it an obligation to speak out on judicial selection and retention."

Yet, all was not smooth—in that very July, neither party bothered to submit to the Association names of nominees for justice of the Illinois Supreme Court—and periodic criticism continued from within and without. Added to these was a flurry of scandals involving lower court jurists—chief among them Circuit Court Associate Judge Cecil Corbett Smith, who resigned amid investigations of his associations with syndicate gangsters, and Circuit Court Judge Richard A. Napolitano, investigated in connection with kickbacks in granting concessions at the Illinois State Fair and subsequently relieved of duties on the recommendation of the Illinois Courts Commission, and Circuit Court Associate Judge Louis W. Kizas, accused of official misconduct for selling bail bonds at $50 each—and the unprecedented case in the summer of 1969 of Chief Justice Roy J. Solfisburg, Jr., and Justice Ray I. Klingbiel of the Illinois Supreme Court. Spurred by demands from Sherman H. Skolnick, a diligent legal researcher and inveterate seeker-out of wrongdoers, the high court took steps for the creation of a special five-man commission, headed by Frank Greenberg, to investigate charges against Solfisburg and Klingbiel in connection with a criminal case involving Theodore J. Isaacs, former state revenue director. Exhaustive hearings disclosed that Klingbiel had received a gift of stock in a bank of which Isaacs was a founder and director—the shares having been paid for by Isaacs and registered in another name—and that Solfisburg was given a favorable opportunity to buy 700 shares of the bank's stock while Isaacs' case was still pending. These shares were put in a trust to conceal ownership and then sold at a profit through a nominee; both purchase and sale had been arranged by Isaacs and their ownership hidden while his case was being considered, thus giving the appearance of impropriety. The inquiry and hearings, on which a corps of young lawyers headed by John Paul Stevens worked ceaselessly without compensation, came to an end with a report recommending the prompt resignation of both justices. Although initially each indicated no inclination to follow that recommendation, they did so on August 2, with the inevitable denials of wrongdoing.

6.

All of these events served to strengthen the resolve of advocates to include in a new state constitution, if ever it became a reality, a provision for nonpartisan merit selection of judges.

By this time, much had been accomplished in the overall drive, led by Samuel W. Witwer and his Illinois Committee for Constitutional Revision, to call a constitutional convention. A $250,000 fund, raised with contributions from individuals and business corporations, was being spent on pamphlets, advertisements, and organization of local campaigns. Assertions of support had been elicited from leaders of both political parties, with Gov. Richard Ogilvie assuring skeptical labor union leaders that the convention would be bipartisan rather than Republican-dominated and with Mayor Daley recommending a door-to-door campaign in behalf of the convention call.

Association activists were sparked by the frequent writings of Peter Tomei in the *Record*. Early in 1968, his influential article detailed the defects of the 1920-22 convention, chief among them the partisan election that resulted in a Republican majority of 5 to 1 and only 3 Democrats named to the 25 committees, thereby alienating party chiefs and Democratic voters. On the eve of the general election of November 3, 1968—at which time voters were asked to approve a call for a constitutional convention—a letter headed "Constitutional Convention or Chaos" from Witwer in scores of the state's newspapers stressed that the Gateway Amendment of 1950 had fallen far short of expectations for meaningful change and concluded, "Illinois will have the chance to throw off the dead hand of the dead past in the future conduct of its government."

The electorate—by a vote of 2,977,977 to 1,135,440—approved the call for a new convention, and almost at once the move began for election of 116 delegates, 2 from each of the 58 state senatorial districts. Tomei, now chairman of the Association's Constitutional Study Committee, was among the first to urge steps to insure an objective convention, the most important of which were the dropping of party labels in the election of delegates and legislation requiring lobbyists at the convention to disclose their identities and the amounts of money they were spending. Nonpartisanship was essential, he stressed in a new *Record* article: "A constitutional convention is the institution through which the people exercise the ultimate power of government—the power to renew and repair the ultimate basic structure and machinery of the government under which we live. . . . The purpose and function of a constitutional convention transcends the normal concerns of partisan politics." Witwer, as Illinois Committee for Constitutional Revision chairman, agreed: "A convention torn by partisan or sectional strife or submissive to any interest other than the public interest will have little chance of success." Tomei's proposal, submitted to the Constitution Study Commission and to the legislature, was accepted, and a primary to elect a slate of convention delegates was set for September 23, 1969, and the election for November 18.

While delegate aspirants campaigned, the Association early in August formally touched off an intensified campaign for a new judicial article. At a press conference, President Frank Greenberg—flanked by former presidents Jerome S. Weiss and R. Newton Rooks—urged adoption of a variation of the Missouri Plan, under which judges were appointed by the governor from names submitted by a high-level nominating commission of lawyers and laymen. "Under the present system," Greenberg said, "some hacks are elevated who have no better qualifications for judicial office than the Brownie points they have accumulated in serving their political parties from precinct captain on up. Judges must be chosen otherwise than out of the political thicket. Not every ounce of politics is out of the system under the Missouri Plan, but it's a very substantial improvement over what we have today."

The statement drew fire. Circuit Court Chief Judge John S. Boyle not only disagreed with Greenberg on the need for a new article but also added: "I haven't found any hacks here in the Circuit Court. We have 253 judges and magistrates and all are capable judges. We have kept politics out of the courts very well." Representative Bernard E. Epton, a Republican who had been on the rival Association candidates' slate in 1961, charged that the system advocated by Greenberg would afford the Association too much influence and produce only judges "secure in the social structure." He threatened to call for a legislative investigation of the Association: "If the spotlight is turned upon them, it will remove the myth that the Chicago Bar Association is a pillar of righteous men."

But Greenberg persisted. In an October speech to the City Club, he called for a massive citizens' effort in behalf of judicial selection. Many judges who had attained their positions through political service and sponsorship were first-rate, he admitted, but he added, "It is high time we adopted a system that had as its primary objective the selection of judges of outstanding quality rather than a system in which judgeships are a reward for political service." In January 1970, a month after Witwer, as president, had convened the Constitutional Convention with a pointed reference to the fears of government among framers of the 1870 constitution ("Let us, unlike the men of that era, not allow mistrust to lead us into temptation. We cannot legislate the detailed solutions for the problems of tomorrow"), Greenberg and Henry L. Pitts, the Illinois State Bar Association's president, announced joint support of the plan for appointive judges. The following week, they and other representatives of both groups journeyed to Springfield to testify on behalf of the proposal before the convention's Judiciary Committee. In three sessions totaling nearly nine hours, they explained in detail what was involved. Laymen on nominating committees, they emphasized, would outnumber lawyers, and eventual nominees would be scrupulously screened.

The system by which judges ran against their record, as provided by the judicial amendment of 1962, would be retained, although the new article would strengthen provisions for retirement, suspension, and removal for cause. The aim was for a judiciary that was independent and yet accountable for its actions. "Please don't indulge in the myth," said Greenberg, "that an election gives the people any say in the choices of judges. In Cook County, judges are selected for us by ward committeemen in private party conclaves on the basis of political considerations." On the railroad trip back to Chicago, Greenberg admitted to Wayland B. Cedarquist, a longtime Association proponent of reform and chairman of the Joint Committee on the Judicial Article, "It's clear we have a long uphill struggle."

He was realistically prophetic. As the convention proceeded with a minimum of the rancorous disputes that had characterized its predecessors and reached its end on September 13, it was decided to offer the judicial proposal not as part of the new constitution but separately as Proposition 2B; other individual propositions included one on capital punishment and another on the vote for 18 year olds. Supporters far outnumbered opponents of the proposed constitution to be voted upon December 15. The Chicago Federation of Labor and the Industrial Trades Council were foremost foes, but there was considerable antagonism to Proposition 2B, principally from the Cook County Bar Association, which maintained that blacks and members of other minorities would have less chance to attain judicial rank, and, of course, from the Daley organization. The mayor withheld any statement until November 30, when he announced that, despite some drawbacks, the constitution merited approval. He was for granting the vote to 18 year olds and strenuously for the election of judges. At a meeting of an organization subcommittee, he pounded the lectern as he cried: "What merit is there in substituting the politics of the statehouse for the politics of the local precinct? They're trying to deceive and fool and hoodwink the people. Sure, there's always room for improvement, but that idea gets my Gaelic up!"

James A. Velde, Greenberg's successor who had earlier led an Association delegation to Daley in a futile effort to gain his support of the proposal, replied, "The Democratic committee leaders know better than anyone the realistic fact that judges are not chosen by the people but by the slatemaking committee of party candidates." Greenberg also could not resist a retort, telling a meeting of the Illinois Society of Certified Public Accountants: "I am sick of the hollow litany that the selective system would take from the people the right to select judges. No amount of the mayor's familiar rhetoric can wash away the obvious truth that the people are as effectively excluded from any participation in the process of selecting judges as if the polls were closed in their faces."

The arguments and counterarguments continued, and the rhetoric resounded. Wayne W. Whalen, one of the convention's ablest delegates and a fervent supporter of the merit plan, undertook to lead the campaign in Cook County, although his hastily formed 2B Committee for Better Courts had limited funds, space, and people. Chester T. Kamin, whose sister, Carole Kamin Bellows, had been the Association's effective representative in advocating progressive articles at sessions of the convention's Civil Rights Committee, led Lawyers for 2-B, comprised of Association members, in a speechmaking campaign. A month before the voting, Velde inaugurated a drive for $1 million desperately needed by the Committee for Modern Courts to carry on its work.

But all the efforts for Proposition 2B were in vain. On the morning of December 16, a *Sun-Times* headline cried, "WE HAVE A NEW CONSTITUTION!" The story enumerated its major elements—increased home rule for cities of more than 25,-000, an income tax, eventual elimination of personal property taxes, establishment of a Judicial Inquiry Board, greater flexibility in the amending process, and civil rights provisions that imposed stronger bans on racial and sex discrimination in employment, promotion, and sale or rental of property. The turnout had been light—about 35 percent of registered voters—with the margin of victory 283,257 out of nearly 2 million votes cast, but those who had worked so hard and so long were quick to agree with the heading on a *Sun-Times* editorial: "Illinois Enters 20th Century." The propositions to abolish the death penalty and to lower the voting age were defeated—and so was Proposition 2B. Even though the proposition had won in Cook County, largely because of a heavy turnout in the suburbs, the votes in Chicago and most of the downstate areas combined to overcome that victory. There were postmortems and second thoughts, analyses and explanations—insufficient funds, minimal involvement of downstate lawyers, too little financial support or active participation by enough members of both the Chicago and Illinois State bar associations, and of course, the concerted assault on the judicial article by the Daley cohorts. And there was some solace in the relatively slight margin of 151,329 opposing votes out of 1,014,000—a "nervous victory" as Rubin G. Cohn, staff counsel of the convention's Judiciary Committee, aptly termed it. Another effort to institute a new way to secure judges had been brought to a standstill, but the future did not appear as bleak as some saw it to be. "Many voters," wrote Velde in the *Record*, "have been persuaded that judges should not be elected but should be appointed under a merit system free from political considerations." Perhaps it might still be possible, he conjectured, to adopt a selection system by an amendment to the new constitution.

Christmas Spirits

For half its lifetime, one of the enduring and pleasurable traditions of the Chicago Bar Association has been the yearly presentation of its Christmas Spirits shows. The productions, written and acted in by talented members, spare no figure of local, national, or international renown. Sometimes good-naturedly and sometimes quite savagely—but always with wit and high humor—the revues gibe at the high and mighty and the politically powerful and at the legal profession.

Here and on the following pages are photographs of some typical productions over the years.

Parole board scandals were among many topics satirized in the 1936 show. In this skit, a parolee, played by John R. Heath, is flanked by Pressly L. Stevenson (left), Jesse H. Brown, and Jerome S. Weiss as members of the board. *Chicago Today*

"Dogmatic Determination" was the title of a skit in the 1943 show, "Lawyers on Parade," with C. Henry Austin as Joseph Stalin, L. Duncan Lloyd as President Franklin D. Roosevelt, and Pressly L. Stevenson as Winston Churchill.

Chicago Daily News

Political figures of past and present delineated in the 1946 production, "State of Confusion," were (left to right) Chicago's famed First Ward alderman John "Bathhouse John" Coughlin (played by John D. Black), Henry Wallace (L. Duncan Lloyd), Harry S. Truman (Thomas L. Underwood), Fiorello La Guardia (Julius H. Miner), and John L. Lewis (Pressly L. Stevenson).

Chicago Daily News

"So long, Harry. Gee, it's nice to see you go!" was a hit song of "Knee Plus Ultra," the 1952 show. Thomas L. McDermand satirized President Harry S. Truman, shown here departing Washington after the inauguration of Dwight D. Eisenhower.

Chicago Daily News

The 1954 production, "Executive Sweetie," featured an imperious Gen. Douglas MacArthur (played by L. Duncan Lloyd) pulled in a Tokyo ricksha by a coolie (Circuit Court Judge Julius H. Miner).

In "Magna Cartage," the 1957 show, three leading judges—(left to right) John J. Lupe, Edwin A. Robson, and Joseph Drucker—formed a musical trio. This number, like scores of others over the years that involved judges, was produced by Arlindo S. Cate.

The opening number of "Heir," the 1969 production, featured John P. Coleman, C. David Howell, Douglas Mitchell, Kenneth Padgham, Jr., Raymond K. Riggs, J. Timothy Ritchie, Michael Saper, and Lee K. Zells, some of them shown here.

Chicago Sun-Times

One of the skits in the 1969 show presented John C. Tucker as a judge who cried "Off with his head!" when defendants' lawyers raised objections. It evoked official criticism for its harsh satire relating to the trial of the "Conspiracy Eight," then in progress before United States District Court Judge Julius J. Hoffman. The Association issued an apology but refused to accede to suggestions that future shows be censored.

Chicago Sun-Times

Mayor Richard J. Daley has been a frequent recipient of barbs. In "The Boys in the Bar," the 1970 show, Robert J. Nye depicted the city's chief executive singing "More."

Chicago Daily News

Tradition was upset in 1971 when Tala Engel was one of two women in that year's show, "New Phases of 1971." In 1970, she had sought unsuccessfully, with a suit in United States District Court, to compel integration of the all-male cast. Since the 1971 breakthrough, other women members of the Association have taken part in productions.

Chicago Sun-Times

In two highly acclaimed numbers in the 1972 show, "The Bench Connection," Julian J. Frazin (top) parodied President Richard M. Nixon and Phillip M. Citrin (bottom) played Henry Kissinger, clad in blue silk pajamas and singing "See What the Boys in the Back Room Will Have."

Chicago Tribune (top); *Chicago Sun-Times* (bottom)

As Rose Mary Woods, President Richard M. Nixon's secretary, Fred Lane tries to explain what happened to 18 minutes of a tape recording made in her boss' Oval Office. The hit number was in the 1973 production, "Planet of the Tapes." *Chicago Daily News*

Heading for a Centennial

1.

DESPITE THE DEFEAT of Proposition 2B, important judicial changes were provided for in the new constitution, among them that retention in office would henceforth require approval by 60 instead of 50 percent of the voters; that vacancies in the Supreme, Appellate, and Circuit courts could be filled by appointment by the high tribunal unless and until specific legislation was passed; and that jurists could hold no outside "position of profit." The last was an especially striking innovation inasmuch as judges had never been barred, ever since Illinois achieved statehood, from receiving compensation from insurance companies, banks, and other financial institutions.

Generally welcomed was the provision for creation of the Judicial Inquiry Board, whose nine members, four of them laymen, had power to conduct investigations and receive or initiate complaints against jurists for possible action by the Illinois Courts Commission. Two of the four lawyers named by Governor Ogilvie were Frank Greenberg and Wayne W. Whalen; and among the nonlawyers were Charles G. Hurst, outspoken black president of Malcolm X College, and Mrs. Anne Willer, a suburban League of Women Voters leader and a well-respected delegate to the constitutional convention. For all the plaudits—"The public has good reason to expect a first-rate performance," wrote a *Sun-Times* editorialist—the board found itself without funds for an office and operating expenses. At the designated start of its activities on July 1, 1971, and for months thereafter, a bill to provide $100,000 for such purposes was bottled up in Springfield amid charges by Greenberg and officers of the Chicago Council of Lawyers that the delay was caused by Democratic legislative leaders. In an exchange with Sen. Thomas G. Lyons, chairman of the state Senate finance committee, Greenberg charged, "The appropriation has been blocked because the Democrats don't want judges investigated," and later the council supported this view. Lyons denied the accusation, asserting that various matters, ranging from the compensation to be paid members to whether lawyers on the board could continue to practice, needed further discussion. Moreover, Lyons maintained that the Illinois Courts Commission retained the primary responsibility for policing the judiciary, a statement quickly denounced by Greenberg as "the most blatant misinformation ever perpetrated on the people of Illinois." Through the summer and fall and into the winter, the squabble continued—at one point, Governor Ogilvie contributed $200 to help finance the board and appealed for public subscriptions—and not until May 1972 did the legislature finally grant the board an initial sum of $47,000 for past and current expenses.

More public disputations were generated in connection with the constitutional mandate for the appointment of magistrates as associate judges of the Circuit Court. Because the new appointees would serve for four years instead of the single year specified in the existing system, the Supreme Court issued directives to each of the 21 judicial districts to screen all sitting magistrates carefully so that any deemed unfit could be sifted out.

In Cook County, a four-judge panel headed by Circuit Court Judge Daniel A. Covelli began its review, and the Association and the Chicago Council of Lawyers initiated theirs. And trouble quickly arose. A substantial majority of the 107 magistrates refused to reply to questionnaires or appear before the Association's Committee on Candidates. Burton H. Palmer, president of the Cook County Magistrates Association, declared, "The Association screening is superfluous and unnecessary." Despite this, the Association continued its hearings and inquiries, and soon Judge Covelli received two lists—the Association's, deeming 38 magistrates unqualified for promotion, and the council's, rating only two fully qualified. Reasons for disqualification were manifold—from general ineptitude, lack of legal knowledge, and erratic behavior to bullying of lawyers and defendants, arbitrary rulings, and old age.

This touched off new disputes. While some members of the council criticized the Association because its recommendations had been far less harsh, the council itself was attacked by Judge Covelli—"The entire report is full of hearsay and reeks of statements that the magistrates are ordered around like a bunch of lackeys"—and, naturally, by some of the magistrates. To add to the turmoil, a group of 23 top Chicago attorneys of diverse political and social hues asked the Illinois Supreme Court to discharge all 107 and set up a nonpartisan process by which the magistrates could be screened, thereby preventing what was envisaged as "a true disaster in terms of the quality of our judiciary." When the high court rejected this request and announced that the county's 69 Circuit Court judges would convene to vote by secret ballot on which of the 107 magistrates would be retained, Milton H. Gray, acting Association president in Velde's absence at a Harvard College reunion, expressed disappointment: "A secret vote is better than a open vote, but I don't think it gets to the real heart of the question, which is that judges should be selected on the basis of merit and not on the basis of partisan politics." State's Attorney Edward V. Hanrahan joined in the public discussion—"It has been our experience that the magistrates, as a group, have performed their important judicial functions extremely well"— and warned that if the appointments were delayed, Circuit courts, already congested with pending cases, would be in a chaotic condition. Judge Covelli asserted that the Association had not made available to him and his aides all available information, including names of complainants, on which its judgment had been based and had rejected a suggestion that there be confrontations to support accusations against specific magistrates.

When the judges met in the new Civic Center to vote, they approved all the sitting magistrates except six who had been found unqualified by both the Association and the council. Velde's instant reaction—"The Circuit Court judges have repudiated the idea, frequently stated by political leaders, that they would not select judges found unqualified by the Association"—was countered by Judge Covelli's reply, "We'll be happy to reconsider if the CBA has any evidence that we acted unconstitutionally." The council's president, Judson H. Miner, denounced the judges' action as "a clear example of the complete contempt in which the people of Chicago and the lawyers of Chicago are held by the controlling political party of the city." A group of 114 lawyers, led by Albert E. Jenner and contending that the upgraded magistrates would constitute more than 40 percent of all trial judges in the county, petitioned the state Supreme Court to block the automatic promotions and allow time for new screening procedures.

The rhetoric and the protests became academic as the Circuit Court judges stood by their decision and the high court turned down Jenner's petition on the grounds that the new constitution barred it from dismissing the magistrates. In due course, the new associate judges took their assigned places amid the complaining organizations' promises to keep close watch on their future activities. And as they did so, all involved might, in less hectic moments, find cause to reflect with philosophic calm on the counsel of Rubin G. Cohn in his *To Judge With Justice*, a scholarly and engrossing account of the history and politics of judicial reform in Illinois: "The 1970 judicial revision had fairly resolved the issues with which the convention had dealt. History teaches, however, that there is no finality to political judgments. As with its predecessors, the 1970 revisions must meet the challenge of reappraisal. This is as it should be."

2.

As in some previous decades, the Association also became embroiled in controversy with yet another Cook County state's attorney, this time as an outgrowth of a violent event on a wintry December day in 1969.

In a predawn raid on an apartment near the headquarters of the Black Panther Party, state's attorney's police killed Fred Hampton, Illinois party chairman, and Mark Clark, a downstate party leader. The raiders maintained after the shooting that their foray had been carried out with a warrant obtained on information that weapons were stockpiled in Hampton's apartment and that their knock on the door was met by a burst of shotgun fire from within. Black Panther leaders denied this and cried, "Murder!" As demands for official inquiries sounded from many sources, State's Attorney Hanrahan, a vigorous and volatile prosecutor, defended the raid and offered to the *Tribune* photographs purporting to show that the holes in doors and walls were made from bullets fired from inside the apartment—a claim quickly refuted by the rival *Sun-Times* with an exclusive story showing that what appeared to be bullet holes actually were nailheads—and granted permission to the local Columbia Broadcasting System television station to film a reenactment of his version of the event.

The Association's initial involvement came shortly thereafter, when President Frank Greenberg proposed that a high-grade jury be named to conduct the inquest into the deaths of Hampton and Clark and that Coroner Andrew J. Toman voluntarily withdraw in favor of a special deputy with a sound legal background. "Only by an investigation open to the press and participated in by representatives of the black community," said Greenberg, "can we hope to restore the public confidence which has been shaken by these events." Toman denied the second request but acceded to the first and named to a five-man jury two blacks, Dr. Theodore K. Lawless, the world-famed dermatologist, and Julian B. Wilkins, a prominent attorney; Philip H. Corboy, member of the Association's Board of Managers and a future Association president; Benedict Mayers, an educator and criminologist; and Dr. James T. Hicks, a pathologist. While on another front a federal grand jury opened a separate investigation, Toman convened the inquest. Testimony was given only by several participating raiders because attorneys for the families of the slain Panther leaders declined to call witnesses, indicating they did not want to disclose defense plans for other Panthers facing possible trial. Basing its decision solely on that evidence, the jury was compelled to rule that the deaths of Hampton and Clark were justified.

In May, the federal grand jury issued its report, indicting no one on either side but filling a 250-page document with strong criticism of Hanrahan's office, the police, and the coroner. This prompted new demands, and shortly before he left the presidency, Greenberg placed the Association alongside the local chapter of the American Civil Liberties Union, the Chicago Council of Lawyers, and Businessmen for the Public Interest in requesting appointment of a special grand jury and prosecutor to investigate the December 4 raid. A petition approved by the Board of Managers was filed before Joseph A. Power, presiding judge of the Criminal Division of the Circuit Court, with the Association's special counsel, Robert F. Cummins, vainly inviting Hanrahan to support the request. In addition, the Chicago Council of Lawyers, noting that two of the city's newspapers, the *Sun-Times* and the *Daily News*, were calling for Hanrahan to resign, petitioned the Illinois Supreme Court to appoint a special commission to investigate Hanrahan's actions during and after the raid, but this plea was denied without comment. Little more than a week later, Judge Power appointed Barnabas F. Sears, a former president of the Illinois State Bar Association and a doughty trial lawyer who had obtained convictions of eight policemen in connection with the Summerdale District burglary scandal a decade earlier, as special prosecutor with a mandate to impanel a special grand jury and begin anew the investigation into the double slaying. "We're going to run a completely independent, objective, impartial investigation," promised Sears. "That's our duty."

While Sears gathered a staff and started investigations before presenting the case to the 23-member grand jury, the Association proceeded with its own inquiry into Hanrahan's post-raid activity. The Committee on Ethics examined his statements to the press and the attendant publicity; then the matter was turned over to the Committee on Inquiry for deeper investigation. The outcome was a decision to file a formal complaint with the Grievance Committee against the state's attorney for alleged violation of professional legal ethics, citing especially his submission of photographs to the *Tribune* and his granting of permission to the television station to recreate his particular account of the raid. Hanrahan not only entered a firm denial but demanded that the Illinois Supreme Court institute a probe of how the Association's action had been leaked to the newspapers. At a tense four-minute press conference, he flayed the Association: "If there is any truth in such published reports they can only have resulted from deliberate disclosure by some members of the Chicago Bar Association, in flagrant disregard by them of Illinois Supreme Court Rule 751, which prohibits publicity about any such charge until after the evidence is received, the truth established and appropriate law applied." Greenberg's successor, James A. Velde, offered an apology for the leak and instituted a search, subsequently futile, for the offender.

The outcome of this phase of the complex case was far in the future. Meanwhile the grand jury gathered in Judge Power's courtroom and began to hear testimony occasionally interrupted by legal arguments. After one such debate, in which Sears was held in contempt and fined $50 an hour for as long as he refused the jurist's order to call certain witnesses, three lawyers representing Hanrahan and two aides sought to quash the inquiry on grounds that the jurors would be "naturally tainted and biased" because of the turbulent hearing. The Association promptly sought to intervene to prevent this from happening. Judge Power turned the Association down but later refused to grant the defense petition also, and the grand jury continued to sit. When it ended its deliberations, Judge Power delayed announcing the findings because he contended that the grand jury had not heard all vital witnesses and that Sears had put pressure on it to return true bills. The Association thereupon joined Sears in asking the Illinois Supreme Court to order that the judge make the indictment public, and, after considerably more legal wrangling, the high court ordered this done. On August 24, 1971, 14 months after Sears had been named special prosecutor, the long-suppressed indictment was handed down. It charged Hanrahan, an assistant, eight of the raiders, and four police officials who conducted investigations into the raid with conspiring to obstruct justice by thwarting criminal prosecution of the raiders and by planting false evidence and conspiring to obstruct the legal defense of seven Panther survivors, against whom Hanrahan had initially placed charges of attempted murder, which were later dropped.

Now began a new assault, led primarily by the Association. Milton H. Gray, Velde's successor, immediately proposed that Judge Power withdraw from the case and assign the trial to a judge without links to the defendants or to the Democratic organization. If Power, a former law associate of Mayor Daley's, were to sit as the trial judge, pointedly commented the *Daily News*, "it would only firm up the cynical belief of a large part of the public that Hanrahan and his co-defendants are likely to go free, regardless of what evidence is marshaled against them." A number of leading law professors, notably Philip B. Kurland of the University of Chicago and Jon Waltz of Northwestern University, agreed, the latter remarking, "The trial judge should be someone beyond the mayor's reach."

Within a few days, Judge Power appointed Judge Philip J. Romiti to preside at the trial. Although Judge Romiti, former dean of the De Paul University Law School, had a solid judicial reputation, the Chicago Council of Lawyers and other reform groups insisted that he too bow out in favor of a downstate judge. But Gray said, "I am sure the step taken by Judge Power was fully considered. The judicial process should be permitted to proceed as expeditiously as possible."

Gray had yet another suggestion: Hanrahan should take a leave of absence until the disposal of the charges against him. "I will not resign nor will I take a leave of absence," Hanrahan promptly replied. "Instead, I intend to fight. I know that I have committed no crime and am supremely confident that I will be completely vindicated." And from an angry Mayor Daley: "I wonder if this is the same thing that the Bar Association does when one of its lawyers is charged with dishonesty or irregularity. Are we arriving at that age where charges will be reduced to accusations and accusations will be reduced to innuendoes and innuendoes and implications are going to be the basis upon which we operate?" The mayor also had harsh words for the Chicago Council of Lawyers: "All these holier than thou guys that are talking about things maybe ought to look into their own procedures. I suggest that as lawyers they reread the Magna Carta, the Declaration of Independence, the United States Constitution and the Constitution of Illinois!"

In spite of the mayor's fervent verbal support, when time came to pick a slate for the March primaries, Hanrahan was cast out as the Democratic organization's candidate and replaced by Judge Raymond K. Berg, who had built a good record in Traffic Court. Hanrahan defied the mayor and ran against Berg and Donald Page Moore. Although the Association classified Hanrahan as "Not qualified," a finding he scornfully labeled "absolutely ridiculous," he won renomination after a hard campaign.

The trial itself started July 10, and it was strident and arduous and marked by Sears' earnest efforts to overcome skillful tactics of a corps of defense lawyers and often hazy and conflicting testimony by prosecution witnesses. On October 13, with the trial approaching its end, the Association once more affixed its "Not qualified" label on Hanrahan. "Mr. Hanrahan's zealousness, vigor and dedication are recognized," read the report issued by Association President Philip H. Corboy. "However, he is lacking in the temperament requisite to the position and is lacking in judgment under stress." The evaluation, retorted Hanrahan, was not surprising. "Everyone knows you can't beat a stacked deck. The Association doesn't speak for the 13,000 lawyers in the county, nor for the voters, who undoubtedly will do what they did in the primary, re-elect Ed Hanrahan. I have never been and never will be a pussy-footing lawyer who doesn't get excited when horrible crimes are committed and injustice is done. I believe in fighting crime and injustice as hard as I possibly can."

This time Hanrahan was wrong. On October 25, he and his

codefendants were acquitted by Judge Romiti, who ruled that it was not even necessary to call defense witnesses ("Evidence is simply not sufficient to establish or prove any conspiracy against any defendant"). But November 7 was a day of defeat for him. Bernard C. Carey, a former agent for the Federal Bureau of Investigation, was elected state's attorney; Carey's relatively close triumph—1,168,000 to 1,040,000—was significantly abetted by the vast number of black voters who split their tickets. Early on election night, it appeared that Hanrahan might win, but as returns continued to arrive from more of the black-ghetto wards, he gradually realized he had lost. Yet even as he conceded, he remained buoyant and combative enough so that political experts looked ahead to his quest of other offices in future elections: "There's nothing I hate more than defeat, but you don't roll over and cry. I shall survive. I believe public service is the finest expression of a legal career. I'll be around in 1974 and I'll certainly be around in 1975."

3.

During these many months of contention, other matters, most of them far less controversial, concerned the Association.

In July 1971, the Younger Members Committee, which had shrunk considerably in size and range of activities, was ordered revitalized by Association President Milton H. Gray, and it was reorganized as the Young Lawyers Section so that the 3,000 members under 36 years of age could more directly participate in Association activities. David C. Hilliard was named chairman, and with its own rules, budget, and staff, the group set as prime objectives an increase in community awareness and involvement in law, the development of law-related educational and training programs in community service and volunteer legal assistance, the stimulation of legal reforms, and the creation of professional and educational programs of service to law students, youthful lawyers, the organized bar, and the judiciary. A month after its organization, no less than 19 committees had been established to deal with such variegated subjects as legal services for the poor, educational sessions for the news media in legal matters, Law Day programs in high schools, relations with the area's law schools, problems of minority groups, continuing education for new lawyers, health care, penal reform, and criminal justice. A *Young Lawyers Journal* offered informative and instructional articles, case notes, and other materials of value; a series of citizens' pamphlets was begun; and a manual was published to help volunteers inexperienced in legal assistance work. Letters were sent to state legislators and Chicago aldermen offering services of members in drafting bills and ordinances. A Creative City Committee undertook a legal aid program for artists and fine-arts organizations and cooperated in establishing a shop for art created by prison inmates.

A major result of study and work by the group's Legal Assistance Committee was the creation in May 1972, in cooperation with the Legal Aid Bureau and with various local and state law offices under the overall direction of Circuit Court Chief Judge Boyle, of the Small Claims Court for people with claims of up to $300 who could not afford or did not want to hire a lawyer. "A victory for the little man," declared Municipal Court Judge Eugene L. Wachowski, one of the plan's earliest proponents, as he outlined the range of minimal fees involved in presenting cases to the court. The Young Lawyers Section prepared a handbook detailing all the steps involved in filing complaints and following through to hearings and offering basic counsel from how to behave in court ("BE EARLY! Sit down in the courtroom and remain quiet. Listen for the clerk to call your name and case number") to how to collect from defendants who refused to heed judgments. This and an ever-expanding list of other projects led, in September 1973, to its selection by the American Bar Association as the outstanding group of young lawyers in the nation. "We were particularly impressed," read the citation, "with the fact that you continued some 30 programs from last year and instituted 26 new programs."

Actions aimed at better public service were also taken by

the Association. A series of bills, some prepared in conjunction
with the Illinois State Bar Association, sought innovations and
beneficial changes in existing statutes. A no-fault automobile
insurance bill supported by the Association and passed by the
legislature was vetoed in September 1973, and another providing for no-fault divorce legislation offered earlier that year
("It will take the hypocrisy and embarrassment out of divorce,"
said Association President Philip H. Corboy) remained mired
in legislative committees. A Consumer Real Estate Protection
Act, drawn in 1969 and calling for increased safeguards for
tenants and contract real estate buyers of residential properties,
finally came before the legislature in 1971 but failed to win
passage. Under Corboy's directive, a study was instituted to
amass statistics and data about the possibility and efficacy of
prepaid legal services similar to medical insurance, and official
support was given to laws for handgun control and to adoption
of the Equal Rights Amendment to the federal constitution.

4.

Long concerned about relations between police and the public,
the Association became more deeply involved in this period in
various moves designed to improve that relationship.

Twice in the preceding years, the Association had been represented in such efforts. In 1966, William A. McSwain, then
president, served on a 23-member committee whose chief purpose was to suggest ways of bettering the police image in communities, and in 1970, the Urban Affairs Committee had gone
on record in favor of setting up a civilian review board; in both
instances, however, little had been accomplished beyond the
discussion stage.

In April 1972, following an increase in complaints about
police brutality, President Gray named a special seven-member
Association committee, with former President John Joseph Sullivan as chairman and including a black, a Latin, a labor lawyer, and a former Federal Bureau of Investigation agent. After
an inquiry into techniques and practices of the police depart-

ment's Internal Affairs Division, the committee, that December, proposed creation of a permanent Police-Community Relations Commission, comprising 15 Association members, to monitor and evaluate the IAD's methods of processing complaints of verbal abuse by policemen or of their use or threatened use of excessive force. In disclosing the committee's 30-page report and recommendations, Corboy noted that only 16 of 987 complaints of brutality had been upheld. "There appears to be," he said, "a lack of public confidence, especially among minority groups, in the department's inability to discipline offending policemen. Formation of this commission will help to restore confidence in the police department." The proposal urged that the Association commission take over the functions of the city's Human Relations Commission in reviewing cases of alleged brutality and issue an annual report of its findings and evaluations to the public, the mayor, and the police superintendent.

Mayor Daley favored the plan but balked at diminishing the role of the Human Relations Commission. In other quarters, opposition was quite strident. "Totally and absolutely unacceptable to the black community," declared United States Rep. Ralph H. Metcalfe, speaking for the Concerned Citizens for Police Reform; he proposed instead a civilian review board, composed primarily of blacks and Latins, with power to investigate discriminatory hiring practices and to discipline offending policemen. Arnold B. Kanter, president of the Chicago Council of Lawyers, expectedly called the proposal "incredibly audacious, preposterous, patronizing and presumptuous."

Without replying to specific criticisms but reaffirming the benefits of the proposed commission, Corboy forwarded the report to Police Superintendent James S. Conlisk, in whose desk it still remained as late as September 1973, when, following the conviction of a high police official and 19 policemen for extorting money from tavern owners and nightclub operators, the superintendent resigned.

Concern over police matters persisted. Late that November, the Association joined with the Chicago Council of Lawyers and the Cook County Bar Association in a call for establishment of an independent civilian agency to investigate complaints of police misconduct. Such an agency, declared Association President James W. Kissel, was needed to combat what he described as "citywide distrust of police" and the general feeling among many segments of the citizenry that prevailing procedures protected policemen instead of weeding out those who were brutal, unfit, or dishonest. The proposed agency would be paid for from the city's budget, and its members would be appointed by the mayor from among candidates selected by a nominating committee that would be broadly representative of the community and even include varied police organizations. It would have a staff of as many as 100 investigators to probe citizen complaints against police and would issue findings of guilt or innocence, with punishment of offenders to be decreed by the police superintendent or the Chicago Police Board. In a joint statement, the three lawyers' groups emphasized, "The good will that should result from the enormous amount of good work done every day by most police officers is dissipated by the fear and distrust of police generally created by the activities of a small percentage of brutal or unfit officers." Amid reactions favorable and unfavorable—the latter mostly from police groups who opposed the idea, saying it was like setting up a "kangaroo court"—Kissel expressed the hope that the agency might be created within the following year.

5.

Interestingly, the Association's long-enduring problem of how most efficaciously to discipline members of its own profession had, by this time, been resolved, while another equally as durable continued to stir arguments.

Few of the Association's avowed functions—first enunciated at its founding in 1874—had proved as vexatious or controversial or had more often been criticized than its disciplinary procedures. Editorialists demanded speedier action, most often after their respective newspapers published articles dealing with ambulance chasing, fraudulent procurement of divorces, shoddy real estate practices, and other kinds of unethical or illegal conduct. Civic organizations periodically made demands that the Association move more swiftly to cleanse the profession's ranks, and occasionally legislative committees were harsh in their condemnation of what they considered the Association's laxity in advocating deserved punishment. Over the many years, accusations were voiced—State's Attorney John E. Wayman, back in 1909, was especially vociferous—that the preponderance of the Association's investigations had been of nonmembers; it was a charge always successfully refuted by enumerating the specific numbers of cases involved, but it continued to persist nevertheless. Litigants who had lost court cases or felt that their lawyers had poorly represented them were high among complainants, and chronic critics of the Association invariably singled out slow disciplinary action or lack of it as evidence of excessive self-interest.

Of little avail were oft-repeated explanations that the Association was compelled by specific rules established by the Illinois Supreme Court to adhere to a detailed, drawn-out procedure: an initial probe of a complaint by a section of the Committee on Inquiry, then successive and lengthy hearings by the full committee and the Grievance Committee acting as commissioners of the high court, and a final review by the Board of Managers. This process meant that it might well take as long as three years before a case could be referred to the state Supreme Court for censure, suspension, or disbarment. Yet, after this procedure had been instituted in 1933 it had been considered by the American Bar Association as a model for other cities to emulate and a notable improvement over the prevailing system in which the Grievance Committee heard statements of unsworn witnesses, and if it thought a lawyer guilty, filed an information with the state Supreme Court, after which the matter was referred to a commissioner or a master in chancery for a hearing and subsequent recommendations. Many who joined in the outcry for increased inquiries and accelerated action overlooked the basic fact that even those charged with the most heinous of offenses were entitled to due process of law, an established right that in a democratic society precluded hasty procedures and guaranteed careful and scrupulous judgmental procedures. Each year, a substantial percentage of complaints failed to reach the Supreme Court because they were initially groundless or the evidence offered did not have the required quality of clear and convincing proof. Moreover, initial investigation and subsequent inquiry kept growing more expensive as the years progressed to a point where an annual expense to the Association of $100,000 was standard and adequate, at that, only to cover employment of one full-time investigator and payment for secretarial services and fees for transcripts and other essential documents and office help and supplies.

But even within the Association, the staunchest defenders of the established disciplinary routine realized its defects. Proposals for basic changes had often been made, but no definitive action occurred until April 10, 1971, when a special committee under the direction of former President Justin A. Stanley issued a report that led to a formal petition by the Board of Managers to the Illinois Supreme Court; it admitted the inadequacy of existing methods, and, in conjunction with the Illinois State Bar Association, asked that a separate commission be set up to handle all complaints and that to finance its operations, each of the state's 22,000 lawyers be assessed an annual fee of $20. On November 17, 1972, approval of the new system was announced by the high court's chief justice, Robert H. Underwood. The following February, Stanley was named chairman of a five-man board, officially known as the Attorney Registration Commission, that included two Chicago lawyers—Lester Asher and George J. Cotsirilos—John Grady of Waukegan, and James H. Bandy of Belleville. Carl H. Rolewick, former deputy director of the Administrative Office of Illinois Courts, was selected to be the commission's administrator. And underscoring the serious intent of the high court that the new system be financially able to conduct investigations and facilitate disposition of complaints was the stipulation that any lawyer refusing to pay the required fee would not be allowed to practice anywhere in the state.

While the greatest share of responsibility now fell on the new commission for making investigations and holding hearings and on a special nine-member board for reviewing its findings before submission to the Supreme Court, the Association still was assigned the role, albeit a much smaller one than heretofore, of establishing an inquiry board—comprised not merely of Association representatives but also those of the Chicago Council of Lawyers and the Cook County Bar Association—to receive complaints and adjudge those worthy of referral to the commission. Although the council's president, Arnold B. Kanter, deplored the lack of laymen on the commission ("Getting rid of the overreaching, unscrupulous and incompetent lawyer is too much a matter of the public interest to be left solely to the lawyers") and some lawyers grumbled at the annual assessment, expectations for the future of the new system generally were high, most Association members agreeing with President Corboy's statement: "This procedure to investigate and prosecute the few lawyers who are errant or erring will help to increase public confidence in the legal profession."

Meanwhile the Association's continuing efforts in connection with the judiciary received setbacks and aroused differences of opinion.

In the months after the defeat of Proposition 2B, a number of bills with a similar aim—nonpartisan merit selection of judges—supported by the Association and others concerned with reform were presented to the legislature, but each died a quick death either in committee or by a negative vote. Furthermore, the retention system in effect since 1964 was evoking unfavorable comment from editorialists and Association critics led by Frank Greenberg. This was especially true when, in the judicial election of November 1972, the 43 Circuit Court and 3 Appellate Court sitting judges, after affirmation by the Association of all but 4 as qualified or well-qualified, kept their seats. "The Judicial Reform Flop," a *Daily News* editorial was headed, and Greenberg proposed, in a long article in that newspaper, that the existing system be abandoned in favor of a return to the old practice of selecting judges under party labels in contested elections.

Recalling that the original intention of the Association's campaign for passage of the 1962 judicial article was that the retention of judges should not be separated from merit selection—an aim quashed in acceptance then of a "half a loaf" compromise—Greenberg sounded a familiar plaint: "The whole idea was that judges would be appointed by the governor from among nominees selected with great care, and after searching examination, by a nonpartisan judicial nominating commission possessed of impeccable credentials. Given that premise and the expectation that only lawyers of exceptional qualifications in terms of legal ability, temperament, integrity and character would be elevated to the bench, virtual life tenure was a logical extension of the concept. The present system, though it masquerades in the guise of popular election, is in reality also an appointive one. The difference is that the appointive power is the head of the dominant machine and that his consultative body consists of the ward committeemen and other politicians who make up the slatemaking organ of the party." A return to the previous system—with judges elected to fixed terms and obliged to run against a candidate of the opposite party at the end of that term—might, Greenberg maintained, bring pressure on the political slatemakers, with ears cocked to growing public sentiment for reform despite the failure to secure binding legislation in its behalf, to drop obviously incompetent judges and build progressively better slates. "I frankly do not believe that the Chicago Bar Association or the Chicago Council of Lawyers or any other organization is even remotely capable of the kind of objective, no-holds-barred evaluation of sitting judges that should inspire great confidence in the electorate."

Greenberg's proposal was opposed by Corboy as "a giant step backward in the battle for judicial reform." In an article also in the *Daily News*, Corboy traced the Association's vital role in the efforts to gain merit selection and the strictures set in the 1970 constitution against the participation of judges in political activity. To require all judges to stand for reelection because a small percentage was demonstrably inept was tantamount, said Corboy, to a situation in which a petulant teacher might punish an entire classroom because a few students misbehaved. "Under such a proposal," wrote Corboy, "judges who have been praised by the bar and by the media would be back in the jungle of partisan politics. They would not be able to devote all their energies to judicial duties, at least not during pre-election times, and they would be forced to compete not only in a general election but perhaps in a primary also. They would be competing against lawyers in private practice who want their jobs and who could be expected to finance campaigns more easily than incumbent judges. Would not the constitutional admonition against holding a position for profit be jeopardized if a judge had to finance a re-election campaign?"

There existed the machinery, Corboy noted, to deal with judges of doubtful integrity, indifferent diligence, poor legal ability, and lack of judicial temperament: the Judicial Inquiry Board, whose mandate provided that it could charge a judge with failure to perform his duties or with conduct prejudicial to the administration of justice or with bringing the judicial office into disrepute. While the fight for merit selection ought to be unceasing, Corboy insisted that the board and not a return to older election methods was the most feasible medium by which to insure proper judicial standards. (Since its creation, the Judicial Inquiry Board has received 50 complaints of varying degrees. One of its most publicized inquiries was into a charge by the Better Government Association that Circuit Court Chief Judge Boyle had derived big profits from a deal in south suburban land. Corboy described announcement of the action by the BGA's executive director, J. Terrence Brunner, as "a grandstand play," while the Chicago Council of Lawyers predictably supported Brunner, alleging in addition that Boyle was unqualified to serve as chief judge. In September 1973, the board cleared Boyle of all charges of impropriety because the investments involved had been made before he was elected a judge and while he held no public office. Another case covered prominently in the newspapers was that of Circuit Court Judge John J. McDonnell. In November 1972, he was involved in a parking lot argument with a suburban couple and was accused by the husband of waving a revolver. Although criminal charges against Judge McDonnell were dismissed, a complaint filed with the Judicial Inquiry Board led to a hearing before the Illinois Courts Commission on charges of improper conduct. Henry L. Mason III argued that McDonnell had shown "an arrogant disregard of the rights and feelings of private citizens" while the judge's attorney, Thomas P. Sullivan, maintained that the incident was sparked by "a minor excess of temper" that had no bearing on McDonnell's judicial integrity. With one dissenting vote, the five-man commission found McDonnell guilty and suspended him from the bench for four months.)

Corboy's position on maintaining the retention system became officially the Association's for the rest of his term and in that of his successor, James W. Kissel. In April 1973, the state Senate passed a resolution presented by Edward McBroom of Kankakee for a referendum in November 1974 on a constitutional amendment that would substitute contested elections of judges for their retention based on merit selection, and in June, the House of Representatives gave the resolution its approval in the hectic closing week of the legislative session; the resolution was heavily supported by Chicago Democrats and by downstate members of both parties. Furthermore, the Senate killed yet another proposed amendment that would have put merit selection into effect in Cook County. Corboy once more deplored the actions: "We think it better to retain those less qualified few rather than the risk of the excellent or good judges being put out of office because of their refusal or inability to campaign effectively." Greenberg again expressed his hopes that the election plan would work ("It is sometimes necessary to go back to Square One and start the game over again"), and Kissel vowed to fight the proposal. Responding to critics unhappy over the failure of spokesmen for either the Association or the Illinois State Bar Association to testify before legislative committees considering the resolution, he emphasized that the Association's opposition had been made firmly known since the inception of the McBroom proposition and that maneuvering by the Chicago-downstate combination for a vote would have been impossible to combat during the session's busy final days: "However, this backward step into judicial politics is still far from becoming law. We intend to vigorously continue this battle with the electorate for a nonpolitical judicial system."

Kissel continued to speak out against the referendum proposal, and soon McBroom and a cosponsor, Rep. George H. Ryan, announced that such opposition and the persuasive arguments of former Governor Ogilvie and State Treasurer Alan W. Dixon had convinced them to ask that the proposal be killed. When the legislature reconvened in November, it rescinded its previous action, although proponents of abolition of judicial retention indicated that their fight was far from over.

6.

And so, at the start of its second century, the Chicago Bar Association finds itself still vitally concerned with a matter it has sought to resolve almost from the day of its inception. It is one that will indubitably continue to be given high priority for many years to come, whatever the resolution of prevailing differences on how best to achieve a long-cherished ambition.

Few of its problems have been of greater importance or have occupied more time and effort throughout the decades than the improvement of the judiciary. "To increase its usefulness in promoting the due administration of justice" read one of the phrases in the Association's 1874 constitution, and year by year, decade by decade, through diverse means and methods, this has remained an aim steadfast and unassailable. At times, the Association's moves in this area have aroused criticism not only from political forces with which it has been compelled to contend but also from segments of its membership and the public. Sometimes, its endeavors have been without major effect or strong impact. But the historical record is clear: Victories and gains have been achieved, and many of these have been of lasting significance. Perhaps even more important—whatever the level of disagreement between members and officials over procedures and theories—the struggle continues and will assuredly persist.

These same historical annals are replete with evidence of other substantial achievements. There have been failures and disappointments, periods of intense activity and relative lassitude, reasons for congratulation and cause for complaint. But if the Association has sometimes seemed laggard or behind the times, it has more often—as is clear from the full record of its first century of existence—been ahead of its times. Whatever the frailties and the strengths of the past, a dispassionate observer must necessarily be impressed with the ever-increasing distance the Association has continued to put between itself and the legal ivory tower in which its critics, inside and outside, have maintained it has spent too many hours. It still may move too slowly for its more impulsive members, but the evidence is ample that it has increasingly injected itself into the realm of public issues in the realization that its obligations as an aggregation of men and women theoretically and ideally considered "ministers of justice" are as much civic as they are professional; as it approached observance of its centennial, fresh signs of its pursuance of the objective stated in its bylaws of promoting "the due administration of justice and the public good" came with its resolution of October 22, 1973, urging Illinois representatives in Congress to investigate and debate the conduct of President Nixon in the firings of the special Watergate prosecutor, Archibald Cox, and Deputy Attorney General William D. Ruckelshaus and the resignation of Attorney General Elliot L. Richardson.

The Association's structure is such that its dozens of committees carry the bulk of responsibility for varied duties and actions, with its Board of Managers as final arbiter in virtually all instances. Yet the Association is no monolithic organization suffused with a high degree of unanimity, and few ultimate decisions are reached without discussion and expressed disagreement. Diverse and viable as its membership is and will be, the Association will, as in the past, always have its critics, and the most serious and earnest of their comments and complaints will rarely stay unheeded. Undoubtedly, the Association will undergo internal changes in hearkening to demands for greater participation by younger members and representatives of ethnic and minority groups. And, as its founders hoped it always would do, it will, at its best, persist in performing essential services for both the profession and the public. Clarence Denning once expressed his views of the Association's function and meaning and of the role and responsibility of the individual practitioner, and at this moment of looking backward and forward, what he said merits consideration and reflection by lawyer and layman alike:

"Those among us who labor for the honor of our profession exceed in number and ability those who degrade it. Those who search for and discover the principles of law which govern eternal justice build permanent monuments in each generation. The true lawyer proves all things and holds fast to that which is good. To the extent that the bar follows that charted course and forgets money, position or power will history record the work of the lawyers of a given period as well done. In the period of world affairs in which we live, bar associations are the channels through which the lawyer achieves his greatest usefulness to society. Among such associations the Chicago Bar Association yields to none in its record of accomplishment."

Acknowledgments

A vast number of persons gave invaluable help of varied kinds in connection with this project.

Enlightening and pertinent information was derived from interviews, correspondence, memorandums, and personal memoirs of past Association presidents: Cushman B. Bissell (1951–52), Jerome S. Weiss (1958–59), William H. Alexander (1960–61), R. Newton Rooks (1961–62), Walter H. Moses (1962–63), Norman H. Nachman (1963–64), Gordon R. Close (1964–65), William A. McSwain (1966–67), Justin A. Stanley (1967–68), John Joseph Sullivan (1968–69), Frank Greenberg (1969–70), James A. Velde (1970–71), Milton H. Gray (1971–72), and Philip H. Corboy (1972–73). The Association's president in 1973–74, James W. Kissel, was equally helpful.

The Association's Centennial Committee was instrumental in making initial plans for this book, and discussions with committee members helped to determine its nature and scope. The committee was composed of Keith I. Parsons, chairman, and James P. Connelly, Appellate Court Judge Robert E. English, David C. Hilliard, Everett L. Hollis, James W. Kissel, John L. Malone, Ray F. Myers, Dean Phil Neal, John A. Nordberg, Francis E. O'Connor, Esther Rothstein, Justin A. Stanley, and Jerome S. Weiss.

Of hundreds of members who responded to my questionnaire, those who proved especially instructive were Ware Adams, Gene L. Armstrong, James W. Ashley, Irwin J. Askow, John P. Barnes, Jr., Benjamin M. Becker, Robert M. Berger, Edgar Bernhard, George E. Bullwinkel, Francis X. Busch,

Thomas Campbell, Henry P. Chandler, John A. Cook, William Cousins, Jr., John L. Davidson, Jr., Philip R. Davis, Leon M. Despres, Jack E. Dominik, Robert T. Drake, Bernard E. Epton, Norman Finkel, Walter T. Fisher, Donald C. Gancer, Criminal Court Judge James A. Geroulis, G. E. Hale, Lee M. Howard, John F. X. Irving, James C. Kellogg, Judge George N. Leighton of the Appellate Court of Illinois, Louis W. Levit, Seymour B. Levy, Charles Liebman, Richard C. Lindberg, Fred Louis, Kenneth McCracken, Harry W. Malm, Richard C. Martin, James F. Oates, Jr., James B. O'Shaugnessy, A. Edmund Peterson, Kenneth C. Prince, Owen Rall, Theodore G. Remer, Esther Rothstein, William L. Ryan, Justice Walter V. Schaefer of the Illinois Supreme Court, Sidney Sherman, Arnold I. Shure, James Sprowl, Anthony W. Summers, Alban Weber, John Williams, Joseph Z. Willner, Bernard Wolfe, William F. Zacharias.

Elmer Gertz, distinguished lawyer and author, permitted me to examine pertinent sections of his autobiography-in-progress. Judge Abraham L. Marovitz of the United States District Court furnished valuable data and anecdotage. Samuel W. Witwer contributed lucid and crucial information about the successful campaign he helped direct for a new state constitution. Donald B. Hatmaker's letters about an earlier era of activities of younger members and David C. Hilliard's detailed memorandums about the revived Young Lawyers Section filled in many gaps. Harry Daley and Julian J. Frazin, among many, were authoritative about Christmas Spirits productions. John S. Lord furnished not only personal recollections about legal practice but also his rare historical volume about the Law Club of Chicago. Harry Barnard, noted biographer-historian, allowed me to read his manuscript about Circuit Court Judge Julian W. Mack. Carl H. Rolewick supplied important materials relating to the Attorney Registration Commission. Of notable assistance in a variety of ways were Richard H. Cain, Clarence Denning's successor; Diann M. Bimmerle, secretary to the Association president; T. M. Murphy, director of the Association's Lawyer Referral Service; Patricia Hanson, former

Association public relations director, and her successor, Theresa Marousek; Rick Kogan, staff reporter of *The Chicagoan;* Hoke Norris of the Chicago Public Library; Mary Frances Rhymer of the Chicago Historical Society; and such newspaper colleagues as Robert E. Kennedy, associate editor of the *Chicago Sun-Times,* and the *Sun-Times'* Burnell Heinecke, Ben Kopriva, Joel Weisman, and Charles Wheeler, Jr.; Fred J. Pannwitt and Gerry Robichaud of the *Chicago Daily News;* and Lloyd Wendt, editor and publisher of *Chicago Today.*

As ever, the reference departments of all the Chicago newspapers allowed me access to thousands of clippings, and for this I express gratitude to Janice Lewis of the newspaper division of Field Enterprises, Inc., Patrick Wilson of the *Chicago Tribune,* and A. G. Wykel of *Chicago Today.* I am also grateful to Herbert Mitgang of the *New York Times'* editorial board and his secretary, Betty Pomerantz, for special research aid.

Bibliography

Printed materials in my research ran into the many hundreds. Most extensively used among Association publications were issues of the *Chicago Bar Record* from 1910 to date, *The Communicator,* the *Young Lawyers Journal,* and a wide assortment of pamphlets, instructional booklets, committee reports, memorials, and manuals. Transcripts of meetings of committees and of the various Boards of Managers were examined, with special attention paid to events dealt with in this narrative. Copies of the *Chicago Legal News,* from 1864 to the final issues in 1925, were carefully read in bound volumes in the Association library for masses of information and data nowhere else available. Other rare legal publications, furnished by the Chicago Historical Society, included the short-lived *Chicago Law Journal* of 1877, whose editor was George L. Barber, and the *Chicago Law Times* of 1886–87, edited by Catherine V. Waite. Of special interest was the 100th anniversary issue of the *Chicago Daily Law Bulletin* of October 27, 1954. Considerable information and data were derived from selective issues of the *American Bar Association Journal; Judicature,* the journal of the American Judicature Society; the *Journal of the Illinois Historical Society;* and *Chicago History.* A partial list of books read and consulted follows:

Arlen, Michael J. *An American Verdict.* New York: Doubleday and Company, Inc., 1973.

Arnold, Isaac N. *Recollections of Early Chicago and the Illinois Bar.* Chicago: Fergus Printing Company, 1882.

Banfield, Edward C., and Wilson, James Q. *City Politics.* Cambridge, Mass.: Harvard University Press, 1963.

Barnard, Harry. *Eagle Forgotten.* Indianapolis and New York: Bobbs-Merrill Company, Inc., 1938.

———. *The Forging of an American Jew: Judge Julian W. Mack and His Times.* New York: Herzl Press, 1974.

Brand, George E. *Bar Associations, Attorneys and Judges.* Chicago: American Judicature Society, 1956.

Brecher, Jeremy. *Strike!* San Francisco: Straight Arrow Books, 1972.

Bright, John. *Hizzoner Big Bill Thompson.* New York: Jonathan Cape and Harrison Smith, 1930.

Brown, Esther Lucile. *Lawyers and the Promotion of Justice.* New York: Russell Sage Foundation, 1938.

Brown, Henry. *The History of Illinois.* New York: New World Press, 1844.

Busch, Francis X. *Casebook of the Curious and True.* Indianapolis and New York: Bobbs-Merrill Company, Inc., 1957.

———. *Guilty or Not Guilty.* Indianapolis and New York: Bobbs-Merrill Company, Inc., 1952.

———. *In and Out of Court.* Chicago: M. A. Donohue & Co., 1942.

———. *They Escaped the Hangman.* Indianapolis and New York: Bobbs-Merrill Company, Inc., 1953.

Carlin, Jerome Edward. *Lawyers on Their Own.* New Brunswick, N.J.: Rutgers University Press, 1962.

Caton, John Dean. *Early Bench and Bar of Illinois.* Chicago: Fergus Printing Company, 1893.

Chester, Lewis; Hodgson, Godfrey; and Page, Bruce. *An American Melodrama.* New York: Viking Press, Inc., 1969.

Cohn, Rubin G. *To Judge with Justice: History and Politics of Illinois Judicial Reform.* Urbana, Chicago, and London: University of Illinois Press, 1973.

Collins, Lorin C. *Autobiography.* Sawyer, Mich.: The author, 1934.

Cook, Frederick Francis. *Bygone Days in Chicago.* Chicago: A. C. McClurg & Co., 1910.

Cornelius, Janet. *Constitution Making in Illinois, 1818 to 1970.* Urbana, Chicago, and London: University of Illinois Press, 1972.

Crossley, Frederic B. *Courts and Lawyers of Illinois.* Chicago: American Historical Society, 1916.

Darrow, Clarence. *The Story of My Life.* New York and London: Charles Scribner's Sons, 1932.

Dedmon, Emmett. *Fabulous Chicago.* New York: Random House, 1953.

Dorsen, Norman, and Friedman, Leon. *Disorder in the Court.* New York: Pantheon Books, 1973.

Fergus, Robert. *John Dean Caton.* Chicago: Fergus Printing Company, 1882.

Fiedler, George. *The Illinois Law Courts in Three Centuries 1673–1973.* Berwyn, Ill.: Physicians' Record Co., 1973.

Friedman, Lawrence M. *A History of American Law.* New York: Simon & Schuster, 1973.

Gerhart, Eugene C., ed. *The Lawyer's Treasury.* Indianapolis and New York: Bobbs-Merrill Company, Inc., 1956.

Gertz, Elmer. *For the First Hours of Tomorrow.* Urbana, Chicago, and London: University of Illinois Press, 1972.

Gilbert, Hiram T. *The Municipal Court of Chicago.* Chicago: The author, 1928.

Ginger, Ann Fagan. *The Relevant Lawyers.* New York: Simon & Schuster, 1972.

Ginger, Raymond. *Altgeld's America.* New York: Funk and Wagnalls Company, 1958.

Goodspeed, Thomas W. *A History of the University of Chicago.* Chicago: University of Chicago Press, 1916.

Gosnell, Harold F. *Machine Politics.* Chicago: University of Chicago Press, 1937.

Gottfried, Alex. *Boss Cermak of Chicago.* Seattle, Wash.: University of Washington Press, 1962.

Harrison, Carter H. *Stormy Years.* Indianapolis and New York: Bobbs-Merrill Company, Inc., 1935.

Howard, Robert P. *Illinois.* Grand Rapids, Mich.: Wm. P. Eerdmans, 1972.

Hoyne, Thomas. *The Lawyer As a Pioneer.* Chicago: Fergus Printing Company, 1882.

Jacob, Herbert. *Justice in America.* Boston and Toronto: Little, Brown and Company, 1965.

_____. *Urban Justice.* Englewood Cliffs, N.J.: Prentice-Hall, 1973.

Johnson, Claudius O. *Carter Henry Harrison.* Chicago: University of Chicago Press, 1928.

King, Willard L. *Lincoln's Manager: David Davis.* Cambridge, Mass.: Harvard University Press, 1960.

_____. *Melville Weston Fuller.* New York: The Macmillan Company, 1950.

Kobler, John. *Capone: The Life & World of Al Capone.* New York: G. P. Putnam's Sons, 1971.

Kogan, Bernard, ed. *The Chicago Haymarket Riot: Anarchy on Trial.* Boston: D. C. Heath and Company, 1959.

Kogan, Herman, and Wendt, Lloyd. *Chicago: A Pictorial History.* New York: E. P. Dutton & Co., Inc., 1958.

Kremer, Charles E. *Mike Monaghan.* Chicago: Law Club of Chicago, 1911.

Kutner, Luis. *I, the Lawyer.* New York: Dodd, Mead & Co., 1966.

Lens, Sidney. *The Labor Wars.* New York: Doubleday and Company, Inc., 1973.

Lewis, Lloyd, and Smith, Henry Justin. *Chicago: The History of Its Reputation.* New York: Harcourt, Brace and Company, Inc., 1929.

Linder, Usher F. *Reminiscences of the Early Bench and Bar of Illinois.* Chicago: The Chicago Legal News Company, 1879.

Lord, John S. *A History of the Law Club of the City of Chicago.* Chicago: The Law Club of Chicago, 1968.

Lukas, J. Anthony. *The Barnyard Epithet and Other Obscenities.* New York, Evanston, and London: Harper & Row, Inc., 1970.

Lyle, John H. *The Dry and Lawless Years.* Englewood Cliffs, N.J.: Prentice-Hall, 1961.

McPhaul, Jack. *Deadlines and Monkeyshines: The Fabled World of Chicago Journalism.* Englewood Cliffs, N.J.: Prentice-Hall, 1962.

————. *Johnny Torrio: First of the Gang Lords.* New Rochelle, N.Y.: Arlington House, 1970.

Marks, F. Raymond with Leswing, Kirk, and Fortinsky, Barbara A. *The Lawyer, the Public and Professional Responsibility.* Chicago: American Bar Foundation, 1972.

Martin, Edward M. *The Role of the Bar in Electing the Bench in Chicago.* Chicago: University of Chicago Press, 1936.

Martin, George W. *Causes and Conflicts: The Centennial History of the Association of the Bar of the City of New York.* New York: Houghton Mifflin Company, 1970.

Masters, Edgar Lee. *The Tale of Chicago.* New York: G. P. Putnam's Sons, 1933.

Mayer, Martin P. *The Lawyers.* New York, Evanston, and London: Harper & Row, Inc., 1967.

Mayers, Lewis. *The American Legal System.* New York, Evanston, and London: Harper & Row, Inc., 1955.

Pierce, Bessie Louise. *A History of Chicago,* 3 vols. New York and London: Alfred A. Knopf, 1937–57.

———— and Norris, J. L., comps. and eds. *As Others See Chicago: Impressions of Visitors, 1673–1933.* Chicago: University of Chicago Press, 1933.

Pound, Roscoe. *The Lawyer from Antiquity to Modern Times.* New York: West Publishing Co., 1953.

Royko, Mike. *Boss.* New York: E. P. Dutton and Co., Inc., 1971.

Schultz, John. *No One Was Killed.* Chicago: Big Table Publishing Company, 1969.

Schwartz, Bernard. *The Life of the Law.* New York: Dial Press, 1973.

Smyth, P. G. *Told Out of Court.* Chicago: The author, 1909.

Spies, August. *Autobiography.* Chicago: Nina van Zandt, 1887.

Stein, David Lewis. *Living the Revolution.* Indianapolis and New York: Bobbs-Merrill Company, Inc., 1969.

Stone, Irving. *Clarence Darrow for the Defense.* New York: Doubleday and Company, Inc., 1941.

Stuart, William H. *The Twenty Incredible Years.* Chicago and New York: M. A. Donohue & Co., 1935.

Walker, Daniel. *Rights in Conflict: A Report Submitted to the National Commission on the Causes and Prevention of Violence.* New York: E. P. Dutton & Co., Inc., 1968.

Weinberg, Arthur M., and Lila, eds. *Clarence Darrow: Verdicts Out of Court.* Chicago: Quadrangle Books, 1963.

Wendt, Lloyd, and Kogan, Herman. *Big Bill of Chicago.* Indianapolis and New York: Bobbs-Merrill Company, Inc., 1953.

————. *Lords of the Levee.* Indianapolis and New York: Bobbs-Merrill Company, Inc., 1943.

Wilkie, Franc B. *Sketches and Notices of the Chicago Bar.* Chicago: Western News Company, 1872.

Zeisler, Sigmund. *Reminiscences of the Anarchist Case.* Chicago: Chicago Literary Club, 1927.

Index

Abbott, Edith, 106
Abbott, Grace, 106
Adamowski, Benjamin S., 232-8
Addams, Jane, 74, 104, 106
Administrative Office of Illinois Courts, 294
Agnew, Spiro, 258
Akers, Milburn P., 235, 241
Alden, William Tracy, 163
Alexander, William H., 237, 248
"Alice Bond in Foreclosure Land," 197
"Alice in Wonderland," 258
Alliance of Business and Professional Women, 189
Altgeld, John Peter, 72, 74, 75-6, 97, 130
American Bar Association, 77, 192, 213, 227, 249, 250, 289, 293
American Bar Association Journal, 240
American Civil Liberties Union, 250, 284
American Legion, 157
American Railway Union, 76
American Red Cross, 75, 124
American Road Builders Association, 131
Anastaplo, George, 230-1
Appellate Court of Illinois, 46, 64, 83, 85-6, 95, 105, 200, 205, 230, 243, 279, 295
Arado, Charles C., 122

Arbeiter Zeitung, 65
Armando, James, 160
Armour, Philip D., 71
Arnold, Isaac N., 21
Arvey, Jacob M., 188, 208, 209
Ashcraft, Edwin M., 116-17
Asher, Lester, 294
Ashland Block, 46
Associated Press, 235
Association of the Bar of the City of New York, 35
Attorney Registration Commission, 294-5
Austin, C. Henry, 272
Austin, Edwin C., 169
Austin, Richard B., 260
Ayer, Benjamin F., 75, 108

Bailey, Joseph, 46
Baker, Frank, 75, 80
Baker, John E., Jr., 230
Baldwin, Matthew S., 118
Balestier, Joseph N., 21-2
Ball, Farlin Quigley, 108, 128
Ball, George, 196
Bancroft, Edgar A., 108-9
Bandy, James H., 294
Bane, Charles A., 227
Banning, Ephraim, 101-2
Barasa, Kay, 196-7
Bar Association Record, The, 122-3
Barnes, Albert C., 102-3
Barnett, Ferdinand L., Jr., 200
Barrett, George F., 196
Bartelme, Mary Margaret, 106, 140

Bean, Edward, 23
Bebb, Herbert, 202
Belcastro, James, 160
Bella Napoli Café, 153
Bellows, Carole Kamin, 268
"Bench Connection, The," 277
Bennett's Tavern, 204
Bentley, Richard, 169
Berg, Raymond K., 287
Better Government Association, 297
Big Bill, 136
Binford, Jessie, 106
Bishop's Criminal Law, 86
Bissell, Cushman B., 227, 241
Bither, William A., 135
Black, Hortensia, 73-4
Black, Hugo L., 231, 255
Black, John C., 67, 169
Black, John D., 169, 273
Black, William Perkins, 39, 44, 67-8, 70, 73-4, 97, 169
Black Panthers, 222, 253, 254, 283-4
Blackstone's Commentaries, 30
Blodgett, Henry W., 47-51, 64, 98
Bloom, David H., 127
Bonney, Charles C., 31, 66
Boodell, Thomas J., 262-3
Booth, Henry, 22
Bowe, Augustine J., 261
Bowen, Mrs. Joseph T., 104
Boyden, William C., 149-50
Boyesen, I. K., 79-80

311

312

319